ITALIAN RENAISSANCE FRAMES
AT THE V&A

ITALIAN RENAISSANCE FRAMES AT THE V&A

by Christine Powell and Zoë Allen

Photography Ian Thomas

Design and Illustration Christine Powell and Zoë Allen

Print Design Clare Johnson

AMSTERDAM • BOSTON • HEIDELBERG • LONDON • NEW YORK • OXFORD
PARIS • SAN DIEGO • SAN FRANCISCO • SINGAPORE • SYDNEY • TOKYO
Butterworth-Heinemann is an imprint of Elsevier

Butterworth-Heinemann is an imprint of Elsevier

The Boulevard, Langford Lane, Kidlington, Oxford OX5 1GB, UK
30 Corporate Drive, Suite 400, Burlington, MA 01803, USA

First edition 2010

British Library Cataloguing in Publication Data
A catalogue record for this book is available from the British Library

Library of Congress Cataloging-in-Publication Data
A catalog record for this book is available from the Library of Congress

ISBN: 978-0-7506-8619-8

For information on all Butterworth-Heinemann publications
visit our web site at books.elsevier.com

Printed and bound in Italy

10   10 9 8 7 6 5 4 3 2 1

CONTENTS

PHOTOGRAPHY & ILLUSTRATION CREDITS

PHOTOGRAPHY

Images of frames and images of tools and materials of gilding

Ian Thomas, Photographer, V&A Photographic Department, V&A Museum, London

Frames 2, 4, 6–12, 15–19, 21, 23, 24, 25–27, 29–36

Ian Thomas, Photographer, V&A Photographic Department, V&A Museum, London

Frame 1 (front)

From VADAR (V&A Digital Asset Repository)

Frame 1 (back)

Victor H. Lopez Borges, Senior Sculpture Conservator, Conservation Department, V&A Museum, London

Frame 3

Colin Harvey, Photographer, Photographic Department, The National Gallery, London

Digitally edited for publication by Ian Thomas, V&A Photographic Department

Frame 4

Detail of inside return of right pedestal. Christine Powell, Senior Furniture Conservator, Conservation Department, V&A Museum, London

Frame 5

Richard Davies, Photographic Department, V&A Museum, London

Frame 13

Colin Harvey, Photographer, Photographic Department, The National Gallery, London

Digitally edited for publication by Ian Thomas, V&A Photographic Department

Frame 14

Colin Harvey, Photographer, Photographic Department, The National Gallery, London

Digitally edited for publication by Ian Thomas, V&A Photographic Department

Frame 17 (back)

Victor H. Lopez Borges, Senior Sculpture Conservator, Conservation Department, V&A Museum, London

Frame 20

Christine Smith, Photographer, Photographic Department, V&A Museum, London

Frame 22

Astrid Athen, Photographer, The National Gallery Photographic Department, London

Digitally edited for publication by Ian Thomas, V&A Photographic Department

Frame 28

Christine Smith, Photographer, Photographic Department, V&A Museum, London

Frame 37

From VADAR (V&A digital asset repository)

All cross-section photographs

Dr Helen Howard, Scientific Department, The National Gallery, London

Illustrations

Joints found on the V&A Renaissance frames

Christine Powell

Mouldings found on the V&A Renaissance frames

Zoe Allen and Clare Johnson

All profiles in individual frame entries

Christine Powell and Zoë Allen

Annotated illustration of a tabernacle frame
    Zoe Allen and Clare Johnson
Illustration naming parts of a frame
    Zoë Allen and Clare Johnson
Digital image reconstruction image of Frame 21
    Clare Johnson
Digital image reconstruction image of Frame 26
    Clare Johnson

Annotated illustration of a Sansovino frame
    Zoë Allen and Clare Johnson
Tables, charts and microphotographs in analysis reports by Dr Brian Singer were supplied by Dr Brian Singer, digitally edited for publication by Clare Johnson and Zoë Allen

ACKNOWLEDGEMENTS

The authors wish to thank Mr Timothy Plaut for the generous funding that made this book possible. His passion for, and appreciation of, Renaissance frames has been an inspiration. His generosity and continuing encouragement throughout the project were invaluable.

The authors also wish to thank:

From the V&A: Marion Kite (Head of Furniture Textiles and Frames Conservation); Ian Thomas, Clare Johnson, Christine Smith, Richard Davies, James Stevenson and Ken Jackson of the Photographic Studio; Victor Borges (Senior Sculpture Conservator), Tim Miller (Senior Furniture Conservator), Dana van Sabben (Furniture Conservator), Donna Stevens (Metals Conservator), Tom Barrow (Contract Frames Conservator), Peta Motture (Chief Curator, Medieval & Renaissance Galleries Project), Meghan Callahan (Kress Curatorial Fellow, Medieval and Renaissance Galleries Project), Melissa Hammett (Curator of Sculpture), Fergus Cannan (Collections Liaison Manager) and Dr Adam Bowett (V&A Research Fellow, British Academy Fellow: British Furniture)

From the National Gallery, London: Martin Wyld (Director of Conservation), Peter Schade (Head of Framing Department), Isabella Kocum (Frames Department), Dr Ashok Roy and Dr Helen Howard (Scientific Department), Astrid Athen, Colin Harvey (Photographic Department) and Carol Hambleton (Communications and New Media)

Satoko Tanimoto (Mellon Fellow, Department of Conservation and Scientific Research, British Museum)

Dr Brian W Singer (Senior Lecturer, School of Arts and Social Sciences, Northumbria University)

Dick Onians (Wood Technology and Carving Tutor, City and Guilds of London Art School)

Roy and Pat Thomson, for editorial assistance

The following individuals generously gave of their time, expertise and opinion: Thomas Knoell (antique frames dealer, Basel, Switzerland), Michael Gregory (Managing Director of Arnold Wiggins and Son, frames dealer), Olaf Lemke (frame restorer, connoisseur and antique frame dealer, Berlin, Germany), Lynn Roberts (artist and picture frame historian) and Achim Stiegel (Curator of the Furniture Collection at the Kunstgewerbemuseum, Berlin).

Thanks also to Gerry Alabone (Head of Framing, Tate Gallery), Richard Hallas (Head of Framing, National Portrait Gallery, London), Caroline Tragett (Head of Framing, Guildhall Art Gallery, London), Stephen Sheasby (Head of Gilding Conservation, The Royal Collection, London), Jennifer Dinesmore (Conservator, Halahan Associates), Jürgen Huber (Senior Furniture Conservator, The Wallace Collection, London) and Hubert Baija (Head of Framing, Rijkmuseum, Amsterdam).

Christine Powell and Zoë Allen

PREFACE
TIMOTHY PLAUT

In 1897, the Italian art dealer Michelangelo Guggenheim published a handsome series of plates illustrating 120 Italian frames of the fifteenth and sixteenth centuries.[1] No collection, with the exception of the stock of that magisterial Florentine mercato, Stefano Bardini, within Italy or without, was more richly represented than that of the South Kensington Museum.[2] Whilst Guggenheim's publication was not the first presentation of illustrations of Renaissance frames, it proved to be easily the most comprehensive and the one that has, in more than the century since its appearance, been recognised as best representing that apogee of late nineteenth and early twentieth century historicist interest in the decorative arts of the Renaissance as manifested in picture frames.[3] For this volume to have singled out a dozen exempla housed in what is now the Victoria and Albert Museum underlines the importance of this museum's collection.

It is the Italian frame of the Renaissance, untrammelled by the standardisation of canvas sizes and the imposition of canons of ornamentation that came to characterise France and England in the course of the seventeenth century, that represents both the font of the disengaged frame and, far and away, its most exuberant range of decorative forms.[4] With Louis XIV's commission to Charles le Brun in 1660 to standardise stock designs, the picture frame starts to lose something of its autonomous aesthetic life.[5] As a result, the claim can be made with confidence that no period in European frame history has seen a comparable corpus of architectural and sculptural forms come into existence, to say nothing of the range of surface treatments and ornamental play, as was the case in Renaissance Italy.

Research into the genesis, commissioning, manufacture and range of Italian Renaissance frames, overwhelmingly a German and Italian domain from the late nineteenth century until it became a broader pursuit in the course of the last few decades, was able to identify two phenomena that indicate the importance attributed to those picture frames utilised for fifteenth and sixteenth century Italian sculpture and painting.[6] The first indication lies in the number of highly prominent painters – including Fra Angelico, Botticelli, Ghirlandaio, Pontormo, Leonardo and Raphael – who designed frames or painted upon frames for their own panels or canvases. A second indication emerges from the sheer number of frames either signed or in which contemporary records secure the name of the master frame maker.[7] These included sculptors of the standing of the de Maiano family.[8] Far from being viewed as a menial craft, the carver along with the gilder were regarded as essential to the formation of a spatial border and context for the enclosed panel or canvas.

Today's perspective is deceptive. It was the eighteenth century that saw the emergence of the artist or name frames (Canaletto, Longhi, Lely, Wright, Morland, Whistler, Pisarro, to name a few).[9] The nineteenth century witnessed dual depredations of the picture frame. Firstly, the triumph of the standardised and uniform gallery frame. This practice was initiated in Mannerist Florence in order to stamp a degree of homogeneity upon the hanging of the Medici collection in the Pitti Palace. In the course of the wave of foundations of national picture galleries before and particularly after 1800, this movement was the occasion for the greatest single destruction of original frames as paintings were rehung in especially commissioned, consistent and formulaic new forms.[10] Secondly, the Industrial Revolution served to commodify and bastardise the art of frame making.

As with the decorative arts as a whole, the post-Vasari world has been characterised by a diminution in the standing of the frame maker and, with the prominent exception of that most visionary of all nineteenth century museum curators, Wilhelm von Bode, a degree of indifference towards original frames in the public hanging of old master paintings.[11,12]

The preceding three decades have been characterised by a modest reversal of this trend. A number of prominent museums have curated exhibitions of their key original frames: Munich's 'Italienische Bilderrahmen des 14.–18. Jahrhunderts' in 1976; the Rijkmuseum's 'Prijst de lijst: De hollandse schilderlijst in de zievendiende eeuw' in 1984; the Art Institute of Chicago's 'The Art of the Edge: European Frames 1300–1900' in 1986; the Metropolitan Museum's 'Italian Renaissance Frames' in 1990; Berlin's 'Schoene Rahmen: aus den Bestaenden der Berliner Gemaeldegallerie' in 2003 and Copenhagen's Staten's Museum's 2008 show 'Frames: State of the Art'. The V&A has yet to show its singular collection of Italian Renaissance frames, although some from this volume are exhibited in the Medieval and Renaissance Galleries. This inclusion is welcome, for as Philippe de Montebello noted, Italian Renaissance frames are now appreciably rarer than paintings, sculpture, drawings or any other comparable category of object from the period.[13]

It is the intention of this publication to bring to light a body of significant frames from this Museum's rich collection of Renaissance *objets d'art*. The authors should be commended for their fine documentation of the collection. In so doing, they recall an earlier era of scholarship in the European decorative arts at the Victoria and Albert Museum, one exemplified by Hayward and Thornton in furniture, Rackham in ceramics, Wigfield-Digby in tapestries and textiles, Ward-Jackson and Reynolds in Prints and Drawings and John Pope-Hennessy in sculpture.

References

1. Guggenheim, M. *Le cornici Italiene dalla meta del Secolo XV allo scorcio del XVI*. Milan, 1897.

2. The Museo Bardini at one stage indicated its intention to publish a volume within its series *L'Archivo storico fotografico di Stefano Bardini* on his stock of frames from the fourteenth to the twentieth century. In Everett Fahy's *Dipinti-Disegni-Miniature-Stampe*. Florence, 2000, within that series, the photographic record does include innumerable paintings sold by Bardini within what are evidently either their contemporary or, in a few cases, historicist nineteenth century frames. Ten of the Bardini frames that have remained with their bequest have been catalogued and published by Marilena Mosco: *Antiche Cornici italiane dal Cinquecento al Settecento*. Florence, 1991.

3. Julius von Falke. *Sammlungen des K.und K oesterreichen Museums fuer Kunst und Industrie; Abteilung Rahmen*. Vienna, 1892; Julius Lessing. *Rahmen, Vorbilderhefte aus dem koeniglichen Kunstgewerbe-museum zu Berlin*, Volume 1: *Italienische Renaissance* and Volume 2: *Italien und Deutschland XVI Jahrhundert*. Berlin, 1888. Alexander Schuetz's *Die Renaissance in Italien: Decoration in Holz*. Hamburg, 1882, deals mainly with architectural ornamentation but includes a number of photographs of significant wooden frames of the period. Adalbert Roeper's *Bilder- und Spiegelrahmen von Albrecht Duerer bis zum Rokoko*. Leipzig, 1897, was published in the same year as Guggenheim's volume.

4. Louis Sambon refers to the frames of the Italian sixteenth century '… debordant de sensualité, a librement mis dans des bordures des tableaux tous les motifs de stylisation dont il disposait.' Louis Sambon, *Exposition de cadre ancien*. Paris, 1924. p. 2.

5. Timothy Newberry. *Frames and framing in the Ashmoleum Museum*. Oxford, 2002. p. 16.

6. On the rather thin scholarly or curatorial literature pertaining to the history of frames, see Jacques Foucart. Etude critique de l'encadrement. *Revue de l'Art*, 76, 1987. p. 8.

7. It was the contribution of Burckhardt's pupil, Elfried Bock, in his doctoral dissertation *Florentinische und venezianische Bilderrahmen aus der Zeit der Gotik und der Renaissance*. Munich, 1902, to initiate the collation of attributions of particular frames to particular craftsmen, based in large parts on contemporary records, notably Vasari. What is striking is how little subsequent research has been pursued on this topic, so that many of the names of frame makers from the Quattro- and Cinquecento still hark back to Bock's work: Bartolomeo da Settignano, Giuliano da Sangallo, Baccio d' Agnolo, Jacobo de Faenza, Antonio Barile, Andrea di Pietro, Giacomo and Giuliano del Maiano. See F. Conzen and G. Dietrich. *Bilderrahmen Stil – Verwendung – Material*. Munich, 1983. p. 50.

8. Renato Baldini, et al. *La cornice Fiorentina e Sienese*. Florence, 1992, p. 14. Patrizia Zambrano observes how in the Quattrocento the articulation of a language of tabernacle frames was inseparable – in development and often in person – from the emergence of architecture and sculpture at the highest level; see her essay in Franco Sabatelli. *La cornice italiana dal Rinascimento al Neoclassico*. Milan, 1992. p. 27.

9. Paul Mitchell and Lynn Roberts. *A history of European picture frames*. London, 1996. p. 13.

10. Marilena Mosco has documented the original seventeenth century reframing projects of the Medici in *Cornici dei Medici: La Fantasia Barocca al Servizio del Potere*. Florence, 2007, while Tobias Schmitz's *Analyse und Bewertung gegenwaertiger Rahmungsmassnahmen ausgewaehlter Museen*, PhD Dissertation. Bonn, 2002, touches on the substitution of original frames in the nineteenth century German museum world in particular.

11. A recent analysis of the initial rupture along the lines of purportedly intellectual rather than manual pursuits between painting, sculpture and architecture on the one hand and the other visual arts on the other around the formation of the Accademia del Disegno in 1563 has been provided by Marina Belozerskaya. *Luxury arts of the Renaissance*. Los Angeles, 2005. Chapter 1.

12. The most detailed recapitulation of Bode's programme of reframing the Berlin collection, particularly in the case of the Italian Renaissance paintings, with original frames bought over a number of decades, is presented in his Die Ausstattung der Gemaelde im Kaiser-Friedrich-Museum mit alten Rahmen. In *Amtliche Berichte aus den koeniglichen Kunstsammlungen*, Berlin XXXIII, No. 9, June 1912. Bode published a number of further essays on the topic, of a less programmatic character, conceived rather as contributions to the nascent art historical enquiry on the topic, of which the earliest was his *Bilderrahmen in alter und neuer Zeit*, in Pan, Berlin, 1898.

13. In his Foreword to Timothy Newberry et al., *Italian Renaissance frames*. New York, 1990. p. 8.

INTRODUCTION

The V&A holds an important collection of Italian Renaissance carved, painted and gilded tabernacle, cassetta, Sansovino and tondo frames. Those featured here represent the majority of this collection and date from the mid-fifteenth century through to the end of the sixteenth century. All are of Italian origin with the exception of one thought to be French and one thought to be Flemish. The V&A also has examples of nineteenth century Renaissance style frames, some of which are included for comparative purposes.[1]

The ideal way to build a more complete picture of a frame's origin is to combine art historical knowledge with technical examination. With this in mind, information is provided on the original materials and techniques used to make frames. This is followed by a discussion about how an understanding of deterioration and alteration of frames combined with scientific analysis can be used to inform the process of authentication.

Each of the frames examined has an individual entry, including images of its front and back. Examination of the rear of a frame can reveal construction, hanging devices, alterations, labels and inscriptions. Additional photographic details offer insight into the nature of the surface decoration and emphasise the sculptural and decorative beauty of these frames. Detailed dimensions of all the elements of the frames are included together with profile drawings. The sight size, rebate size and object accommodation size are given, as these may enable a frame to be linked to the object for which it was originally designed.

In each entry, a description of the structure and decoration enables the original appearance of each frame to be described and later additions and alterations to be identified. In some cases, digital reconstruction has been used to give an impression of how the frame would have appeared without alterations. Each entry also contains a description of ornament using terms from architecture and framing nomenclature. The description of ornament helps to navigate around the frame and identify the parts described when discussing the frames, structure and decorative finish. Annotated illustrations of frame types and a glossary are provided to aid the reader.

According to Bisacca and Kanter, 'Very few frames can be independently documented to a time or a place, and fewer still to a particular artist or artisan. Only a small number of surviving frames remain together with the object they originally contained and of these only a fraction are still visible in their original context ... having been removed from the sites they were intended to embellish'.[2] Most of the frames in this volume were acquired by the Museum in the nineteenth century. The majority were acquired empty as decorative art objects in their own right, a few came with original sculptural reliefs and some came with paintings and reliefs that were not original to the frames. Since acquisition, some non-original objects have been removed from the frames with which they were acquired.

It is hoped that this volume will facilitate the comparison of frames from public and private collections with those at the V&A. Recognition of similarities of style, material and technical characteristics may allow more detailed attribution of the frames. The images, illustrations and the descriptions of finish and structure of the frames in this publication will add to the broader knowledge and understanding of the subject and will assist curators, collectors, conservators and frame makers.

References

1. Information on frames at the V&A can be found at www.vam.ac.uk
2. Bisacca, G. & Kanter, L. *Introduction to Italian Renaissance frames.* Exhibition Catalogue. New York: Metropolitan Museum, 1990. p. 30.

PART I
RENAISSANCE MATERIALS AND TECHNIQUES

A BRIEF BACKGROUND TO RENAISSANCE FRAMES

The widespread demand for both religious and secular images during the fifteenth and sixteenth centuries resulted in a growing market for frames to house them. Painted or sculpted images of Christ, the Virgin and saints adorned every altar, and both traditional and new forms of altarpiece required framing solutions. Christian imagery was also not just confined to the church, but was found in a variety of public and more intimate settings. For example the small relief with Eve on the base, that was originally part of a triptych Frame 9 (6867-1860), probably belonged to a woman who would have used it in her devotional practice at home or perhaps when travelling. In addition to prompting devotion, such images often carried talismanic associations. In fifteenth century Florence, for instance, Fra Dominici suggested that an image of the Virgin and Child should be kept in every bedchamber as an example. Virgin and Childs were also set up on street corners as neighbourhood protectors.[1]

These Madonnas often took the form of sculptural reliefs made of terracotta (fired clay) or stucco (a type plaster), which were then painted and gilded to create colourful and naturalistic images see Frame 4 (57:2-1867) and 7 (93-1882). One of the advantages of these materials, which were cheaper than stone or marble, was their malleability, allowing them to be cast in moulds to produce replicas of the same scene. Although little is known about workshop practice, it is clear that such reliefs were reproduced widely: a vast number of Virgin and Childs survive, testifying to their popularity and significance. Five frames in this volume still contain what appear to be their original sculptures.

Tabernacle frames were used to house many of these religious subjects. Sansovino, tondo and cassetta frames were also used in this way, but equally housed secular images, such as the portraits and mythological scenes that increasingly decorated public buildings and the homes of the nobility and growing merchant classes.

Although many of these sculptures or pictures and their frames were commissioned, Renaissance artists also produced a stock of uncommissioned works to sell.[2] It is also possible that they kept a supply of the separate elements needed to make the frames, such as lengths of uncarved mouldings and a selection of moulds for ornamental cast work.

Research has suggested a close relationship between painters and wood workers.[3] They were employed to produce or decorate a range of images and objects, from altarpieces and portraits to candlesticks and furniture.[4] Thus comparisons can be drawn between the materials, techniques and practice used in the fabrication of altarpieces, panel paintings, furniture and related objects of the time and those used on frames.[5]

References

1. Currie, S. & Motture, P. *The Sculpted Object 1400-1700*. Aldershot: Scholar Press, 1997. pp. 1–24.
2. Dunkerton, J., Foister, S., Gordon, D. & Penny, N. *Giotto to Dürer: Early Renaissance Painting in the National Gallery*. London: National Gallery, 1991. p. 128.
3. Gilbert, C. Peintres et menuisiers au debut de la Renaissance en Italie. *Revue de l'Art*, 37, 1977. pp. 9–28; Newbery, T., Bisacca, G. & Kanter, L. *Italian Renaissance Frames Exhibition Catalogue*. New York: Metropolitan Museum, 1990. Dunkerton et al., op cit. pp. 122–141.
4. Dunkerton et al., ibid. p. 122.
5. Thanks to Peta Motture for her valuable contributed to this section.

WOOD

Definitive identification of wood usually requires microscopic identification of anatomical features and typically requires a cubic centimetre of sample to be removed from the object.[1] Such interventive sampling was considered inappropriate for this project, particularly for the smaller frames. Identification of the hardwoods listed in the frame entries was therefore based on visual examination of gross anatomical characteristics.[2] Accretions or coatings often obscure the characteristics required for identification and limit the accuracy of visual identification. Softwoods, for example pine and spruce, are relatively easy to distinguish from hardwoods but cannot reliably be distinguished from each other without microscopic identification. Whereas walnut and oak have distinctive characteristics that are visible to the naked eye, lime and poplar can be difficult to distinguish from each other by eye alone. In some instances, both woods are suggested in the frame entry, with the most probable wood listed first.

Woods used by Italian Renaissance frame makers and craftsmen are discussed elsewhere.[3] Mitchell suggested that the identification of species of wood used in frames can, as for furniture, be an important guide to a likely region of origin. Analysis of woods in seventy Italian frames in a 1976 exhibition suggested that Venetian frames were generally made of pine or fir with fir backs. Florentine frames generally had walnut for carved mouldings, as well as poplar and lime, with poplar or pine back frames, whereas in Bologna and Naples poplar was normally used.[4] Woods found on the V&A frames include the following softwoods and hardwoods.

Softwoods

Found on the back of several frames, softwoods have distinctive early and late-season growth rings that produce alternating soft pale and harder dark stripes in the wood.

Hardwoods

Poplar (*Populus* spp.) is a creamy white to pale brown, medium-density and comparatively lightweight timber. It is straight grained with a fine uniform texture. Poplar was an abundant, relatively cheap wood in Italy. Its texture made it a suitable substrate for painted and gilded decoration. White poplar (*Populus alba*), which grew to a size from which large planks could be obtained, was the wood most commonly used for panel paintings.[5] Poplar was observed on many of the frames and was used for structural work, simple mouldings or carving.

European lime (*Tilia* spp., principally *T. vulgaris*) is a pale yellow wood that turns light brown on exposure to light. It is soft and has a fine uniform texture that makes it an excellent wood for carving detailed and delicate work. Lime was observed on the more intricately carved parts and front mouldings on some of the frames.

European walnut (*Juglans regia*) is a chocolate to grey–pink brown medium-density timber, in which dark streaks and patches are often observed. The sapwood is pale in contrast to the heartwood, which fades when exposed to sunlight. Walnut has visible growth rings and a medium texture. Italian walnut is paler than English. Walnut was valued for its rich colour and was generally used where its appearance could be seen and appreciated. It is good for carving and was often partially gilded, as seen on Frames 20 (7694-1861) and 23 (682-1883).

Fruit woods, such as pear or plum, were sometimes substituted for walnut, either because their particular colour and texture were preferred or simply because they were more readily available.[6]

Pear (*Pyrus communis*) is typically a pinkish-brown colour with a straight grain and a fine, even texture. Pear was thought to have been used for the finer detailed carving on Frame 10 (1079–1884).

European oak (*Quercus robur, Q. pedunculata, Q. petraea, Q. sessiliflora*) is yellowish-brown, with light coloured sapwood. It darkens with age. It is generally straight grained but varies with growth conditions. It has a characteristic coarse grain, and distinct growth rings with alternating zones of open-pored early wood and dense late wood. Distinctive broad silvery rays are present in quarter-sawn material. Oak is very rarely encountered in Italian frames. The two frames made of oak are thought to be French (Frame 12, 649-1890) and Flemish (Frame 27, 1605-1855), partly for this reason.

Tools

Renaissance craftsmen had an extensive range of woodworking tools, similar to those found in specialist carving, framing or cabinet-making workshops today. Olga and Wilmering provide a detailed account of woodworking tools used in Renaissance Italy.[7]

Wood Finishes

Oils, varnishes and stains were in use in the sixteenth century to adjust tone, to enhance colour or to give a shiny or matt finish to wood. Juniper resin, walnut and linseed oil have been mentioned as ingredients for varnishes.[8] Original wood finishes can be difficult to distinguish from varnishes and waxes applied during later repairs and restorations.

Wood had been left deliberately exposed on Frames 20 (7694-1861) and 23 (682-1883), which are sixteenth century partially gilt walnut. A stain, wax or varnish may have been applied to enhance the colour of the wood on these frames.

References

1. Hoadley, B. *Identifying wood*. Newtown, CT: Taunton Press, 1990.
2. Thanks to Dick Onians and Dr Adam Bowett.
3. Olga, R. and Wilmering, A. *The Gubbio Studiolo and its conservation*. New York: Metropolitan Museum of Art, 2001. pp. 3–26; Mitchell, P. Italian picture frames, 1500–1825: a brief survey. *Journal of the Furniture History Society*, 20, 1984. p. 20; Bomford, D., Dunkerton, J., Gordon, D. and Roy, A. *Art in the making: Italian painting before 1400*. Exhibition Catalogue. London: National Gallery, 1992. pp. 11–13.
4. Mitchell, P. Italian picture frames, 1500–1825: a brief survey. *Journal of the Furniture History Society*, 20, 1984. p. 20.
5. Dunkerton, J., Foister, S., Gordon, D. and Penny, N. *Giotto to Dürer: early Renaissance painting in the National Gallery*. London: National Gallery, 1991. p. 152.
6. Newbery, T., Bisacca, G. and Kanter, L. *Italian Renaissance frames*. Exhibition Catalogue. New York: Metropolitan Museum, 1990. p. 28.
7. See Olga, R. and Wilmering, A. *The Gubbio Studiolo and its conservation*. New York: Metropolitan Museum of Art, 2001. pp. 43–59. This section is rich with illustrations of tools and their use.
8. Ibid. pp. 40–42.

METHODS OF CONSTRUCTION

Most Italian tabernacle, Sansovino and cassetta frames were made of a joined back frame that formed a rigid structure onto which the decorative elements, for convenience called the front frame, were applied. The back frame usually consisted of four wooden members, two vertical sides and a horizontal top and bottom. The wood used for the back frames was smoothed flat, although not highly finished. The back frames utilised simple joints such as the corner bridle or T-bridle joint, which were sometimes pegged through (*cavicchio*). Alternatively, a lap or halved joint (*mezza pialla*) was used.[1] The keyed dovetail half lap was also found. Larger parts of the decorative fronts of the frames were usually butted up to each other and fixed on to the back frame with glue and nails. Butt mitre joints were used for the corners of the sight mouldings.

Mouldings

The sight edge mouldings, whether integral or applied, were mitred at the corners. Other running mouldings, for example the cornice moulding applied to an entablature, were shaped in lengths, cut to size, mitred to fit the frame and then fixed with glue and nails.

The profiles of the moulding most commonly found on the frames were:

- Astragal: a small semicircular moulding, sometimes ornamented by bead or reel
- Cavetto: a concave moulding of more or less quarter round profile
- Cyma recta, or ogee: a moulding of S-shaped profile, concave over convex
- Cyma reversa, or reverse ogee: a moulding of S-shaped profile, convex over concave
- Fillet: a small, flat component, rectangular in section, separating one moulding from another

- Ovolo: a convex elliptical or quarter round moulding
- Quirk: a small channel or recess between mouldings
- Torus: a large convex moulding, sometimes called a round, generally used in column bases.

Tabernacle Frames

In most cases, regardless of size, the front frames of the tabernacle frames were constructed following architectural models, with separate parts for pediment, entablature, capitals, columns or pilasters, plinth and predella. Imposts and pedestals were often made from additional pieces of wood with vertical grain, as opposed to the horizontal grain direction of the main parts of the entablature and predella to which they were fixed. Running mouldings, and the frieze relief could be integral or applied and were often mitred at the corners. In contrast to this model, Frame 11 (7820-1861) utilised half lap joints and did not have a back frame.

Sansovino Frames

The front frames of the Sansovino frames were generally made up of four main pieces. Like the tabernacle frames from which they were loosely architecturally and structurally derived, the sides were butted between the top and bottom pieces, relying on the joined back frame to which they were attached for stability. The corner-mitred sight edge moulding was integral or applied.

Most of the Sansovino and tabernacle frames used a single depth of wood for the main parts of the carved front frame. Where this was not the case, additional wood was added to create a thicker dimension. Smaller pieces of wood were often

5

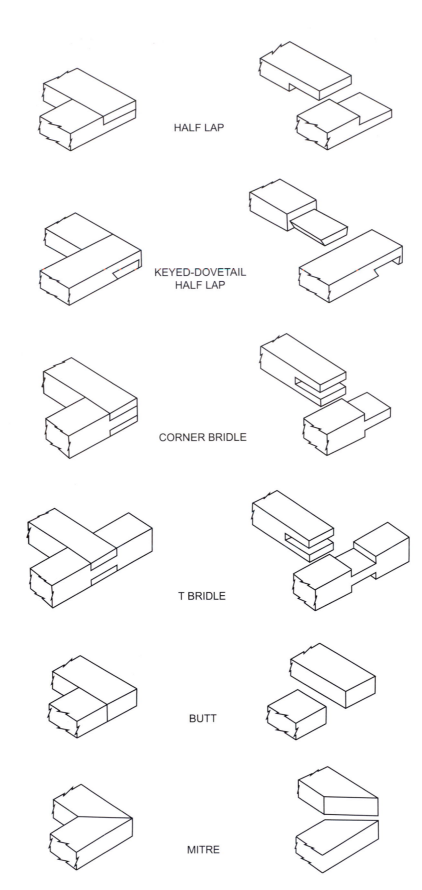

HALF LAP

KEYED-DOVETAIL
HALF LAP

CORNER BRIDLE

T BRIDLE

BUTT

MITRE

Some joints found on Renaissance frames.

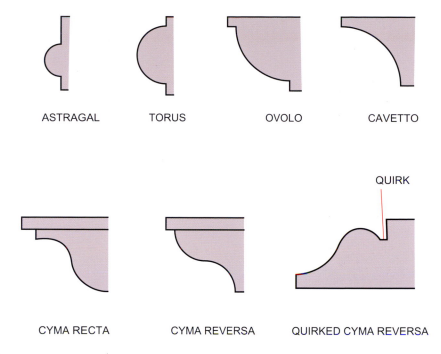

ASTRAGAL	TORUS	OVOLO	CAVETTO

QUIRK

CYMA RECTA	CYMA REVERSA	QUIRKED CYMA REVERSA

Some mouldings found on the V&A Renaissance frames.

added (nailed and probably glued) to give extra height or width for the carved work or for the higher relief parts of the carving, for example protruding masks or festoons.

Cassetta Frames

These utilised half lapped back frames with mouldings added at the front and sides. The more richly carved examples had additional frieze, decorative corners and centres inset or applied.

Tondo Frames

The large tondo frame 14 (76-1892) was made from several pieces that appeared to have been butt jointed. Mouldings were added at the front and sides, with additional wood for the carved frieze and paterae. The small tondo frames 19 (10-1890) and 20 (7694-1861) were turned on a lathe, and were decorated with carved or pastiglia ornament. Of the two round mirror frames, one had stucco applied on to a wooden frame (Frame 18, 5887-1859) and the other was made from carta pesta (Frame 17, 850-1884).

Reference

1. Joyce, E. *The technique of furniture making*. London: B.T. Batsford, 1987. pp. 158–159.

CARVING (INTAGLIO)

Carving the Parts

Running mouldings were often enriched with carving, such as egg and dart or other repeating ornament. The positioning of the ornament was tailored to fit the lengths used so that one element of the carved ornament completed the design. At a corner mitre, for example, the sculptural surface was continuous, with one element of the running ornament, such as an egg or a dentil, with the join through its centre. Alternatively, a separate motif was carved on each end of the length of the running moulding to complete the design at the corner. However, on entablature and predella it is quite common to see the frieze decoration end in the middle of a decorative element.

Order of Carving and Assembly

It is probable that in most cases, the components of the front frames of tabernacle and Sansovino frames were carved before being fixed to the back frame. This can be deduced by examining the carved festoons on the Sansovino frames. On Frame 24 (765:2-1865), gaining access to carve the underside of the festoons would have been very difficult once they were assembled. Finishing touches were added once the parts had been fixed to the back frame. Occasionally, evidence suggests a different approach. The continuity of the surface between the two pieces of wood forming the hippocampus and leaf detail on the restello frame (21, 7150-1860), for example, suggests that these were carved after assembly.

Frieze decoration, such as scrolling leaves, was generally carved together with the background from one piece of wood. Only on Frames 2 (594-1869) and 33 (4242:1-1857) was the decorative relief carved separately and then applied on to the flat background. In this process, it is likely that a thin piece of wood was glued or nailed to paper on a piece of sacrificial wood and then carved. The carved relief was then removed and applied to the flat background of the frame.

Generally the carving on the frames was well finished, though not crisp, even for pieces that were painted and gilded. The carving on most of the frames displays a bold yet soft fluidity, undulating and unconstrained. The carving on sophisticated examples, such as cassetta Frame 13 (7816-1862), is fine in execution and intricacy, yet retains fluidity and confidence, the product of experienced craftsmen. Carving relief decoration was more time consuming and skilful than making simple running mouldings, so increased the cost of an object.

Modern carving tools: wooden mallet and gouges with different profiles.

Glues

Olga and Wilmering refer to the use of casein glue and animal glue in Renaissance Italy.[1] Casein glue was made from cheese and quick lime. It allowed a longer assembly time but tended to discolour the wood. Animal glue was produced from skin, bones and sinew. It was applied hot, gelled quickly, had high tack and did not discolour the wood. There is no clear evidence of the type of glue used on many of the frames. Some exposed joints show glue, but it is not clear whether it was original or had been applied during later repairs.

Wrought Nails

Wrought iron nails *(chiodi)* were often found securing joints on the frames. These nails are faceted along the shank rather than the round or oval shape associated with modern drawn nails. The majority of the nails observed were small (~3 mm) and medium (~5 mm) sized with rectangular heads. Occasionally larger circular facet-headed nails, approximately 10 mm in diameter, were observed. Similar nails have been observed on Italian Renaissance cassoni at the V&A.[2]

On the frames, the nails were commonly driven from the front through into the back frame. Their angular heads are usually concealed under the painting and gilding, but they can be seen where they have come loose or where they have rusted and caused loss of the overlying finish.

Hanging Fittings

Wrought iron crossover hanging loops were found on many of the frames, fixed to the back of the frame with wrought nails. Another common hanging device consisted of two holes drilled diagonally from the back top centre of the back frame and emerging on the top edge. These holes presumably allowed ribbon, cord or perhaps metal fittings to be passed through the frame.

References

1. Olga, R. and Wilmering, A. *The Gubbio Studiolo and its conservation*. New York: Metropolitan Museum of Art, 2001. pp. 38–40.
2. For example cassone 8974–1863, Tuscany, c.1430–1460.

GILDING

Introduction

Gold leaf may be applied using water, oil or mordant gilding. These processes use distinct methods of preparation and application that result in surfaces with differing qualities and appearance. In the case of Italian fifteenth and sixteenth century gilding on wood, water gilding was used for larger areas, while oil gilding was used for specific decorative elements, such as spots or line drawn patterns. Frames were assembled before being painted or gilded. Both the frame and the framed object were often coated with a continuous white ground layer, painted, gilded and given the same punch work decoration.[1] This continuity was observed on Frames 6 (A.45-1926) and 7 (93-1882).

Cennino d'Andrea Cennini's *Il libro dell' arte* (*The craftsman's handbook*), written c.1390, provides invaluable historical insight and informs research into the materials and techniques of early Italian painting and gilding.[2] The workshop inventory of the Sienese painter Neroccio De' Landi (1445–1500) includes a gilder's cushion, several burnishers and other related tools and equipment.[3] These sources provide evidence that gilding tools and processes have changed relatively little since the Renaissance.

Some gilders' materials: 1. Parchment glue size with a hog hair brush. 2. Wet parchment clippings. 3. Dry parchment clippings. 4. Powdered gypsum in glue size and hog hair brush. 5. Powdered gypsum. 6. Powdered yellow ochre in glue size with hog hair brush. 7. Powdered yellow ochre. 8. Red bole in glue size with squirrel hair mop. 9. Powdered Armenian bole. 10. Cone and lump of bole.

Modern gilders' tools: 1. Gilder's tip made from long soft hairs such as squirrel, glued between two pieces of card. 2. Gilder's cushion, with a gold leaf laid flat on the cushion and a gold leaf crumpled at the back of the cushion. In front are leaves of gold in a tissue book. 3. A metal punch and two burnishers made of agate stone, set in metal ferrules on a wooden handles. 4. Gilder's brush or mop, made with soft hair such as squirrel, and gilder's knife, with a smooth fine edge blade, but no sharp edge.

Water Gilding

Water gilding is used to apply gold leaf on to wood. The wood is coated with glue size, followed by a white ground, then bole (often orange–red) to which gold leaf is applied. The gold leaf can then be burnished to a high shine.

Sample of water-gilded wood, showing the preparation layers. Left to right: wood covered with glue size, white ground, red bole, gold leaf, burnished gold leaf, artificially aged gold leaf.

Glue size (*Colle animale*)

Cennini wrote that the glue was made from the neck parts of goat and sheep parchment, which were soaked in water and then boiled. He also described the application of strips of linen soaked in glue size over the joints and knots in the woodwork. It has been suggested that this stage began to be omitted during the fifteenth century.[4] Linen was not observed on any of the frames described in this book.

The ground (*Il gesso*)

The ground was used to fill the wood grain and provide a smooth foundation for subsequent layers. Gypsum and/or chalk were added to warmed animal glue. Clay either could be naturally present in gypsum or chalk or was sometimes added to impart smoothness and hardness to a ground. Pigments, ashes or charcoal could also be added. The warmed mixture was then applied to the sized wood.

Gesso is the Italian name for both gypsum (calcium sulphate) and the white ground found underneath painting and gilding on wood. Gypsum in its raw form is dihydrate of calcium sulphate ($CaSO_4 \cdot 2H_2O$). The white ground may consist of a coarse layer (gesso grosso) followed by a fine layer (gesso sottile), or the fine layer alone.

According to Cennini, gesso grosso was 'coarse plaster of "Volterra" reduced to powder, sifted and then mulled on a slab with the warmed glue size. The gesso grosso was applied to the wood with a knife or bristle brush. Application of a finer ground, gesso sottile, followed'.[5] In his translation of Cennini, Thompson likens coarse plaster of Volterra to plaster of Paris. Mactaggart, however, comments that the use of plaster of Paris grounds has not been supported by analysis and it seems likely that Cennini's gesso grosso was in fact a builder's plaster (anhydrous calcium sulphate, $CaSO_4$).[6]

Gesso sottile was made from coarse plaster that had been soaked ('slaked') in water for several days. The mixture was stirred from time to time to prevent it from setting. After further processing, which is described by Cennini, this was mixed with warm glue. If applied over gesso grosso, the sottile glue mixture was weaker (slightly more dilute) than that used for the underlying layer. If applied on top of gesso grosso, the first coat of sottile could be applied with a hog's hair brush, although Cennini advised the use of fingers. Thereafter it was applied with a hog's hair brush in several coats, each applied while the previous coat was still somewhat damp.[7]

Once fully dry, the white ground could be smoothed with scrapers, metal hooks (*raschietti*) and damp linen rags. Italian Renaissance carved and gilded work is characterised by a general softness about the form, with few hard edges. The sculptural form of Italian frames is largely created in the carved wood, with the white ground softening the form. Although there is generally little obvious carving of the white ground to redefine the form, some more intricately carved examples, such as Frame 14 (76-1892), suggest that carving of the white ground layer may have been used to achieve finer definition.

Gypsum occurs most frequently in the white grounds of paintings and gilding from Italy, Spain and the south of France. Analysis of the grounds of fourteenth century Tuscan panel paintings at the National Gallery identified the presence of both gesso grosso and gesso sottile layers. The grounds of fifteenth century paintings in Florence and Siena tended to consist of the anhydrate form of calcium sulphate (builder's plaster). North of the Apennines, particularly in Venice and Ferrara, the gesso was nearly always of the dihydrate form, suggesting that either gesso sottile or raw gypsum was used.[8] Analysis of the white grounds on the frames in this book identified gypsum, or a mixture of gypsum and chalk.

Chalk (calcium carbonate, $CaCO_3$) has been used in the grounds of paintings and gilded artefacts throughout Europe, including Italy. However, it is more commonly found in northern European countries and is the typical component of the ground layer found in English gilding. 'Gesso' has been adopted as a generic term in English for the white ground for gilding, whether it is made from gypsum, chalk or other materials. To avoid confusion in terminology, the term white ground will be used in this book.

Bole (*Bollo*)

Bole is predominantly made of clay. Its colour can be a result of naturally occurring iron oxides or the deliberate addition of pigments. Colour can range from the yellows, oranges, browns and reds of natural iron oxides, to pink, purple, blue, green, grey, black or white. The colour of the bole affects the tone of the gilding. Gold leaf can look slightly green if laid over white bole, while red bole will impart a warm tone. Gold leaf takes on the texture of the surface to which it is applied, so the choice of a matt (pigment rich) or shiny (clay rich) bole will affect the final appearance. The clay in the bole enables the gold leaf to be burnished.

Bole was applied over the white ground before the application of the gold leaf. The bole was ground in water and the resulting paste mixed with animal glue or glair (whipped egg white left to stand and liquefy, then diluted with water) as the binding medium. The bole could be applied with a soft brush or sponge and once dry, could be polished smooth.

Italian Renaissance frames often have quite a bright orange–red bole. The boles most frequently used on the original gilding on the frames examined in this book were shades of orange, red and red–brown.

Gold leaf (*l'oro*)

Painters were usually contracted to use pure gold. The leaf was manufactured from coinage, for example the gold Florentine florin, that was beaten with hammers, cut, trimmed and beaten again until the required thin leaf was obtained.[9] It is interesting to note that gold beaters were part of the same guild as painters.[10] Cennini discusses how many leaves of gold leaf should be obtained from a ducat (gold coin) for different uses in gilding.[11] Italian Renaissance gold leaf was thicker than that used today. Alloying gold with silver or copper altered the colour of the leaf. Contracts for gilding and painting work sometimes specified that gold alloys, silver or even tin leaf were to be used for minor parts of the painting and the frame.[12] The gold leaf observed on the majority of the frames discussed in this book was of consistently good quality and in some cases, clearly thicker than modern leaf.

Laying gold leaf for water gilding

Before applying the gold leaf, an area of bole was first brushed with water containing a little glair or animal glue size. Cennini instructed that the gold leaf was to be picked up with tweezers, transferred to a sheet of parchment and then slid on to the wetted bole. The water was absorbed into the ground, reactivating the layer of glair or size to which the gold leaf adhered. The next leaf was laid slightly overlapping the previous one. Pieces of cut gold leaf were used to patch minor imperfections in the gilding.

Burnishing (*brunitura*)

Water gilding can be burnished so that the gold surface, in its entirely or in selected areas, takes on a highly reflective shine. Early Italian gilding was extensively and highly burnished. Cennini mentions the use of haematite, sapphires, emeralds, balas rubies, topazes, rubies and garnets or 'teeth from any flesh eating animal' for burnishing.[13] The burnisher needed to be perfectly smooth and was used before the preparation layers below the gold were completely dry.

Punch work (*punzonatura, bulinatura*)

Metal punches were used to indent or punch decoration into the gilded surface. This type of decoration appears on several of the frames, for example the background to the candelabrum decoration on Frame 8 (5893-1859).

Oil or Mordant Gilding

Oil gilding derives its name from the use of an oil-based adhesive. In gilding terminology, mordant refers to any material that has adhesive properties. Cennini referred to the use of varnish, linseed oil with the addition of lead white, or garlic juice with lead white and a little bole.[14] Oil or mordant gilding can be applied to any substrate provided that the surface is non-porous or has been coated to make it non-porous. Mordant gilding can sometimes be recognised by the texture of brush strokes or runs in the mordant.

The oil size or mordant, which could be coloured with pigment, was applied to the area to be gilded. It could be a thin layer or bulked with fillers or pigments to create raised patterns. The gold leaf adhered only to the mordant and thus allowed very fine decoration to be applied to selected areas. Oil gilding usually has an even, matt finish. It should not be assumed, however, that all oil gilding was matt as it could be bright and reflective if the ground prepared for it was smooth and glossy. The longer the drying time of the mordant, the more reflective the finish produced, although the greater the risk that particles of dust would become attached to the mordant and affect the texture of the gilded surface.

Shell gold/powdered gold

Powdered gold can be mixed with a binder such as gum arabic to make a gold paint. The name shell gold derived from the practice of using and storing the paint in shells. Shell gold has a fine granular texture and appears quite dull. It was applied with a brush, usually only for areas of fine decoration.

Partial gilding (*luminolegno*)

While most of the frames described in this book were fully gilded, some, mainly made from walnut, were partially gilded. On these frames, selected ornament was highlighted with water or mordant gilding. Frame 23 (682-1883) utilised both types of gilding. Fine gilded detail was used on Frame 22 (535:A-1870) to create an impression of carved ornament, for example fluting in the cornice.

Coatings

Gilding could be decorated with varnish or transparent coloured finishes. Analysis of some of the frames showed the presence of lakes that may have imparted colour to glazes, for example the red lake on Frame 8 (5893-1859). Gilding could also be coated with transparent materials, such as glair or glue size, to protect the surface or modify its appearance.

References

1. Dunkerton, J., Foister, S., Gordon, D. and Penny, N. *Giotto to Dürer: early Renaissance painting in the National Gallery.* London: National Gallery, 1991. p. 174.
2. Cennini, Cennino d'Andrea *The craftsman's handbook, 'Il libro dell' arte'.* c.1390. Thompson, D. V. (trans.), 1960: Dover Publications. New York; Bomford, D., Dunkerton, J., Gordon, D. and Roy, A. *Art in the making: Italian painting before 1400.* Exhibition Catalogue, London: National Gallery, 1992. Dunkerton et al., ibid.
3. Dunkerton et al., op. cit. p. 141.
4. Dunkerton et al., op. cit. p. 163.
5. Cennini, op. cit. pp. 70–71.
6. Mactaggart, P. and Mactaggart, A. *A pigment microscopists's notebook.* 7th rev. Somerset: unpublished paper by the authors, 1998. p. 43.
7. Cennini, op. cit. pp. 70–73.
8. Dunkerton et al., op. cit. p. 163.
9. Bomford et al., op. cit. p. 22.
10. Dunkerton et al., op. cit. p. 174.
11. Cennini, op. cit. pp. 84–85.
12. Dunkerton et al., op. cit. pp. 131 and 175.
13. Cennini et al., op. cit. p. 82.
14. Cennini et al., op. cit. pp. 96–97.

CAST WORK

Low relief cast ornament, often with intricate designs, was frequently applied to Renaissance objects including caskets, cassone and frames. It had a different character to carved work but was quicker and cheaper to produce. Cast work was left plain or coated with white ground and then painted and/or gilded.

Pastiglia

Pastiglia was made by mixing a powdered bulking material such as chalk, gypsum or lead white with a binder such as animal glue or egg white to make a malleable paste. This was cast in moulds, removed, trimmed as required and then attached to the surface of the object. Analysis of pastiglia found on Frames 10 (1079-1884), 16 (11-1890) and 19 (10-1890) showed that the cast work on all three frames contained similar materials.

The presence of straight cracks crossing the length of the ornament is usually indicative of joins between lengths of applied cast decoration. If joins are found at regular intervals in the design, this can indicate the repeat length of the mould from which the ornament was cast. The lines of the join may not appear perfectly straight, as a result of ageing cracks in the gilded or painted finish, but the lines of such joins should be distinctly straighter than other ageing cracks in the decorative finish or cast work. Joins between the lengths of applied casting can be seen on Frames 16

(11-1890) and 19 (10-1890). These lines help to distinguish pastiglia from aggetti.

The term 'aggetti' has been used to describe the 'low relief designs [that] were made by freehand brush application of a heavy gesso before gilding'.[1] According to Cennini, raised work applied with a brush was made from gesso sottile.[2] The term pastiglia is commonly used to describe aggetti work, although the techniques are very different.

Carta Pesta

Carta pesta, also known as papier mâché, is a general term used to describe crushed paper mixed with glue or glued paper applied in layers in a mould. Frame 17 (850-1884) was made from carta pesta.

Stucco

Stucco describes a slow-setting gypsum plaster mixed with sand, slaked lime and other substances. Different mixtures have different uses. It was used for internal and external decorative architectural work and for sculpture. Frame 18 (5887-1859) incorporates stucco decoration.

References

1. Brettel, R. and Starling, S. *The art of edge: European frames 1300–1900*. Exhibition Catalogue. Chicago, IL: Art Institute of Chicago, 1986. p. 30.
2. Cennini, Cennino d'Andrea, *The craftsman's handbook, 'Il libro dell' arte', c.1390*. Thompson, D. V. (trans.). New York: Dover Publications, 1960. p. 76.

PAINTED DECORATION

Techniques

Decorative paintwork was found on several of the frames. Painted decoration was often used in combination with gilding, in roughly equal proportion. Paint could be applied over the same ground as the gilding, over the bole or over the gilding. This last technique was identified on smaller frames, where the small amount of gold saved by avoiding gilding the areas that were to be painted did not justify the extra time involved.

Although Sansovino frames are commonly gilded or partially gilded against show wood, painted decoration has been found on some Sansovino frames, such as an Italian sixteenth century frame painted green in recessed areas[1] and those with painted cherubs or caryatid figures.[2]

Trompe l'oeil

Trompe l'oeil is a painting technique used to give the impression of three-dimensional decoration, such as carving, on a flat surface. Black paint can be used to indicate recessed areas, with washes of grey skilfully applied to imitate the depth of carved relief. Frames 5 (5768:2-1859) and 11 (7820-1861) were decorated with trompe l'oeil decoration.

Marbling

Marbling describes the painted imitation of the veined or mottled appearance of marble or stone and is common on sixteenth century frames and altarpieces.[3]

Imitation porphyry was observed on the back edge of Frame 3 (19-1891) and possibly on the sloping floor area of Frame 8 (5893-1859).

Sgrafitto (*Il graffito*)

In this technique, paint was applied over burnished water gilding. When this had nearly dried, a softly pointed stylus, made of material such as bone, was used to scrape a decorative pattern through the paint to reveal the gold. Sgrafitto work was seen on Frame 4 (57:2-1867), on the antependium of Frame 3 (19-1891), on the pedestal return of Frame 5 (5768:2-1859) and on the frieze of Frame 9 (6867-1860).

Binding Media

On Renaissance Italian polychrome sculpture and paintings, egg tempera was prepared by grinding pigments in water and then adding about an equal measure of egg yolk. The paint dried to a velvety sheen. Binding media analysis of a sample taken from the sgrafitto work on Frame 9 (6867-1860) identified the presence of an egg-based binder.

Alternatively, pigments ground in water could be mixed with glue size. Although not as common the use of oil as a binder is mentioned by Cennino Cennini[4]

Pigments

The following is a list of pigments in use in the Renaissance that were identified on the frames. These pigments have also been identified on other examples of painted Italian sixteenth century frames.[5]

Azurite (basic carbonate of copper, $2CuCO_3 \cdot Cu(OH)_2$)

Azurite was used in Italy and northern Europe between the fourteenth and seventeenth centuries and was seldom used in Europe after the middle of the seventeenth century. It was the most common blue identified on the frames described in this book. Azurite was an expensive pigment.

Coarsely ground, it produces a bright blue, while finely ground azurite is lighter in tone. The large particle size and consequent low covering power of azurite meant that several layers were necessary to produce a saturated blue when it was applied over a white ground. It was therefore often applied over a coloured underpaint both to enhance the colour and to reduce cost. A coloured layer under azurite was found on several of the frames, including Frame 2 (594-1869). This practice is consistent with the use of azurite on panel paintings and polychrome sculpture.[6]

Carbon black, charcoal, ivory and bone black

Carbon black is known by a variety of names that reflect the traditional method for producing a particular pigment. Charcoal was made by burning wood with a very restricted air supply. Even-grained woods such as beech and willow were used, as well as other organic materials such as peach stones or almond shells. Charcoal could be ground to form carbon black, which was used in oil or watercolour media. Vine prunings were used to produce vine black. Ivory and bone black were made from charred ivory and animal bones.

Earth pigments

Earth pigments have been used since prehistoric times. The iron oxides present in naturally occurring minerals produce a range of yellow, red and brown colours. Pigments found on the frames include yellow ochre (hydrated iron oxide, $Fe_2O_3 \cdot H_2O$, plus a range of mineral impurities) and red ochre (anhydrous ferric oxide, Fe_2O_3, plus a range of mineral impurities), also known as terra rossa. Boles used for gilding were coloured by iron oxide, although the proportion of clay-like minerals exceeded the iron oxide content. Earth pigments are often named after their geographical region of origin.

Indigo

Indigo, a blue pigment, was obtained from a wide range of plants. India and the near East were the main sources of indigo in Renaissance Italy. Indigo was produced from the shrub *Indigofera tinctoria* and imported into Europe in the form of dry cakes. An inferior pigment could be extracted from woad (*Isatis tinctoria*). Indigo was observed in the underlayer for azurite on Frame 3 (19-1891). The use of indigo in the underpaint below azurite is consistent with other works of this period.[7]

Lead white (basic lead (II) carbonate, $2Pb(CO_3)_2 \cdot Pb(OH)_2$)

Lead white has been produced since antiquity by exposing metallic lead to vinegar.

Malachite (basic copper (II) carbonate, $2CuCO_3 \cdot Cu(OH)_2$)

Malachite is a mineral usually associated with azurite. Coarsely ground, it produces a bright green pigment, whereas finely ground, it produces a paler green. Malachite has been in use since Egyptian times. Particles of malachite were found mixed with azurite on some of the frames, for example Frame 3 (19-1891).

Orpiment (arsenic sulfide, As_2S_3)

Orpiment is a naturally occurring yellow mineral prepared as a pigment by grinding or levigation. It is highly toxic owing to the presence of arsenic and has been found on objects and paintings for over 2000 years.

Red lakes

Lakes are dyestuffs precipitated on to a colourless base material with a low refractive index. Lakes are translucent and often used to colour glazes. The natural red dyes that have been used in this manner include madder, kermes, lac, carmine. Red lake was identified on Frame 8 (5893-1859).

Smalt (K Co (Al) silicate (glass))

Smalt was made by roasting a cobalt-containing mineral to form cobalt oxide, CoO, and adding this to molten glass. The glass was ground to form the blue pigment. Smalt has been in use in Europe since the fifteenth century and it has been identified on a number of sixteenth century objects.[8] Smalt was identified in the original blue layer on Frame 8 (5893-1859).

Vermilion (mercuric sulfide, HgS)

Vermilion is found naturally in the form of the mineral cinnabar, the principal ore of mercury. It can be crushed and used directly as a red pigment and has been used since Egyptian times in this manner. The dry process of combining mercury

and sulphur to form artificial cinnabar was known by the eighth century AD.

References

1. This frame is pictured in Penny, N. *Frames*. National Gallery Pocket Guides. London: National Gallery, 1997. Plates 56 and 57.

2. See Mitchell, P. and Roberts, L. *Frameworks*. London: Merrell Holberton Publishers, 1996. p. 63; Newbery, T. *Frames in the Robert Lehman Collection*. Princeton, NJ: Metropolitan Museum of Art in association with Princeton University Press, 2007. Plate 32, p. 59.

3. For example, Smith, A., Reeve, A., Powell, C. and Burnstock, A. An altarpiece and its frame: Carlo Crivelli's 'Madonna Della Rondine'. *National Gallery Technical Bulletin,* 13, 1989. p. 28–43.

4. Cennini, cennino d'Andrea. The Craftsman's handbook, 'Il libro dell'arte, c.1390. Thompson, D.V. (trans). New York: Dover Publications, 1960. p. 198.

5. Ravenel, N. Painted Italian picture frames in the Samuel H. Kress Foundation Collection at the National

Some pigments found on the V&A Renaissance frames.
Left to right: Green malachite in raw state and powdered malachite, two lumps of blue azurite with areas of associated green malachite in raw state and powdered azurite, pale powdered blue smalt, dark blue smalt, indigo and bone black.

Gallery of Art. In V. Dorge and F. Carey Howlett, eds. *Painted wood – history and conservation.* Los Angeles: Getty Conservation Institute, 1998. pp. 100–109.

6. Pandolfo, A. Aspetti technici e conservative della scultura lignea policroma. *Kermes*, 1:1, 1988. p. 12, cited by Ravenel, ibid.; Galassi, A. G., Fumagalli, P. and Gritti, E. Conservation and scientific examination of three Northern Italian gilded and painted altarpieces of the sixteenth century. In D. Bigelow, ed. *Gilded wood: conservation and history.* Madison, CT: Sound View Press, 1991. p. 200; Olga, R. and Wilmering, A. *The Gubbio Studiolo and its conservation.* New York:

Metropolitan Museum of Art, 2001. p. 169; Smith et al., op. cit.

7. Martin, E. and Bergeon, S. Des bleus profonds chez primitifs Italiens. *Techne*, 4, 1996. pp. 74–89. Smith et al., op. cit.

8. Stege, H. Out of the blue? Considerations on the early use of smalt as blue pigment in European easel painting. *Zeitschrift für Kunsttechnologie und Konservierung*, 18, 2004. pp. 121–142; Spring, M., Higgitt, C. and Saunders, D. Investigation of pigment–medium interaction processes in oil paint containing degraded smalt. *National Gallery Technical Bulletin*, 26. p. 6.

UNDERSTANDING DETERIORATION AND ALTERATION

Many of the tools, materials and techniques utilised for joinery, carving, casting, gilding and painting in the Renaissance have remained in continuous use to the present day. However, there are often differences in execution, materials and ageing characteristics that enable Renaissance work to be distinguished from later work.

In general, nineteenth century makers of reproduction frames did not attempt an exact match of the original materials and techniques. They often employed different methods of construction, mouldings not seen in the Renaissance period, different carving styles and finishes. Marks from tools not available in the Renaissance may also be visible. Present day replica frame makers and their clients have a much more thorough and sophisticated knowledge of Renaissance materials and techniques. As a result, modern replica frames and repairs can be more difficult to recognise.

A key part of the process of understanding Renaissance frames is to interpret changes that have occurred, in order to identify original material and distinguish later additions. It is therefore important to understand the effects of natural ageing and how frames may be altered over the course of time.

Deterioration
Wood
Fluctuations in relative humidity cause wood to expand and contract and can cause glue to fail. When relative humidity is low and the movement of the wood is restrained, for example in cross-grained joints or by fixings, wood may split. Small gaps may appear in joints, for example in corner mitres. High relative humidity is conducive to mould growth and fungal and insect attack.

Damage caused by wood-boring beetles is common in Renaissance frames. The larvae bore within the wood and, if infestation is severe, can create a network of tunnels that weakens the wood. The larvae develop into beetles that bore their way through the surface, creating a flight hole. The extent of damage may not be immediately apparent. Insect-damaged wood is susceptible to breakage and loss, as for example in Frame 21 (7150-1860).

Poor handling and storage can result in dents and breakage. Applied parts can detach, especially if wood movement has loosened fixings.

Decorative surface
Decorative surfaces consist of one or more layers on a substrate. Fluctuations in relative humidity cause the layer(s) and substrate to expand and contract, often at different rates and in different directions. This causes cracking, distortion and separation of finishes from each other and the wood. Gaps in wood joints will cause cracks in the finish. With age, pastiglia decoration can shrink, crack and detach.

Water gilding
In a water-gilded finish, although cracks form both along and across the wood grain, cross-grain cracking is predominant. The animal glue within the preparation layers of the gilded finish expands and contracts equally in all directions in response to fluctuations in relative humidity. The wood expands and contracts across the grain but not along the grain. As a result, the movement of the preparation layers in this direction is restrained by

the wood. This incompatibility leads to the formation of cross-grain cracks in the gilded finish.[1] As cracks form, the decorative surface becomes susceptible to flaking. Loss of decorative surface often occurs from the porous end grain of wood.

If wood has shrunk considerably, this may result in the complete separation of the ground layers from the surface of the wood. The resulting shell of painted or gilded finish is very vulnerable to compression damage, for example by handling.

The reflective effects of burnished gilding lessen in time, as a result of fluctuations in relative humidity, handling and accretions of dirt. As water gilding wears, the places where the laid gold leaf had slightly overlapped appear as brighter bands or stripes. As wear continues, the clay bole is revealed, and then the white ground.

Water gilding is particularly susceptible to damage caused by water and abrasion. Inappropriate cleaning can cause much damage, as seen on Frame 9 (6867-1860), where a wet absorbent material has been wiped over the surface, dissolving and smudging the layers.

Mordant gilding

Depending on the mordant, the finish can stay soft for some time after gilding and is easily damaged during the drying period. The mordant can, in time, develop a craquelure and, in turn, the appearance of the gilding becomes more matt.

Silver

Silver leaf tarnishes, eventually completely blackening, as it oxidises owing to the effects of sulphur-based pollutants.

Coatings

Coloured glazes and coatings can fade, darken or become opaque, resulting in loss of subtlety in the original design.

Alteration

Alteration of a frame can occur as a result of repair or replacement of damaged and lost parts, modernisation or change of use.

Wood

Damage and loss of wood due to insect infestation can result in the need to rebuild parts of a frame. If the wood loss was extensive, a reproduction frame may have been made incorporating salvaged parts, for example Frames 29 (163:2-1910) and 33 (4242:1-1857).

In some cases, parts of frames, such as the pediment and antependium, were removed. This could occur if the part was damaged, to modernise the frame, to appeal to a different taste or simply to reduce the overall height to fit into a new setting. Lunettes painted with a religious theme were often removed if the frame was reused for a non-religious painting. Similarly, an antependium might be removed if it had an inappropriate coat of arms for a new owner. In other cases, fragments from several frames may have been incorporated into a new frame. Frame 8 (5893-1859) is thought to have been altered by adding and removing parts to make it fit into a new location.

Change of sight size

Frames were often adapted to fit different objects and such changes might occur more than once. This often required the alteration of the sight size. Wood was added or removed at the corner joints to alter sight size dimensions. Additional mouldings could be used to reduce the sight size and could be set in the rebate. Slip mouldings have a plain or rectangular profile. These project into the aperture of the frame, reducing the sight size dimensions and holding the new, smaller object. Frame 4 (57:2-1867) appears to have had a sight edge moulding added to make the sight size smaller. The frame is thought to be later than the relief, and may have been reused. Another method of reducing the sight size was to cut through the sides of the frame, remove the required length and rejoin the sections.

To make the sight size larger, the sight size moulding could be removed or the frame could be cut through and additional lengths of wood inserted. Sometimes the frame was dismantled, individual parts were cut through at different points and then the whole was reassembled. This made the alterations less obtrusive, as for example on Frame 13 (7816-1862).

Unconventional proportions may betray alterations to the size of a frame. Other clues include mis-aligned or lost carved corner ornament. The carved ornament on Frame 30 (148-1869), for example, does not meet at the corners of the sight edge.

The presence of straight cut edges through the finish and wood indicates that cuts have been made after gilding was completed. On Frame 10 (1079-1884), for example, the pilaster mouldings have been cut through at the mitres. Close inspection often reveals where carving repairs have been carried out by a different hand, for example the later egg-and-dart carving on Frame 8 (5893-1859).

Examining the back of a frame may reveal later additions that are not apparent from the front, where overpainting or gilding may have been carried out to conceal the alterations. Evidence of structural alterations can include joints that do not relate to original construction or a different colour or type of wood. Sections of wood unaffected by wood-boring beetle in a frame that has suffered attack can indicate later additions. Coatings may have been applied to tone down or obscure such additions.

Later hanging fittings and nails

Non-Renaissance hanging fittings made from cast iron are more regular in shape and have a smoother surface than the original wrought iron hanging loops, which were attached with cut nails. Mirror plates, a common later fitting, are often made of polished brass or chromed.

Cut nails are available today, wrought iron hanging fittings can be reproduced and age can be simulated on both. Modern wrought iron can be identified by chemical analysis of its composition.[2]

Decorative surface

It is common to find alterations to the decorative surface on Renaissance frames carried out to blend in structural repairs to reflect a change in taste. Changes range from retouching small losses to complete overpainting and/or regilding. Careful examination of the decorative finish will often reveal these changes. In fewer cases, the original finish may have been stripped and the object completely repainted and gilded. Occasionally original decoration may survive in good condition. Frame 9 (6867-1860) retains parts of the original gilding on the sight edge moulding under glass that give a good indication of the original appearance of the gilding. On Frame 4 (57:2-1867) original sgrafitto work survives on the inside return of the pedestal.

The more skilful a repair, the more difficult it may be to detect. On Frame 19 (10-1890), repairs have been carried out to areas of gilding and the wooden structure. Although the materials and techniques of the original gilding have been copied faithfully, the repair can be distinguished because the punch work is slightly different.

Retouching of small losses and repairs often overlaps adjacent earlier finishes. In the case of repairs to losses of ground or replacement parts, the thickness, texture or colour of the white ground, bole or gold may differ from the original, as may the method of gilding. An attempt may have been made to blend the repair with the surrounding original surface by rubbing through the gold, the bole, white ground and wood. The natural crack pattern found in a gilded finish may be simulated with a scalpel. Fine scratches may be made in the gold to imitate craquelure, as observed in areas of repair on Frame 14 (76-1892).

Areas of lost or worn finish may be coloured out using paints or stains, including bronze paint, which has also been used to overpaint gilded frames completely. It has a fine grainy appearance and although gold-coloured when first applied, it darkens with age.

Total repainting and regilding may be undertaken because of changes in fashion or to blend in repairs. The decorative scheme may be reinterpreted, fields of colour may be lost and different colours used. Sometimes a darker shade of an original colour may be used, for example on Frame 8 (5893-1859). The original decorative scheme on Frame 26 (771: 2-1865) combined black painted and gilded areas. At some point the whole frame was overgilded, although the original decorative scheme is visible where the later finish is delaminating. An image of this frame has been digitally reconstructed to give an indication of the probable original scheme.

The spandrels on Frame 28 (5633:2-1859) are nineteenth century additions. These were probably added to accommodate the relief it now frames. The spandrels were gilded over a Victoria-plum coloured bole over a brick-red coloured bole. These bole colours are associated with nineteenth century gilding. In order to blend the new and old parts, the nineteenth century scheme was applied over the whole frame.

Overpainting and gilding may soften the sharpness of the original carved sculptural form, as seen on Frame 26 (771:2-1865). The floral detail in the scrolls at the base of each side, for example, is almost completely obscured. Even relatively thin overpainting or gilding can result in loss of detail such as punch work. This has been avoided on Frame 8 (5893-1859) where the front pilaster with earlier gilding has not been overgilded, although other parts have.

In some cases damage to the original surface was not made good before overpainting and gilding. On Frame 22 (535:A-1870), for example, the original surface had shallow craters in areas of loss and the later painting was applied directly over these.

Later coatings

Pigmented coatings are often used to tone in areas of repair, to give the impression of age and natural accretions. These may be applied locally to the repair but often the toning layer extends over adjacent earlier finishes or may be applied all over the frame, front and back. Coatings were commonly made with glue size, linseed oil paint or shellac.

Later varnishes can alter and darken the original colour. The blue background to the female figure on Frame 17 (850-1884), painted with azurite, was once very bright but has dulled to almost black.

Later gilding was sometimes coated with a thin layer of glue size. Dirt can become embedded in this coating over time, resulting in the gilded surface losing its brilliance and becoming dull and opaque, as has occurred on Frame 21 (7150-1860).

The cupping of finishes is often caused by an application of a stronger coat over a weaker one, which causes the weaker finish below to pull away, as seen on Frame 16 (11-1890). Usually this is associated with later coatings or finishes being applied over earlier ones.

References

1. Michalski, S. Crack mechanisms in gilding. In D. Bigelow, ed. *Gilded wood conservation and history*. Madison, CT: Sound View Press, 1980. pp. 171–181.
2. Selwyn, L. *Metals and corrosion: a handbook for the conservation professional*. Ottawa: Canadian Conservation Institute, 2004. pp. 89–112.

SCIENTIFIC ANALYSIS

Scientific analysis is an important tool in the authentication of Renaissance frames. It has been used to add to the body of knowledge of original materials and techniques, and to identify fakes, such as those produced by Icilio Federico Joni (1866–1946) of Siena.

Many of the materials used for painting and gilding today, such as iron oxides, the clays in bole and the chalk and gypsum found in grounds, are indistinguishable from those used in the past. However, many pigments introduced after the Renaissance can be used for dating purposes. The presence of pigments appropriate to a given historical period is not in itself proof of authenticity, as many have remained available through to the present day. Results of scientific analysis must, therefore, be considered in conjunction with an overall examination of the execution, materials and ageing characteristics of the frame.

Analytical Methods

Scientific analysis was used to collect further evidence where later decorative schemes had been identified by visual examination. Although non-destructive methods are preferable, many of the analytical techniques used required the removal of a small sample of material from the frames. A limited number of samples was taken and these were as small as possible.

Optical microscopy of samples viewed in cross-section shows the stratigraphy of the layers of paint and gilding, and can be used for pigment identification. Samples can be used to identify later additions where a frame has been overpainted or regilded. On Frame 8 (5893-1859), for example, the original parts of the frame have two decorative schemes whereas later additions have only one.

Samples of the surface decoration, usually including the ground layers, were analysed by the National Gallery Scientific Department. The samples were mounted in polyester embedding resin and ground and polished to reveal the edge of the sample. These were examined in reflected (incident), ultraviolet and polarised light at magnifications up to 500 $\times$.

Pigment particles were taken from existing samples, treated with dichloromethane to soften any binding media, crushed between glass slides to separate the particles, mounted on microscope slides with Meltmount 1.66 resin and examined with a Swift polarising microscope by Dr Brian Singer.

Scanning electron microscopy (SEM) can elicit information on morphology and provide very high-magnification images with a three-dimensional appearance. SEM may be combined with **energy-dispersive X-ray microanalysis (EDX)** to identify the elemental composition of a single paint layer or even a single pigment particle. Although EDX can identify the presence of an element (e.g. iron, arsenic, mercury), it does not indicate the molecular form in which it exists. Therefore the data must be interpreted in conjunction with the examination of paint samples by optical microscopy and other techniques in order to specify whether a particular pigment is present.

Samples were analysed by the National Gallery Scientific Department using a Cambridge Stereoscan 200 SEM with an Oxford Instruments X-ray detector and Inca software. Elemental analysis of paint samples was carried out on loose samples attached to carbon stubs on a Rontec ESEM system fitted with a Rontec analyser by Dr Brian Singer.

Cross-section of an original Italian Renaissance gilded scheme from the gilded area in the entablature frieze of Frame 2 (594-1869).

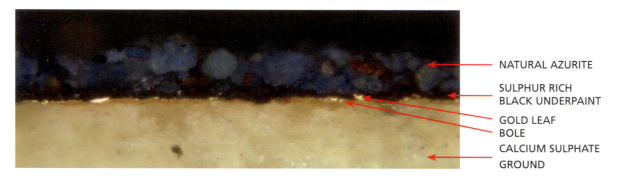

Cross-section of an original blue painted finish from the background of the pilaster frieze of Frame 2 (594-1869) showing an azurite paint layer on top of a black underpaint.

Cross-section of an overpainted finish from Frame 13 (7816-1862). The original azurite paint layer has been covered with yellow orpiment overpaint, and there is overlying varnish.

Fourier transform infrared spectroscopy (FTIR) can be used to identify or characterise the binding medium and pigments in each layer. Samples were analysed by the National Gallery Scientific Department using a Nic-Plan FTIR microscope coupled with a Nicolet 5700 FTIR spectrometer. Samples were prepared in a diamond cell and scanned in transmission, 128 times at $4\,cm^{-1}$. Data was manipulated using OMNIC software.

Samples were also analysed by Dr Brian Singer, Northumbria University, using the following method. A sample of each paint, adhesive, coating or plaster was placed on to the diamond window of a Durascope diamond ATR attachment linked to a Perkin Elmer 1000 Fourier transform infrared spectrometer. Each sample was pressed down against the window using a metal anvil and scanned sixteen times. The background scan was automatically subtracted. Each sample was thus analysed by reflectance FTIR.

Raman spectroscopy is a non-destructive analytical technique used for pigment identification. The presence of indigo in a sample taken from Frame 3 (19-1891) was confirmed by Satoko Tanimoto, Mellon Fellow, Department of Conservation and Scientific Research, British Museum. A green (532 nm) laser was used.

Gas chromatography–mass spectrometry (GC-MS) can be used to identify binding media. It can determine the amino acids derived from proteins, thereby identifying which protein is present in the binder. It is also possible to distinguish fatty acids from lipids, oils or resins.

Samples were analysed for the presence of oils, proteins, waxes and resins by Dr Brian Singer, Northumbria University. A portion of samples from Frames 9 (6867-1860), 19 (10-1890), 16 (11-1890) and 10 (1079-1884) was derivatised by acid hydrolysis and then treatment with propan-1-ol and dry hydrochloric acid followed by treatment with pentafluoropropanoic acid anhydride. This procedure gave an opportunity to analyse the amino acids from proteins present as their propyl ester/pentafluoropropanoyl (PFP) derivatives, and also fatty acids derived from any lipids, and oils and resin acids derived from any resins present as their propyl esters.[3]

Samples were transferred to a Reacti-vial and hydrolysed with concentrated hydrochloric acid at 90°C for 3 days. The acid was removed under vacuum and the residue treated with propan-1-ol, dry hydrochloric acid mixture at 110°C for 45 minutes. The excess reagent was evaporated under nitrogen at 50°C and the residue dissolved in 5% solution of pyridine in dichloromethane. Pentafluoropropionic anhydride was added and the mixture was heated to 100°C for 15 minutes. The excess reagent was evaporated under nitrogen at room temperature and the residue dissolved in dichloromethane. This procedure yielded the propyl esters of the *N*-pentafluoropropanoyl derivatives of the amino acids in the proteins and also propyl esters of the fatty acids released by hydrolysis of any drying oil present, which were then analysed by GC-MS. The GC-MS instrument used was a Thermo Focus fitted with a DSQ mass detector.

A layer from a sample was transferred to a Reacti-vial and derivatised by heating to 60°C with two drops of 5% methanolic solution of 3-trifluoromethylphenyltrimethylammonium hydroxide for 4 hours. The mixture was then subjected to thermal decomposition at 250°C before analysis by GC-MS in order to look for evidence of oils, waxes and resins in the sample. The GC-MS instrument used was a Focus GC fitted with a DSQ mass detector. The column used was a Thermo 15m column. The temperature of the column was raised from 90°C to 250°C within the run.

Pigments

The earliest finishes on the frames believed to date from the Renaissance were analysed. Pigments appropriate to the period are listed with information about painted decoration. Pigments found on the V&A frames that came into use at a later date are described below.

Prussian blue (iron (III)-hexacyanoferrate (II), $Fe[Fe^{3+}Fe^{2+}(CN)_6]_3$)

Prussian blue has been widely used in Europe since it was discovered in Berlin in 1704. Prussian blue was found in a later decorative scheme on Frame 1 (5-1890).

Synthetic red iron oxide

Synthetic red iron oxide pigments were manufactured from the eighteenth century. Synthetic red iron oxide was found in the uppermost decorative scheme on Frame 1 (5-1890).

Synthetic (French) ultramarine

Genuine ultramarine is a deep, purple–blue pigment made by grinding lapis lazuli and, in the Renaissance, was more expensive than gold. Synthetic ultramarine, developed in 1826, cost around one-tenth of the cost of genuine ultramarine at that time. Synthetic ultramarine was identified in the uppermost decorative scheme on Frame 8 (5893-1859).

Zinc white (zinc (II) oxide, ZnO)

Zinc white has been in use as a pigment since the late eighteenth century. It was found on Frame 12 (649-1890).

Chrome yellow (lead (II) chromate, $PbCrO_4$)

Chrome yellow was discovered in the form of a natural mineral in the eighteenth century. A number of factories in Europe and the USA were manufacturing synthetic chrome yellows by the beginning of the nineteenth century. Chrome yellow was found on Frame 15 (415-1882).

Naples yellow (lead (II) antimonate, $Pb(SbO_3)_2$ or $Pb(SbO_4)_2$)

Naples yellow is thought to have originated as a by-product of the glass-making industry in the seventeenth century and to have been used widely throughout the eighteenth century. A mixture of Naples yellow and orpiment was used to overpaint original schemes on Frame 13 (7816-1862) and Frame 14 (76-1892).

Bronze paint

Bronze paint is a generic name used to describe paint made with metal powders, usually pulverised brass, mixed with a painting medium. Bronze paint has often been used to colour out losses or abrasion on gilded surfaces since the nineteenth century. When first applied it appears gold in colour but, as the copper element in the metal powder oxidises, it darkens to a dull brown. Bronze paint was found over gold leaf on Frame 10 (1079-1884).

Reference

1. Singer, B. and Mcguigan, R. The simultaneous analysis of proteins, lipids, and diterpenoid resins found in cultural objects. *Annali di Chemica*, 97, 2007. pp. 405–416.

PART II
THE FRAMES

READERS' NOTES

Titles

V&A curatorial staff provided information on the date and origin of the frames. Acquisition numbers are provided alongside the V&A collection that holds curatorial responsibility for the frame.

Dimensions

Overall maximum refers to the largest dimensions found on a frame. The depth does not include any obvious later build-ups that have been added to the back of the frames. The rebate width and depth sizes given are the mean average, unless the dimensions vary greatly, in which case these are listed individually. Where a category of dimension is not included in a frame entry this is due to its being inaccessible. Dimensional variations occur across similar parts on such frames owing to their handcrafted nature, the age and distortion of wood, and the presence of overpainting and gilding.

Profiles and Dimensional Annotated Black and White Images of the Frames

Profiles of top, bottom and sides are provided for most of the frames. Where these were not included this was due to limited access or the fragility of the object. Profiles were taken using profile gauges, rulers and set squares. The original pencil drawings were then scanned into a computer and traced by the authors using a drawing package. Overpaint and overgilding affect the crispness of the profile. Where this occurs, for example, on running moulding where the moulding is so obscured by finish that it is otherwise indiscernible, the authors have indicated the form of the wood below.

The profile outline is drawn in black, with the finer internal grey line indicating joins between wood components or between wood and cast work. Where the line does not connect with another line, for example, on the internal fine grey line, this indicates that the line of the internal joining was less certain or unknown. When this occurs on the black outline, this indicates that full access to take the whole profile was not possible. A green line represents an indication of a part that is now missing.

Where there is a running moulding with carved repeating ornament, such as egg and dart, the highest point is usually represented, for example the carved egg. Where there is carving or cast applied work on a frieze, the profile reproduced is that of the relief at that point. Cast applied ornament is shaded in grey. A dark blue line above the carving or cast work indicates the highest point and greatest width the carving or cast work reaches.

On the small black and white image of the frame, the arrows outside the image at right and bottom denote the overall height and width of the frame. The red lines annotated AA, BB, CC and DD crossing the frame represent the point from which the drawn profiles/sections drawings were taken. The arrows pointing at the red line indicate the viewpoint of that section/profile, not the length of the section.

The dimensions of each profile/section are shown to the right and below each profile/section.

Structure

When describing the front of a frame, left and right are used as seen from the front, and when describing the back, left and right are used as seen from the back.

The grain direction runs along the length of the wood. For some pieces where grain direction may be unclear, this information is provided. Wood identification was based on visual examination of gross anatomical characteristics and is not definitive.

Ornament and Frame Parts

Many of the ornaments used are classical and architectural in origin and descriptions of ornament are therefore based on this terminology. Ornament is generally described in the following order: sight edge, sides, top (entablature and pediment) and base (predella and antependium). Definitions of the terminology used are given in the Glossary. Annotated illustrations, naming the parts of the frames, precede each of the frame groups. Typical moulding sections are illustrated in Methods of Construction.

Decorative Finish

The thickness of the white grounds is defined as: thin, less than 1 mm; medium, 1–2 mm; or thick, greater than 2 mm.

Comparable Frames

Comparable frames are included at the end of the frame entries with full bibliographical references. The selection of comparable frames has been limited to those having similarities to those illustrated in books listed in the bibliography. Where available, the dimensions of these comparable frames are given. Scholarship has progressed since the publication of many of these books and the dates assigned to particular frames in these publications may now not be correct. These frames were not examined by the authors and their structure, profiles or surface decoration may not be identical.

Previous Citations

Details are listed of where the frames appear in other selected publications.

In some cases the image used in a previous publication shows parts of the frame that are now missing, details of which are provided.

TABERNACLE FRAMES

The term tabernacle describes a frame where structure and ornamentation were inspired by classical Graeco-Roman architecture. The style was symbolic, elevating the image and acting as a shrine. Tabernacle frames were commonly used to frame the Virgin and Child and other religious images. They varied greatly in size, some were immovable fixtures such as those found on altarpieces in churches, while others were intended to be portable.

Renaissance tabernacle frames were designed in accordance with the patron's wishes and means. The Florentine painter Neri di Bicci listed the features demanded by his patrons in his workshop logbook. For a painting of the Virgin and Child, for example, one patron requested a complex tabernacle frame 'with columns on both sides and a corbel underneath, and above, an architrave, frieze, cornice, and pediment'.[1]

The V&A's fifteenth century marble tabernacle *Virgin and Child with God and Angels* (316-1894), attributed to Giovanni di Antonio Buora (c.1450–1513) and illustrated opposite, is a good example of the type of tabernacle found in churches and chapels, beneath porticos and on house exteriors. This marble tabernacle shares many architectural elements with wooden tabernacle frames: pilasters, an entablature with architrave and cornice supporting a pediment, the base supported by consoles and an antependium. This particular relief remains faithful to the trend of using an architectural device to place the image of God the Father in the uppermost section of the altarpiece,

Fifteenth century marble tabernacle, Virgin and Child with God and Angels, attributed to Giovanni di Antonio Buora (c.1450–1513).

reminding the viewer of his heavenly, unworldly realm. The format of the tabernacle frame separated God the Father in the 'heavenly sphere' of the lunette from the image of the Virgin and Child beneath. This format can also be seen on Frames 1 (5-1890) and 7 (93-1882).

References

1. *Exhibition of Tabernacle Frames from the Samuel H. Kress Collection at the National Gallery of Art*. Exhibition Catalogue. Washington, DC: National Gallery, 2007. *Ricordanze* (1453–75; Florence, Uffizi, MS.2) I. B. Santi, ed. Pisa: Marlin, 1976.

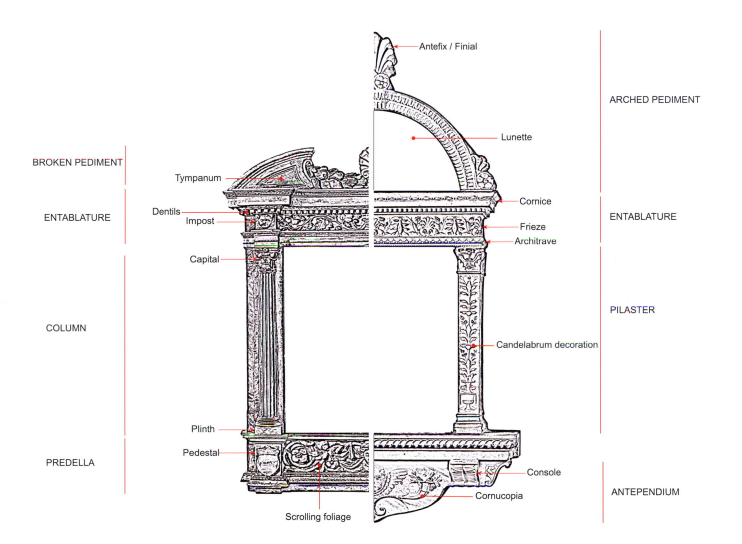

Antefix / Finial

ARCHED PEDIMENT

Lunette

BROKEN PEDIMENT

Tympanum

Cornice

ENTABLATURE

Dentils

Impost

ENTABLATURE

Frieze

Architrave

Capital

PILASTER

COLUMN

Candelabrum decoration

Plinth

PREDELLA

Pedestal

Console

ANTEPENDIUM

Cornucopia

Scrolling foliage

Annotated illustration of a tabernacle frame.

1

CARVED AND ORIGINALLY WATER GILDED AND PAINTED TABERNACLE FRAME WITH LUNETTE

Italy (Florence), about 1475–1500
Original frame for the painted and gilded terracotta relief of the Virgin and Child after
Benedetto da Maiano (1442–1497), the painting of the lunette attributed to Bartolomeo di
Giovanni (c.1475–c.1500/05)
Bought in Florence (Bardini) for £116
5-1890 (Sculpture Collection)

1110 mm

683 mm

Dimensions (mm)
H: 1110; W: 683; D: 80 (overall maximum)
Terracotta relief: H: 20; W: 445; D: 50

Ornament

Fluted and stopped fluted pilasters with Corinthian capitals and bases support an entablature of an architrave, suppressed frieze and dentil cornice. A semi-circular arched pediment carved with an interlocking chain decoration supports a scroll and half anthemion at either side and a pair of scrolls at the top. The lunette is painted with the Trinity flanked by two adoring angels. There is a piece of ornament missing at the top, possibly an anthemion. The predella frieze is inscribed 'AVE SOLA VIRGO PARENS' (Hail alone the Virgin Mother).

Structure

The main hardwood back frame has been assembled with glue and nails. The mouldings and ornamental carvings, such as the capitals, have been applied to the back frame. The frame has suffered significant damage from wood-boring beetle and several areas at the back of the frame have

AVE·SOLA·VIRGOPARENS·

been repaired. The arched top has been reinforced by replacing the area with a new piece of wood that is attached to the frame with nails. The lower panel, bearing the weight of the terracotta relief, has been supported by placing additional pieces of wood between the panel and the main frame. The original system supporting the relief within the frame has been replaced. Nail holes indicate that, originally, a large plank of wood would have covered the whole of the back of the relief. This was removed and two strips of wood were placed horizontally across the terracotta, fixed to the frame with screws, and four support blocks glued to the bottom. All replacement pieces are discernible by their lighter colour, visible in the image of the back of the frame.

Decorative Finish

There have been three decorative schemes. The present scheme is red and gold. The red is overpaint that has been poorly applied and overlaps on to the adjacent gilded areas. Paint samples were analysed to try to establish the original decorative scheme and to identify possible links between the frame and the terracotta relief.[1] Two decorative schemes were identified below the current red and gold scheme. Originally, the frame was entirely gilded except for the inscribed area of the predella frieze.

First decorative scheme

Analyses of samples taken from the original scheme found water gilding applied over a bright orange bole, over a thick ground layer of anhydrous calcium sulphate rich in binding material. A thick layer of glue was observed on top of the wood, which was probably applied as a preparation layer.

Azurite was found in the inscribed area of the pradella frieze.

The majority of the gilded elements visible today retain their original gilding with some small areas

of repair. In some of these repairs, silver can be seen under a layer of varnish, identified as shellac owing to its characteristic fluorescence under ultraviolet (UV) light. Silver could have been used either in the form of silver particles blended in shellac or as a very irregular silver leaf layer.

Second decorative scheme

At some point, the original gilded scheme was partially overpainted with blue. Analysis of samples taken from this blue scheme found two preparation ground layers of calcium sulphate applied over the original gold, followed by a layer of Prussian blue paint. Prussian blue was widely used in Europe after its discovery in Berlin in 1704. The blue layer can be seen where there are losses and wear to the uppermost red finish. Prussian blue found on the Virgin's cloak and on the lettering on the predella frieze are probably contemporaneous.

Present decorative scheme

Results of analyses of samples taken from the uppermost red scheme, applied over the blue, found synthetic red iron oxide over a thin ground layer of calcium sulphate. Synthetic iron oxide was manufactured from the eighteenth century. The uppermost paint layer was therefore applied sometime after that date, while the use of calcium sulphate implies that this probably occurred in Italy.

Hanging Device

There are holes from mirror plate fixings on the back of the modern replacement arch. The top of the back of the original frame is not visible.

Observations and Conclusions

Examination and analysis of the paint layers revealed links between the original scheme on the painted terracotta relief and that on the frame. The same two original preparation layers, animal

glue and anhydrous calcium sulphate, were found on both. The original gilding on the frame is the same as the gilding on the terracotta. The cross-sections are identical, with the same colour and thickness of orange bole and the same quality of gold leaf. The layer of azurite found in the earlier layers near the lettering on the predella frieze was prepared in exactly the same way as the blue areas of the Virgin's cloak. Both have an extra preparation layer containing carbon black particles and both have the same azurite layer on top.[2]

Further analysis would the required to establish the original appearence of the inscribed frieze.

The frame appears to date from the later fifteenth century and is undoubtedly the original frame for this painted and gilded terracotta sculpture relief. There is a possibility that relief and frame were painted by the same hand. The painted lunette has been attributed to Bartolomeo di Giovanni (c.1475–c.1500/05).[3]

Comparable Frames

This frame is stylistically similar to Frame 37 (6-1890).

Original Italian tabernacle frame for *Madonna and Child* by Jacopo del Sellaio (c.1442–1493) with similar form in the Museo d'Arte Sacra, Florence. See Sabatelli, F. *Le cornice Italiane dal Rinascimento al Neoclassico*. Milan: Electa, 1992. pp. 30, 33, Figure 31.

Italian tabernacle frame, c.1470, with similar form and columns. See Newbery, T., Bisacca, G. and Kanter, L. *Italian Renaissance frames*. Exhibition Catalogue. New York: Metropolitan Museum, 1990. p. 22, Figure 16.

Tabernacle frame with similarities in form. See Bock, E. *Florentinische und Venezianische Bilderrahmen aus der Zeit der Gotik und Renaissance*. Munich: F. Bruckmann, 1902. p. 65.

Previous Citation

Pope-Hennessy, J. *Catalogue of Italian sculpture in the Victoria and Albert Museum*, Volume 1.

References

1. Analyses of pigment dispersions and observations of cross-sections with natural and ultraviolet light were carried out by Victor Borges (V&A Sculpture Conservation) and Lucia Burgio (V&A Conservation Science).
2. Observations noted in V&A Conservation Report 5-1890 by Victor Borges, June 2003.
3. See Pope-Hennessy, J., assisted by Lightbown, R. *Catalogue of Italian sculpture in the Victoria and Albert Museum*. London: Her Majesty's Stationery Office, 1964. pp. 161–162.

2

CARVED, PAINTED AND WATER GILDED TWO-SIDED PROCESSIONAL TABERNACLE FRAME WITH LUNETTE AND ANTEPENDIUM

Italy, early sixteenth century
The panel painting depicts the Virgin and Child with
God the Father in the lunette and on the reverse
St Anthony Abbot with St Paul the Hermit and
St Anthony in the Desert in the lunette
Bought for the frame in 1869 for £12
594-1869 (Paintings, Drawings and Prints Collection)

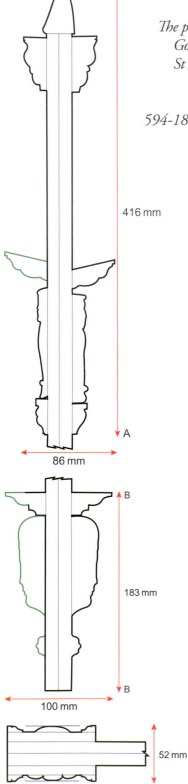

416 mm

86 mm

183 mm

100 mm

52 mm

83 mm

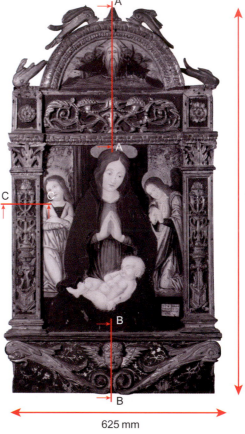

1145 mm

625 mm

Dimensions (mm)
H: 1145; W: 625; D: 110 (overall maximum)

Ornament
The pilasters with Corinthian capitals are enriched with candelabrum decoration. The pilasters support a leaf-and-tongue and bead-and-pearl architrave.

The entablature frieze comprises a central figure with arms terminating in scrolling foliage, flanked by overflowing cornucopia. The imposts are decorated with a single rosette. The cornice, missing on one side, is decorated with simplified egg-and-dart and leaf-and-tongue and supports the arched pediment. The pediment is decorated with the same leaf-and-tongue moulding on the outer edge and egg-and-tongue on the inside and is surmounted by four dolphins. The predella is decorated with a central winged cherub head flanked by two dolphins with bodies terminating in scrolls.

Structure

The two paintings have each been applied to separate large panels of wood, probably poplar, and the panels then sandwiched together. The frame is made up of separate pieces of wood that appear to be walnut and are attached with nails on to the main painted panels. The seperately applied carved detail also has the appearance of walnut. The lengths of each of the pilasters are made from one piece of wood onto which the mouldings and carved candelabrum decoration are applied. The Corinthian capitals, carved from one piece of wood, are also applied. The architrave moulding, carved with both leaf-and-tongue and bead-and-pearl decoration, is mitred and applied. The background of the entablature frieze is part of the main painted panel. The carved figure, flanked by overflowing cornucopia, is applied, as are the imposts on to the main panel. The single rosette and framing mouldings, applied in four lengths, have been applied separately on to the imposts. The cornice, decorated with both simplified egg-and-dart and leaf-and-tongue, is mitred and applied. The central length of architrave is missing on one side and the two smaller lengths, on the top of each impost, are missing from both sides. The arched semi-circular section of the pediment is applied separately and each of the four dolphins is applied and nailed on

to the top of the main painted panel. The winged cherub head and the two flanking dolphins have been carved and applied separately, on top of the lower part of the main painted panel, and form the predella. The winged cherub head and the two flanking dolphins are missing from the side of the panel painting depicting St Anthony. Several small pieces of applied carved ornament and mouldings are missing. There is damage caused by wood-boring beetle throughout.

Decorative Finish

The painted and gilded scheme on the frame appears to be original. A sample of the gilding and recessed blue background was taken from each side of the object.[1] The gilded areas are water gilded, with possibly two layers of gold leaf, over an orange–red bole on a white preparation consisting of calcium sulphate with a few inclusions of calcium carbonate. The blue pigment was identified as natural azurite. Azurite was applied over a sulphur-rich black underpaint, which would have enhanced the colour of the azurite and reduced the quantity required. The black underpaint was applied directly over the red bole on the calcium sulphate ground. The background of the base of the frame is decorated in sgrafitto with a foliate pattern.

Hanging Device

It has been suggested that this may have been a processional panel carried on a pole or mounted on a float for religious parades, and that the imagery may have represented a particular Guild.[2] There are the remains of what may be an old metal hanging device with remnants of string around the top. There are holes through the frieze at the bottom that may have been used to attach the frame to a wall.

Observations and Conclusions

The gilded finish on the frame has flaked away revealing the wood in several areas and there are losses to the blue painted areas. Nonetheless this is a very good example of an original decorative surface that has not been repaired, overgilded or painted. The construction and materials used for the decoration are consistent with those used on other sixteenth century frames and related objects.

Kauffmann describes the frame as early sixteenth century and says the painting is thought to be a later imitation, describing it as 'in Manner of the Italian School, perhaps 18th century with a false inscription on the lower right of the panel painted with The Virgin and Child PFr Stefanus … die ultimo. Ap (ri) lis 1515'.[3] It has been suggested that the date inscribed on the panel may read 1545 rather than 1515.[4] The gilded scheme on the frame appears to be exactly the same as that on the panel painting and is continuous between the two, indicating that the panel is in fact part of the same object. Many of the painted areas on the panel are crude, but these are restorations over the worn original. While samples of the decorative surface were being taken, it was suggested that the painting may be sixteenth century.[5] Further investigation is needed to assess whether the painting is contemporaneous with the frame.

References

1. SEM/EDX analysis of the gilded and blue painted areas on the frame was carried out by Dr Helen Howard, Scientific Department, The National Gallery, London.
2. Lynn Roberts, personal communication, February 2008.
3. Kauffmann, C. M. *Victoria & Albert Museum catalogue of foreign paintings before 1900*. London: Eyre & Spottiswoode, 1973. p. 152.
4. Lynn Roberts, personal communication, February 2008.
5. Dr Helen Howard and Dr Ashok Roy, The National Gallery, London, personal communication, October 2008.

RESULTS OF ANALYSIS
SAMPLE 6/1
LOCATION

Frame surrounding St Anthony, attached floral motif at upper right side: blue background, blue over red.

PAINT CROSS-SECTION IN INCIDENT LIGHT

UV LIGHT

Earliest/original decoration

- natural azurite
- sulphur-rich black underpaint
- gold leaf
- red bole
- calcium sulphate preparation with some calcium carbonate inclusions.

SEM/EDX

- SEM/EDX analysis of the ground confirmed the presence of: Ca, S, Cl
- SEM/EDX analysis of inclusion in the ground confirmed the presence of: Ca, O

- SEM/EDX analysis of the metal leaf confirmed the presence of: Au
- SEM/EDX analysis of the pink bole confirmed the presence of: Al, Si, Ca, Cl, K, Fe, Mg
- SEM/EDX analysis of a blue particle confirmed the presence of: Cu, O, (Ca, Cl, Si)
- SEM/EDX analysis of a green particle confirmed the presence of: Cu, O, (Si, Cl, Ca)
- SEM/EDX analysis of the black underpaint confirmed the presence of: Si, Ca, Al, Fe, Mg, S, K, Cu.

SAMPLE 6/2
LOCATION

Frame surrounding St Anthony, attached floral motif at upper right side: original gilding on floral motif.

PAINT CROSS-SECTION IN INCIDENT LIGHT

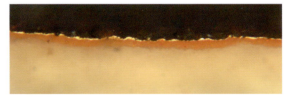

UV LIGHT

- surface accretions

Earliest/original decoration

- gold leaf
- red bole
- calcium sulphate preparation with some calcium carbonate inclusions.

SAMPLE 6/3
LOCATION

Frame surrounding the Virgin and Child. Frieze, left side, under vase motif: blue background, blue over red.

PAINT CROSS-SECTION IN INCIDENT LIGHT

UV LIGHT

Earliest/original decoration
- natural azurite
- black underpaint
- red bole
- calcium sulphate preparation.

SAMPLE 6/4
LOCATION

Frame surrounding the Virgin and Child. Frieze above the Virgin, central figure: original gilding.

PAINT CROSS-SECTION IN INCIDENT LIGHT

UV LIGHT

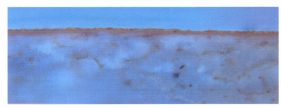

Earliest/original decoration
- gold leaf
- red bole
- calcium sulphate preparation.

CARVED AND WATER GILDED TABERNACLE FRAME WITH PAINTED ANTEPENDIUM DECORATED WITH SGRAFITTO

Italy (Tuscany), 1480–1550
Bought in Florence (Stefano Bardini) for £35 7s 0d
19-1891 (Furniture and Woodwork Collection)

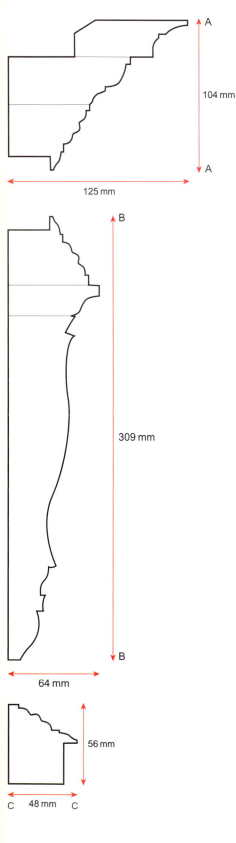

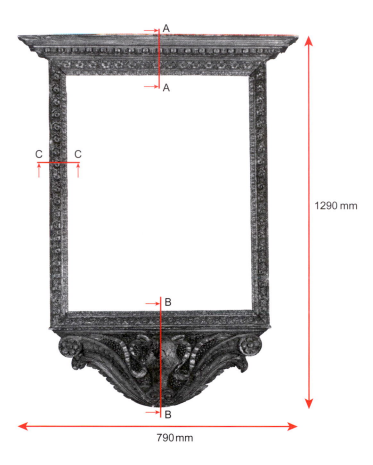

Dimensions (mm)

H: 1290; W: 790; D: 270 (overall maximum)

Sight size: H: 713; W: 524

Rebate: W: 9; D: 30

Object accommodation size: H: 730; W: 538

The dimensions above do not include the recent addition sight edge moulding in the rebate.

Ornament

A leaf-and-tongue cyma-reversa moulding borders the sight edge, followed by an ovolo moulding enriched with rosettes. The cornice is enriched with an egg-and-dart ovolo moulding. The antependium carries a shield, with a fluttering ribbon, flanked by fluted scrolls terminating in patarea and caulicoli. The shield appears to bear the arms of the Chigi family, important Sienese bankers, with a jelly and crossed halberds.

Structure

The frame is made of hardwood. The back frame is corner bridle jointed, with the tongue on the vertical members. At the front, the leaf-and-tongue cyma-reversa moulding and rosette enriched ovolo mouldings are mitred and applied on to the back frame.

The cornice egg-and-dart ovolo moulding is made in one piece. Above this, the remainder of the cornice is made up of two pieces, one at the front and one behind, which has been hollowed out at the centre back and so does not appear in the profile drawing. The reason for the hollowed area is not known. The moulding between the bottom of the main frame and the antependium is made from a separate piece. The antependium is made of one piece, now warped. The frame has extensive wood-boring beetle damage.

Later Additions

At the back, a modern build-up frame has been screwed on behind the rosette enriched ovolo moulding. The top and bottom are half lapped over the left and right pieces and the edges of the frame are chamfered. A slip frame has been added behind the sight edge moulding to decrease the sight size. It is painted brown at the front and is clearly evident at the back because of its light colour. Black velvet ribbon has been glued on the front of the rebate to cushion the surface of the painting. There are two packing strips of wood placed inside the left and right rebate to fill the gap between painting and the side edge of the rebate. These are also evident because of their light colour. These packing strips are held in with two mirror plates on each side. These additions, which were probably made in order to fit the current painting, are not included in the profile drawings and have been digitally removed from the image of the front of the frame.

Decorative Finish

There is one early, probably original, painted and gilded decorative scheme. The mouldings are water gilded on an opaque brown–red bole over a medium to thin calcium sulphate ground. The antependium is water gilded and then painted blue with sgrafitto gold spots. The back edge sides of the frame are painted a blue–red–brown, possibly in imitation of porphyry. Both the blue–red–brown and the blue paints have gritty textures. Analysis of the original paint from the right side of the frame identified vermilion applied over a ground of calcium sulphate with a little yellow earth pigment.[1] Analysis of a sample of blue paint from the antependium identified azurite applied over an underpaint of indigo and lead white, on top of the gold leaf.[2]

Hanging Device

On the back of the frame, near the bottom at left and right, are two modern mirror plate fittings applied over later addition blocks of wood.

Observations and Conclusions

This frame has been on loan to the National Gallery, London, since 1938, where it frames *The Virgin and Child with an Angel* (*No. 589*) by an imitator of Fra Filippo Lippi, c.1480.[3] Penny suggested that the frame was probably originally

designed for a terracotta relief, which would have been hung high on a wall, with a candle on a separate bracket below.[4] Newbery supports this idea, mentioning that marble and terracotta reliefs by Guiliano's brother, Benedetto da Majano (1442–1497), have nearly identical mouldings.[5]

There may originally have been a lunette or a pediment, which is now missing. The original gilding, though much worn, would have imitated solid gold. The original blue paint would have appeared a brighter, lighter blue.

Comparable Frames

Newbery compares this frame to a tabernacle frame, Florence, c.1480–1500, workshop of Giuliano da Maiano, that has a very similar rosette moulding and the same general form but retains its lunette and has no antependium.[6]

Previous Citations

Guggenheim, M. *Le cornici italiane dalla metà del secolo XV o allo scorcio del XVI; con breve testo riassuntivo intorno alla storia ed al'importanza delle cornice.* Milan: U.Hoepli, 1897. Plate 78, where is it referred to as Tuscan, first half of the sixteenth century.

Penny, N. *Frames.* National Gallery Pocket Guides. London: National Gallery, 1997. pp. 31–33, Figure 24, where the frame is described as sixteenth century Florentine, perhaps from the workshop of Giuliano da Maiano 1470.

Newbery, T. *Frames in the Robert Lehman Collection.* Princeton: Metropolitan Museum of Art in association with Princeton University Press, 2007. p. 46, Figures 27.1 and 27.2.

Newbery, T., Bisacca, G. and Kanter, L. *Italian Renaissance frames.* Exhibition Catalogue. New York: Metropolitan Museum, 1990. p. 43.

References

1. Cross-section and SEM/EDX analyses of paint samples were carried out by Dr Helen Howard, Scientific Department, The National Gallery, London.
2. Raman spectroscopy was undertaken by Satoko Tanimoto, The British Museum.
3. Furniture and Woodwork Collection records.
4. Penny, N. *Frames.* National Gallery Pocket Guides. London: National Gallery, 1997. pp. 31–33, Figure 24.
5. Newbery, T. *Frames in the Robert Lehman Collection.* Princeton, NJ: Metropolitan Museum of Art in association with Princeton University Press, 2007. p. 46, Figures 27.1 and 27.2.
6. Ibid.; Newbery, T., Bisacca, G. and Kanter, L. *Italian Renaissance frames.* Exhibition Catalogue. New York: Metropolitan Museum, 1990. p. 43, No. 11.

RESULTS OF ANALYSIS
SAMPLE 3/1
LOCATION

Antependium, lower left side of shield with heraldic decoration: blue paint over gold.

PAINT CROSS-SECTION IN INCIDENT LIGHT

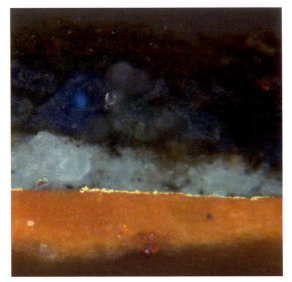

- surface accretions

Earliest/original decoration

- azurite
- lead white combined with indigo
- gold leaf
- red bole with dark iron-rich inclusions
- calcium sulphate.

SAMPLE 3/2
LOCATION

Right side of frame, inner moulding, fourth motif from bottom: original gilding.

PAINT CROSS-SECTION IN INCIDENT LIGHT

- surface accretions

Earliest/original decoration

- gold leaf
- red bole with dark iron-rich inclusions
- calcium sulphate with yellow earth.

SEM/EDX

- SEM/EDX analysis of the metal leaf confirmed the presence of: Au
- SEM/EDX analysis of the bole confirmed the presence of: Si, Al, Fe, Ca, K, Mg
- SEM/EDX analysis of the substrate confirmed the presence of: Ca, S, Fe, K, Si, Al.

The presence of indigo was confirmed by Raman microspectroscopy.

SAMPLE 3/3
LOCATION
Outer edge of frame, right side, just above large loss and one-third distance from front edge: painted decoration in imitation of porphyry.

PAINT CROSS-SECTION IN INCIDENT LIGHT

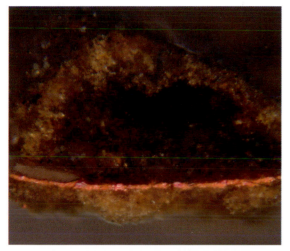

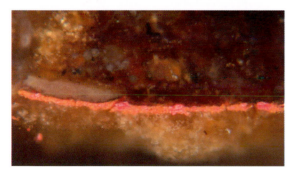

UV LIGHT

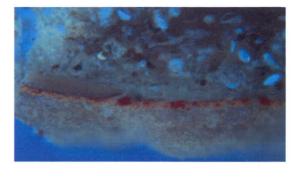

- surface accretions

Earliest/original decoration
- vermilion
- calcium sulphate with yellow earth.

SEM/EDX
- SEM/EDX analysis of the red pigment confirmed the presence of: Hg, S
- SEM/EDX analysis of the substrate confirmed the presence of: Ca, S, Fe, K, Si, Al
- SEM/EDX analysis of the material on top of the red pigment confirmed the presence of: Ca, S, Si, C, Fe.

4

CARVED AND WATER GILDED TABERNACLE FRAME WITH BROKEN PEDIMENT PAINTED WITH GLAZES AND SGRAFITTO DECORATION

Italy (Venetian) late sixteenth century[1]
Framing a gilded terracotta relief of the Virgin and Child,
Donatello or follower, 1450–1500,
Italy (Florence) 57:1-1867
Bought in Florence (Gagliardi) for £100
57:2-1867 (Sculpture Collection)

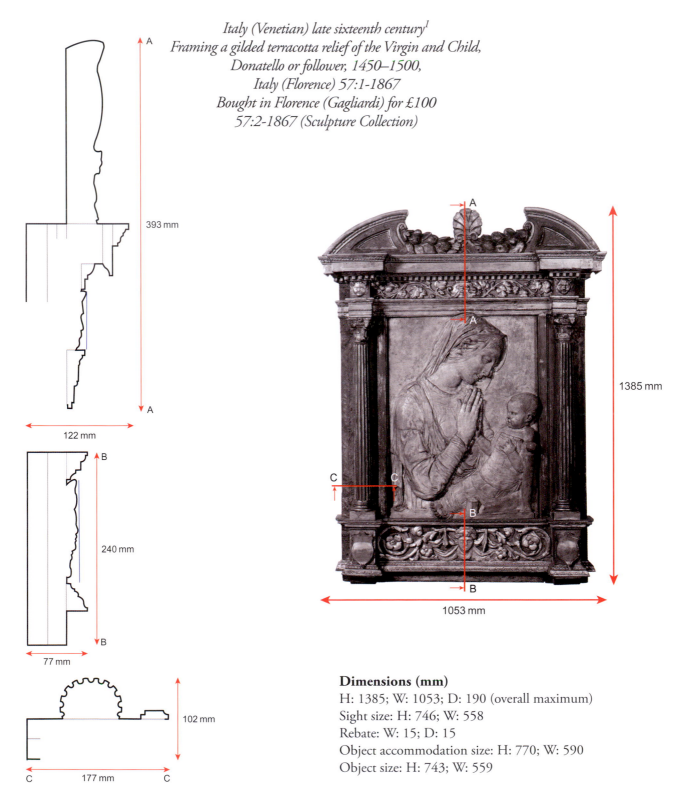

393 mm

122 mm

240 mm

77 mm

102 mm

177 mm

A

B

C

1385 mm

1053 mm

Dimensions (mm)
H: 1385; W: 1053; D: 190 (overall maximum)
Sight size: H: 746; W: 558
Rebate: W: 15; D: 15
Object accommodation size: H: 770; W: 590
Object size: H: 743; W: 559

Ornament

Fluted columns support an entablature, architrave mouldings are decorated with leaves and two rows of beads, and the cornice is also decorated with leaves, beads and dentils. The frieze is enriched with vine leaves and grapes springing from a central mask, with imposts decorated with a single winged cherub head. A palmette, supported by volutes emerging from fruit and foliage festoons, is set within a broken arched pediment. Scrolling leaves and rosettes springing from a central female mask with drapery decorate the predella frieze and a blind shield decorates each pedestal.

Structure

The back frame is partially obscured by a later build-up. The vertical members of the hardwood back frame are half lapped over the horizontals. The insides of the back frame form the depth of the rebate. In front of the back frame, at the top edge, there is a horizontal piece that, at left and right, is joined on to vertical pieces below by a T-bridle joint. The tongue of the joint is on the horizontal piece. In front of this is more wood, largely concealed below the applied arched pediment. The pediment is made from one piece of wavy figured hardwood, possibly lime. Beneath the pediment, there is a length of wood that forms the main part of the overhanging cornice. At either end, there are blocks with vertical grain that form the imposts above the columns. To the outside of each of these, there are wooden blocks and a horizontal grained piece of wood that form the overhanging cornice. Another horizontal grained piece forms the overhanging cornice at the sides. Over these, the cornice mouldings are mitred and applied, the flat first and then the leaf moulding. The dentils and leaf mouldings are applied below. The carved frieze is probably made of a length of wood set between the imposts.

The depth of the sides is composed of the vertical members of the back frame and a piece of wood in front, seen along the back edges of the sides, that is probably the verticals of the T-bridle jointed frame seen from the top. There are joins across the depth of the front piece near the top and bottom that can be seen behind the columns, which are applied to these pieces. The columns are almost round in section and have one-quarter of their depth cut away at the back.

Although the bottom edge was not accessible for examination of the construction, it is probable that the construction of the pedestals and the frieze is much the same as those of the imposts and frieze at the top. The shields on the pedestals are applied. The predella mouldings are mitred and applied.

Later Additions and Alterations

There is a recent softwood build-up on the back of the frame, with the top and bottom pieces butted between the side pieces, and a strip of wood across the bottom quarter of the relief. These are screwed into the back of the original frame.

The plain strips of wood at the sight edge on the left and right sides may have been added to cover the space between the sides of the relief and the frame, indicating the frame is not original to or made for the relief. Pope-Hennessy notes that the interior of the late sixteenth century frame of carved, gilded and painted wood appears to have been modified and the frame was not, therefore, made for the present relief.[2] The sight edge has been cut out around the figures. This might indicate that a frame not originally intended to house this relief was adapted to fit it; however, a similar characteristic exists on Frame 37 (6-1890), in which frame and relief are believed to be contemporaneous.

Inside return of right pedestal.

Decorative Finish

The single painted and water gilded scheme appears to be mostly original. The painted areas are quite worn and have several areas of retouching. The gilded areas have several areas of repair such as new patches of gold leaf, infills and retouching of areas of loss. A dark toning layer has been applied with the result that the surface now appears quite dull and the decoration is partly obscured.

The original water gilding was applied over an orange bole on a medium white ground. On the fruit festoons, the apples are painted red and, at the centre of the left festoon, yellow can be seen on the lemon, which is also textured with lines inscribed in the surface. The fruit has been further decorated with short, narrow, wavy gold lines carried out in sgrafitto, for example the pomegranates. This sgrafitto pattern is repeated elsewhere on the frame below the central palmette, on the background to the acanthus leaf capitals and on the fronts of the pedestals. The foliate and fruit festoons have been further embellished with the addition of a darker colour applied to recessed areas on the leaves to emphasise the relief.

On the flat areas of the broken arched pediment are the remains of painted husks and beads, and on the recessed area there is a sprig of three-lobed leaves. The painted backdrop to the columns is worn, but a painted vertebrate band of foliage, with a stem of laurel leaves with berries, is clearly distinguishable.

On the inside returns of the pedestals, the original painted scheme survives in remarkable condition. There is a foliate design outlined in blue–grey with black definition painted over burnished gilding (see detail image of inside return of right pedestal).

Hanging Device

Modern hanging fittings have been attached to the later build-up.

Observations and Conclusions

The frame is later than the relief. The frame may have been reused or may have been commissioned in the late sixteenth century to house this relief.

The carvings have a soft, fluid quality. The cherub heads have round, low-relief faces. These and the carving on the frieze and festoons are similar in general style to carving on Frame 21 (7150-1860). The central palmette at the top is slightly set off-centre towards the right, and the right side of the broken pediment is narrower than the left. Had the frame been made for the relief later, then the carver of this frame may have chosen to offset these in accord with the compositional bias of the Virgin and Child.[3]

The original painted and gilded finish would have appeared colourful and sumptuous. The gilded areas were probably burnished. Close visual examination revealed several colours and decorative patterns in sgrafitto.

Although the frame and relief do not belong together, as evidenced by the alterations to the frame to accommodate the relief, it is possible that they were gilded at the same time. The frame is water gilded over an orange bole on a white ground. The terracotta relief is oil gilded, though this is not original. Pope-Hennessy noted that 'The gilt surface of the relief is described by Maclagan and Longhurst as partly rubbed. From cleaning (1949), it transpires that old (possibly original) gilding is preserved in the recesses of the relief'.[4]

Further investigation is required to establish the nature of the earlier gilding on the terracotta and to identify any similarities with the early gilding on the frame. Results could indicate that the terracotta was gilded when the frame was fitted.

Comparable Frames

The use of short, narrow wavy gold lines carried out in sgrafitto can also seen on a tabernacle frame,

Lombardy, late sixteenth century, in Newbery, T., Bisacca, G. and Kanter, L. *Italian Renaissance frames.* Exhibition Catalogue. New York: Metropolitan Museum, 1990. p. 75, Figure 49.

Previous Citation

Pope-Hennessy, J., assisted by Lightbown, R. *Catalogue of Italian sculpture in the Victoria and Albert Museum.* London: Her Majesty's Stationery Office, 1964. p. 77, Cat. No. 64.

References

1. Date of frame based on notes from a brief survey of V&A of Italian frames and furniture, carried out December 1992 by Larry Kanter, Curator Lehman Collection, Metropolitan Museum of Art, New York.
2. Pope-Hennessy, J., assisted by Lightbown, R. *Catalogue of Italian sculpture in the Victoria and Albert Museum.* London: Her Majesty's Stationery Office, 1964. pp. 77–78, Cat. No. 64, Figure 80.
3. Tim Miller, personal communication, January 2008.
4. Pope-Hennessy, J., assisted by Lightbown, R. *Catalogue of Italian sculpture in the Victoria and Albert Museum.* London: Her Majesty's Stationery Office, 1964. pp. 77–78, Cat. No. 64, Figure 80; referring to Maclagan, E. and Longhurst, M. H. *Catalogue of Italian sculpture.* London: Victoria and Albert Museum, 1932. pp. 22–23.

5

CARVED TABERNACLE FRAME PAINTED WITH TROMPE L'OEIL DECORATION, TRIANGULAR PEDIMENT AND ANTEPENDIUM

Italy (Florence), 1475–1500
Probably original frame for Virgin and Child
relief after Benedetto da Maiano (1442–1497) 5768:1-1859
Bought in Florence (vendor not recorded) for £3
5768:2-1859 (Sculpture Collection)

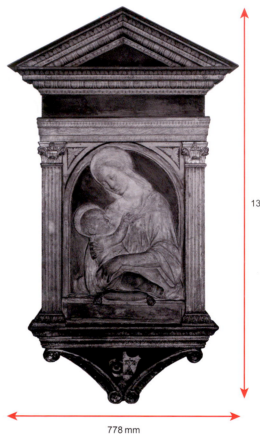

1378 mm

778 mm

Dimensions (mm)
H: 1378; W: 778 (overall maximum)
Relief: H: 632; W: 429

Ornament

The spandrels have painted tri-form foliage. Fluted pilasters with Corinthian capitals and carved leaf-and-dart bases support an entablature with architrave, frieze and cornice and a triangular pediment. The mouldings on the frame are painted in trompe l'oeil to give the illusion of carving. The architrave is painted with fluting, Vitruvian scroll and leaf-and-dart. The cornice is decorated with a leaf-and-tongue cyma, egg-and-dart ovolo, dentil fillet and leaf-and-dart cyma. These are repeated in the upper part of the pediment. The entablature frieze is inscribed 'GLORIA IN EXOLSE' (gloria in excelsis) and the tympanum is undecorated. The antependium, formed by fluted scrolls terminating either end with rosettes, is decorated with a shield bearing arms. Pope-Hennessy describes these as sable, two concentric annulets argent,

64

impaling another coat argent, a sextuple mount with a rose bush in chief. He also notes the annulets correspond with those of Albizzi save in the substitution of argent for gold.[1]

Structure

The depth of the pilasters is made up of two pieces of wood. The capitals are applied separately and the carved detail continues around their sides. The carved bases of the pilasters are mitred and applied and the carved detail continues around the side. The pediment and antependium are made of separate pieces, which are applied. The mouldings of the architrave, cornice, pediment and those above the antependium are mitred and applied. The wood could not be visually identified.

Decorative Finish

The painted and gilded finish appears to be original. The mouldings are painted beige and grey stone. The illusion of depth is emphasised in dark grey and the high relief is highlighted in pale grey. The pilasters appear to be painted to imitate marble. The background to the tympanum, entablature, frieze and antependium is painted dark blue. The capitals and scrolls in the antependium are water gilded. The recessed fluting on these scrolls is painted in dark blue. The sides of the frame are a dark, speckled red, possibly painted in imitation of porphyry. Imitation porphyry is also found on Frame 3 (19-1891).

Hanging Device and Fittings

The back of the frame was not accessible to observe any hanging device. There is a metal flower in the crux of the antependium, below the painted shield, which may be part of a candleholder. The sacred presence could be signalled through light and many images of the Virgin and Child were provided with prickets for candles. A frame with candleholder and hanging device for a holy water vessel and sprinkler can be seen in *The Dream of St Ursula* by Vittore Carpaccio.[2]

Observations and Conclusions

The frame does not appear to have been altered and the relief fits well within it, suggesting that it may be original. Construction and surface decoration appear consistent with the other fifteenth century tabernacle frames examined. However, Maclagan and Longurst suggest that although the frame is old it is not necessarily the original frame.[3] Further investigation is required to confirm whether frame and relief are contemporaneous.

Comparable Frames

Tabernacle frame 11 (7820-1861) is also decorated with trompe l'oeil and has similar colours and painted mouldings.

Tabernacle frame, Italian, original to polychromed stucco relief of *Madonna and Child* attributed to Neri di Bicci, with similar pediment. See Sabatelli, F. *La cornice Italiana dal Rinascimento al Neoclassico.* Milan: Electa, 1992. p. 32, Figure 30.

Previous Citations

Maclagan, E. and Longurst, M. H. *Catalogue of Italian sculpture.* London: Victoria and Albert Museum, 1932. p. 57.

Pope-Hennessy, J., assisted by Lightbown, R. *Catalogue of Italian sculpture in the Victoria and Albert Museum.* Her Majesty's Stationery Office, 1964. pp. 162–3, Cat No. 138.

References

1. Pope-Hennessy, J., assisted by Lightbown, R. *Catalogue of Italian sculpture in the Victoria and Albert Museum.* London: Her Majesty's Stationery Office, 1964. p. 163, Cat. No. 138.

2. Cooper, D. In M. Ajmar-Wollheim and F. Dennis, eds. *At home in Renaissance Italy.* London: V&A Publications, 2006. p. 192.

3. Maclagan, E. and Longurst, M. H. *Catalogue of Italian sculpture.* London: Victoria and Albert Museum, 1932. p. 57.

6

PAINTED AND WATER GILDED TABERNACLE FRAME WITH TRIANGULAR PEDIMENT AND ANTEPENDIUM

Italy, c.1435–1440
Original frame for stucco relief of the Virgin and Child, after Donatello
(1386/7-1466) and probably painted by Paolo di Stefano (1397–1478)
Presented by The Art Fund with the aid of
a body of subscribers in memory of Lord Carmichael of Skirling
A.45-1926 (Sculpture Collection)

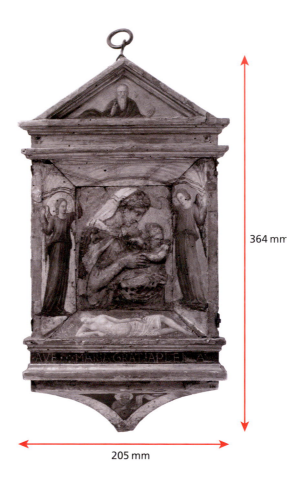

364 mm

205 mm

Dimensions (mm)
H: 364; W: 205; D: 48 (overall maximum)
Sight size: H: 117; W: 94

Ornament

The main frame surrounding the Virgin and Child is painted with two angels, one either side, holding a cloth, and Eve reclining at the bottom. Above, a plain entablature supports a pediment with God the Father, and below, the predella frieze bears the inscription 'AVE MARIA GRATIA PLENA' (Hail Mary Full of Grace). The antependium is painted with a prophet holding a scroll.

Structure

The frame is made from walnut. The back of the frame appears to be made of one piece from which the two chamfered sides are carved out, leaving a flat surface between, to which the stucco relief is applied. The flat surface extends at the top and bottom. However there are circular cracks in the finish on the flat top edges of the chamfers indicating that there are pegs or large nail heads underneath, suggesting that

the chamfered sides are applied. The top chamfer and entablature are made from one piece that is applied to the upper surface. The bottom chamfer and predella, with mouldings, are made from one piece that is applied to the bottom lower flat surface. The cornice and architrave mouldings at the front and back edges are mitred and applied. The pediment is made from one piece with a diagonal grain direction, with applied mouldings. The pediment is applied on the top of the entablature and held with wrought nails, one inserted through the top on the left and one on the right. The antependium is made from one piece and is applied on to the base with wrought nails inserted from the bottom, one on the left and one on the right. The cast stucco relief is applied to the flat area at the centre of the frame. There is some damage caused by wood-boring beetle.

Decorative Finish

The frame and stucco retain the original painted and gilded finish. The gilding on both the frame and the stucco is water gilding on an orange–red bole applied over the thin, white ground. The painted and gilded finish is continuous over both frame and stucco relief. The gilding has been decorated with punch work and incised lines around the halos of the figures, which continues on the chamfered sides of the frame. The lettering on the predella frieze has been carried out in sgrafitto. The top of the pediment, sides of the entablature mouldings and sides of the antependium are painted off-white. The sides of the entablature frieze are painted blue. The sides of the central area and the predella frieze are red.

Hanging Device and Fittings

There is a metal ring at the top from which the object would have been hung. There are holes on the back caused by nails from previous hanging fittings. The remains of two hinges on each outside edge indicate that there were originally two doors or that this was originally a triptych that has now lost its wings.

Observations and Conclusions

The size of this tabernacle frame indicates that it was probably placed in a domestic setting or was a portable devotional image. The inscription provides a prompt for the recitation of the rosary, while the cloth held by the two angels on either side recalls the veils used to cover paintings.[1]

The soft sheen of the paint has the appearance of egg tempera. The appearance of the paint, particularly of the sgrafitto work, is very similar to Frame 9 (6867-1860), where analysis showed the paint to include egg. The bole colour on these two objects is also very similar. Although not analysed, there is little doubt the object retains an original water gilded and egg tempera painted finish and that the relief and frame are integral. This conclusion is based on the continuous painted and gilded surface and tooling of the gilding, which confirms that the image and frame were painted and gilded at the same time.

Comparable Frames

Frame 7 (93-1882) also has stucco relief surrounded by a painted wooden frame.

Previous Citations

Pope-Hennessy, J., assisted by Lightbown, R. *Catalogue of Italian sculpture in the Victoria and Albert Museum*. London: Her Majesty's Stationery Office, 1964. p. 77.

Sabatelli, F. *La Cornice Italiana dal Rinascimento al Neoclassico*. Milan: Electa, 1992. pp. 30–31.

Evans, M. *The painted world from illumination to abstraction*. London: V&A Publications, 2005. p. 36.

Cooper, D. In Ajmar-Wollheim, M. and Dennis, F. *At home in Renaissance Italy*. London: V&A Publications, 2006. p. 192.

Reference

1. Cooper, D. In M. Ajmar-Wollheim and F. Dennis, eds. *At home in Renaissance Italy*. London: V&A Publications, 2006. p. 192.

7

WATER GILDED TABERNACLE FRAME WITH TRIANGULAR PEDIMENT DECORATED WITH SGRAFITTO AND PUNCH WORK

Italy (Florence), about 1430–1440
Original frame for stucco relief of the Virgin and Child
with Saints and Angels after Donatello (1425–1446)
Bought in Florence (vendor not recorded) for £80
93-1882 (Sculpture Collection)

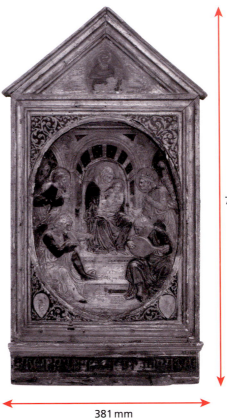

762 mm

381 mm

Dimensions (mm)
Frame: H: 762; W: 381
Relief: H: 406; W: 305

Ornament

An oval sight edge is surrounded by four spandrels decorated with scrolling leaf work and two vacant shields at the bottom. The surrounding main frame consists of a cavetto and fillet. The same moulding is repeated in the triangular pediment, which is painted with the figure of the Redeemer. The predella frieze is inscribed 'AVE MARIA GRATIA PLENA DO MINUS TECUM' (Hail Mary Full of Grace the Lord is with you).

Structure

The main body of the frame is made from one piece of hardwood, approximately 70 mm thick, which has an oval recess for the stucco. The stucco relief has a flat border that is roughly level with

the surrounding spandrels of the wooden frame. The lowest point of the stucco, the background to the Virgin and Child, is of some depth, which explains the need for such a thick back frame. The outer moulding is mitred and applied and held with nails. The pediment is applied on top of the main body of the frame, the front mouldings are applied, capped by a separate top moulding that covers the full depth of the pediment. The front of the predella is a separate piece with horizontal grain and is applied on to the main body of the frame. The top predella moulding is applied. The bottom predella moulding is missing. Bands of bare wood on the front and back edges indicate where mouldings, now missing, would have been applied. A large, roughly circular, facet headed nail, used to secure the front wood of the predella to the main body of the frame, can be seen at the bottom left of the predella.

Decorative Finish
The gilding is original water gilding on an orange–red bole over a thin, white ground. The spandrels and predella frieze are painted in dark blue with sgrafitto. The gilded scrolling foliate design is decorated with punch work.

Hanging Device and Fittings
The back was not accessible. There was no evidence of hinges or fittings to indicate that the frame had wings or doors.

Observations and Conclusions
This frame and stucco relief have been on loan to the National Gallery, London, since June 1938. The gilded finish on the frame and on the edge of the central painted stucco panel is continuous, indicating they were decorated at the same time. It can therefore be concluded that the frame retains its original stucco relief. Its form and scale suggest that it was a private devotional image. The inscription provides a prompt for the recitation of the rosary.

Comparable Frames
Frame 6 (A.45-1926) also has a stucco relief with painted and gilded wood, sgrafitto and punch work. The bole colour is similar to Frame 7 (93-1882).

Previous Citations
This frame is referred to as the original frame for the stucco relief and is attributed to the workshop of Donatello in Sabatelli, F. *La cornice Italiana dal Rinascimento al Neoclassico*. Milan: Electa, 1992. p. 30.

The frame is described as the original frame for the stucco relief in Pope-Hennessy, J. *Catalogue of Italian sculpture in the Victoria and Albert Museum*, Volume I. London: V&A Publications, 1964. Cat. No. 74, pp. 93–94.

8

CARVED, WATER GILDED AND ORIGINALLY POLYCHROMED TABERNACLE FRAME WITH PERSPECTIVE ARCH

Italy (probably Tuscany), 1475–1500
Bought for £19
5893-1859 (Furniture and Woodwork Collection)

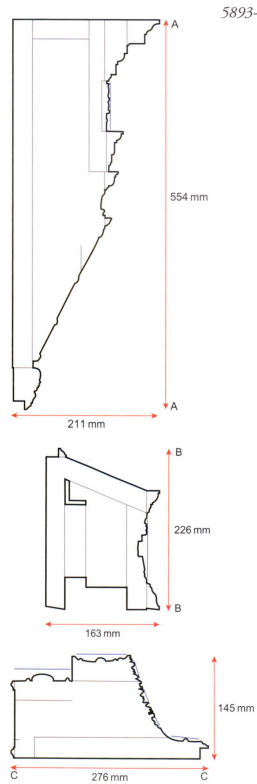

554 mm

211 mm

226 mm

163 mm

145 mm

276 mm

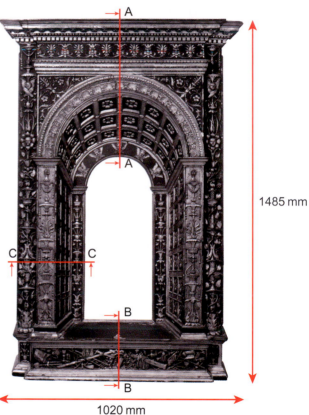

1485 mm

1020 mm

Dimensions (mm)

H: 1485; W: 1020; D: 235 (overall maximum)
Sight size: H: 695; W: 285
Rebate: W: 15; D: 16
Object accommodation size: H: 725; W: 310

Ornament

This perspective tabernacle frame consists of pilasters, each decorated with classical candelabrum, supporting an arch enriched with scallop shells and an egg-and-dart ovolo moulding, with spandrels either side decorated with scrolling leaves

terminating in a flower and an anthemion. The entablature consists of an architrave made up of a succession of pearls, bead-and-pearl and leaf mouldings, a frieze embellished with anthemia and a cornice consisting of dentils, egg-and-dart and acanthus-leaf modillions. The arch and pilasters frame a receding-perspective coffered niche, decorated with rosettes. At the sight edge there are pilasters, each with classical candelabrum supporting an arch decorated with five winged cherub heads. At the base of the frame, the predella frieze is carved with the instruments of Christ's passion: the cross, the dice, cock, clothes, sponge, open tomb and flag of the Resurrection. Recessed pilasters at the sides of the frame are also decorated with classical candelabrum and embellished with flowers with faces, wheat, ivy leaves and winged cherub heads.

Structure

The frame is mostly made of poplar, with some oak. The back is made from four wide, full-height boards with an arched aperture rebated at the back. There are several large wrought nails with roughly round faceted heads, approximately 10 mm in diameter, which hold the back parts of the frame to the front. There are also several later countersunk holes for modern screws. There is a horizontal piece of wood inserted at the top edge that conceals some of the construction.

At either side of the four pieces on the back, various pieces form the back and back edge of the outermost pilasters. The joints have opened up along the back edges. The small mouldings on the back edge of the pilasters are applied, and have joins along their length. The pilaster's left back edge is made from three pieces joined along the length to form most of the depth. There is a thin piece of wood between the carved front of the pilaster. The right pilaster's back edge is made from two

pieces, the back piece is made of two pieces of oak joined across the length, and there is another piece of wood further in, which appears to have been inserted from the top. A slightly different arrangement of wood can be seen when looking at the bottom of the frame.

The carved fronts of the outer pilasters are each made from one piece. Between these, above the arch are four wide vertical-grained pieces from which the spandrels are made. The cornice and architrave are applied over the top of these pieces. The cornice mouldings are applied in two layers. The egg-and-dart and dentil moulding is applied first, followed by the cyma and modillions. Most of these mouldings are mitred at the corners, except for the front piece of the egg-and-dart and dentil, which is set between the return pieces. On the front of the cornice, at the top left and right, there is a join across the moulding just before the mitres. The carved frieze panel in between is applied.

The niche is made from several pieces. The front third of the niche, including the protruding carved pilasters and the shell-carved part of the arch, is divided centrally into two halves and each half appears to be carved from a single piece. The mouldings above and below the shell carvings are applied. The remaining depth of the niche, also divided centrally, appears to be made of one piece. The sight edge pilasters, with rebate behind, are made of the same type of wood as the back of the frame. The inset arch with winged cherub heads is made in two halves, butt joined at the centre and held in with modern nails. The impost mouldings along the base of the arch are mitred and applied.

The sloping floor is made from a single piece of wood applied on to the top of the predella. The front of the predella is made from one piece of wood, applied on to the side pieces. The mouldings at top and bottom are mitred and applied. The

predella is hollow. Internally, there are several sharp ends of wrought nails visible that have been used to hold the pieces together. On the underside of the slope, at left and right, there are lighter coloured areas and remains of glue, where supporting blocks were once attached. A length of wood is applied across the inside back of the frame. At the centre front there is a large block of wood that, at the top, is shaped to support the floor above and is fitted over the length of wood applied across the back. The wood applied across the inside back of the frame and the wood of the slope are much lighter and more orange coloured than other nearby wood and have not suffered from wood-boring beetle damage. These pieces are held with nails with roughly round faceted heads. On the outside front, at the centre of the predella, a large nail head holding this block can be seen in the carved entry to the cave tomb. There are several small pieces of wood applied at the base of the pedestals.

Later additions

The following parts are probably later additions: the whole length of the back edge of the outer pilasters and the rectangle of small applied mouldings at the base of the pilaster, the applied cornice and predella mouldings on the outermost pilasters, the small pieces of wood at the bottom below the pedestals and some of the associated structural pieces behind the earlier carved front of the outer pilasters.

Decorative finish

There are two decorative schemes. The present finish consists of dark blue overpaint and gilding. The dark blue overpaint, which consists of French ultramarine combined with lead white and a sulphur-rich black pigment, has been thickly applied and overlaps the adjacent carved relief. French ultramarine was developed in the early nineteenth century, so this paint scheme must have been applied after that time. Under the cornice,

above the outer pilasters, the blue pattern over gold between the acanthus modillions is created with a brush, while at the front, above the spandrels, it is mainly created in sgrafitto.

The original scheme, also painted and gilded, is visible where there are losses in the dark blue overpaint layer. Analysis and visual examination indicate that the frame was originally decorated with a rich and complex scheme.[1] The original brilliant blue consists of smalt sometimes combined with a little natural azurite (samples taken from the right outer pilaster, entablature frieze and the predella frieze). This particular combination of pigments has been identified in a number of contemporary panel paintings.[2] In the sample taken from the entablature frieze, the blue pigment was applied over a pinkish ground of red lake and lead white, possibly to produce a warm purple cast to the blue layer. This may also have been done to simulate natural ultramarine.[3]

On the sloping floor above the predella, an earlier red paint is visible with brush strokes in a darker colour on the surface, which may have been applied to imitate marble or porphyry. It has been suggested that linear details may have been painted in perspective to indicate receding floor tiles, similar to a perspective effect used on a marble tabernacle at San Lorenzo, Florence, by Desiderio da Settignano.[4] A sample of the red paint from the floor area confirmed the presence of vermilion combined with a yellow earth pigment, producing a bright orange–red, over a calcium sulphate preparation. The back edge of the protruding pilasters and the arch are also painted red but samples from this area did not provide clear evidence of the original finish.

The gilded areas are largely original water gilding with several areas of later repair overgilding.

The earlier water gilding, applied over a dark red bole on a white ground, can be seen on the fronts of the protruding pilasters, which are enriched with punch work on the background. Punch work is also seen on the dividing mouldings in the coffered niche and some details of the carved symbols of Christ's Passion on the predella frieze. These areas were possibly not overgilded in order to retain the original punch work.

Analysis of the original water gilding indicates that the gold leaf was applied over a red bole on a calcium sulphate ground. In the sample taken from the carved moulding of the predella, a red lake glaze is apparent over the gold leaf, applied to provide subtle variation in colour. In addition, in a sample from the plinth base of the left protruding pilaster, a large, copper-rich particle, possibly azurite, was identified combined with surface accretions on the surface of a red lake glaze over gold leaf. This may represent the remains of a semi-translucent purple layer used to embellish the gilding in this area.

The overgilding is apparent in several areas such as the bases to the pilasters, where the original gilded finish can be seen below. The shell-decorated arch appears to have later oil gilding.

A sample of paint taken from the bottom of the right outermost recessed pilaster, lower section, showed only the presence of the most recent scheme. This consisted of French ultramarine combined with lead white and a sulphur-rich black pigment, over a white preparation layer.

Hanging Device

There are two later metal fixings at the top and various modern fixing holes. There are no remnants of hinges or holes to indicate that there could have once been a door.

Observations and Conclusions

The original setting for this frame was likely to have been a church or private chapel. It possibly framed a relief or a painting of the Crucifixion, Pieta, or other associated subject.[5] It has also been suggested that this could equally be the framework or front piece for a cupboard or niche to store the ciborium. The lower panel is carved with the instruments of the Passion, perhaps picking up the theme of the painting or the ciborium the frame may have contained.[6]

The cornice mouldings on the outer pilasters have a very different character of carving from the cornice above the main frieze. Further evidence to support the suggestion that these are later additions is found through close visual examination of their painted and gilded surfaces. Here, only the later painted and gilded finish was found with no earlier scheme below. They also have a different character of sgrafitto work.

The rest of the frame retains the original painted and gilded finish; overpainted areas have the same dark blue paint that was found on the later parts. In many areas, the original gilding is overgilded with the same gilding found on the later parts. It would appear that the overpaint and overgilding were applied when these later parts were added.

There is little evidence to imply that these later pieces of wood were applied as repairs to a damaged wooden structure. It is more likely that they were added to adapt the frame to create a stand-alone object after it was removed from its original setting where, perhaps recessed into the architecture of a room, it may not have had back edges or a flat base.

Comparable Frames

Marble tabernacle at San Lorenzo, Florence, by Desiderio da Settignano (1408–1464) illustrated in Bock, E. *Florentinische und venezianische Bilderrahmen aus der Zeit der Gotik und Renaissance*. Munich: F. Bruckmann, 1902. p. 63.

Venetian tabernacle frame, end of fifteenth century (Edmond Foulc Collection, Paris) in Guggenheim, M. *Le cornici Italiane dalla metà del secolo XVo allo scorcio del XVI.; con breve testo riassuntivo intorno alla storia ed all'importanza delle cornice.* Milan: U.Hoepli, 1897. Plate 36.

Masaccio's Fresco of *The Trinity* in St Maria Novella in Florence depicts a similar coffered ceiling decorated with paterae. See Bock, E. *Florentinische und venezianische Bilderrahmen aus der Zeit der Gotik und Renaissanc.* Munich: F. Bruckmann, 1902. p. 35.

Girolamno Romanino's *The Virgin and Child with Saints Benedict, Giustina, Prosdocimo and Scolastica* (1513–1514) depicts a coffered ceiling decorated with paterae. The frame is painted blue and gold and is similar to this frame's original colouring (Padua, Museo Civico). See Penny, N. *National Gallery Catalogues. The Sixteenth Century Italian Paintings*, London: National Gallery, 2004. p. 314.

Previous Citation

This frame is referred to as Italian (Lombardy), end of the fifteenth century in Guggenheim, M. *Le cornici Italiane dalla metà del secolo XV allo scorcio del XVI; con breve testo riassuntivo intorno alla storia ed all'importanza delle cornice.* Milan: U.Hoepli, 1897. Plate 16.

References

1. Cross-section and SEM/EDX analysis of paint samples were carried out by Dr Helen Howard, Scientific Department, The National Gallery, London.

2. Stege, H. Out of the blue? Considerations on the early use of smalt as blue pigment in European easel painting. *Zeitschrift für Kunsttechnologie und Konservierung,* 18, 2004. pp. 121–142; Spring, M., Higgitt, C. and Saunders, D. Investigation of pigment–medium interaction processes in oil paint containing degraded smalt. *National Gallery Technical Bulletin,* 26, 2005. p. 63; Smith, A., Reeve, A., Powell, C. and Burnstock, A. An altarpiece and its frame: Carlo Crivelli's 'Madonna della Rondine'. *National Gallery Technical Bulletin,* 13, 1989. pp. 28–43.

3. Galassi, A. G., Fumagalli, P. and Gritti, E. Conservation and scientific examination of three Northern Italian gilded and painted altarpieces of the sixteenth century. In D. Bigelow, ed. *Gilded wood conservation and history.* Madison, CT: Sound View Press, 1991. p. 200.

4. Lynn Roberts, personal communication, February 2008.

5. V&A Furniture Curatorial Records.

6. John Kitchen, former Head of V&A Furniture Conservation, from curatorial records.

RESULTS OF ANALYSIS
SAMPLE 5/1
LOCATION

Right column, background: dark paint next to gilded droplets.

PAINT CROSS-SECTION IN INCIDENT LIGHT

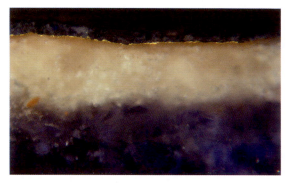

UV LIGHT

- surface accretions
- French ultramarine combined with lead white and a sulphur-rich black pigment
- gold leaf
- thin layer of bole
- calcium sulphate preparation.

Earliest/original decoration
- smalt with a few particles of azurite.

SEM/EDX

- SEM/EDX analysis of a glassy blue particle in the lowest layer confirmed the presence of: Si, K, Ba, Fe, Co, As, Cl
- SEM/EDX analysis of a copper-rich blue particle in the lowest layer confirmed the presence of: Cu, O, Si, Cl, K, S, Al
- SEM/EDX analysis of the white ground over the glassy blue layer confirmed the presence of: Ca, S, Cl, Mg
- SEM/EDX analysis of the metal leaf confirmed the presence of: Au
- SEM/EDX analysis of bole beneath gold confirmed the presence of: Ca, S, Si, Al, Fe, Cl
- SEM/EDX analysis of a large black particle in the uppermost layer confirmed the presence of: S, Cl, K, (Pb)
- SEM/EDX analysis of a blue particle in the uppermost layer confirmed the presence of: Si, Al, S, K, Na, Cl, Ca
- SEM/EDX analysis of the matrix of the uppermost layer confirmed the presence of: Pb, Cl, (K).

SAMPLE 5/2

LOCATION

Antependium, front, edge of loss: red and flake next to this.

PAINT CROSS-SECTION IN INCIDENT LIGHT

UV LIGHT

- dark organic layer on surface
- red layer of vermilion combined with yellow earth
- calcium sulphate preparation.

SEM/EDX

- SEM/EDX analysis of brilliant red inclusions in paint layer confirmed the presence of: Hg, S, Ca, Fe, Cl
- SEM/EDX analysis of yellow inclusions in paint layer confirmed the presence of: Fe, Cl, Si, Ca, K, S, Al
- SEM/EDX analysis of red paint layer generally confirmed the presence of: Hg, S, Ca, Fe, Si, Cl
- SEM/EDX analysis of the white ground confirmed the presence of: Ca, S, Cl.

SAMPLE 5/3

LOCATION

Front carved panel, near centre: original gilding.

PAINT CROSS-SECTION IN INCIDENT LIGHT

UV LIGHT

INCIDENT LIGHT

- organic layer on the surface

Earliest/original decoration

- red lake
- gold leaf
- red bole
- calcium sulphate preparation.

SAMPLE 5/4
LOCATION
Base of left-hand carved inner column, plain moulding: original gilding.

PAINT CROSS-SECTION IN INCIDENT LIGHT

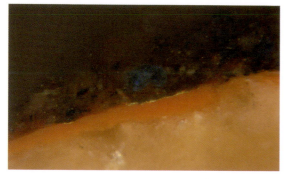

UV LIGHT

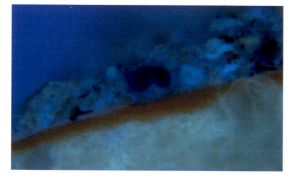

- surface accretions including large copper-rich blue particle

Earliest/original decoration

- red lake
- gold leaf
- red bole
- calcium sulphate preparation.

SAMPLE 5/5
LOCATION
Coffered inner arch next to carved 'rose' left side: dark background.

PAINT CROSS-SECTION IN INCIDENT LIGHT

UV LIGHT

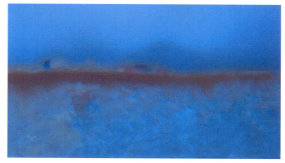

- surface accretions

Earliest/original decoration

- red lake
- gold leaf
- red bole
- calcium sulphate preparation.

SAMPLE 5/6

LOCATION

Frieze of architrave, left side: dark background.

PAINT CROSS-SECTION IN INCIDENT LIGHT

UV LIGHT

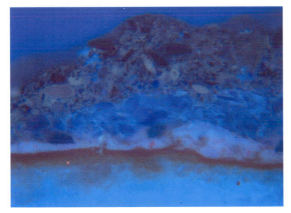

- surface accretions
- French ultramarine combined with lead white and a sulphur-rich black pigment.

Earliest/original decoration

- smalt with a few particles of azurite at the base of the layer
- lead white combined with red lake
- red bole
- calcium sulphate preparation.

SEM/EDX

- SEM/EDX analysis of blue particle in the uppermost dark blue paint layer confirmed the presence of: Si, Al, K, Na, Cl, Pb
- SEM/EDX analysis of glassy particle in lower blue layer confirmed the presence of: Si, K, Co, Fe, Ba, As, Cl
- SEM/EDX analysis of copper-rich blue particle in lower blue layer confirmed the presence of: Cu, O
- SEM/EDX analysis of a red lake particle confirmed the presence of: Al, S, Ca, Cl, K, Pb
- SEM/EDX analysis of the red preparation confirmed the presence of: Si, Al, Fe, K, Cl, Ti
- SEM/EDX analysis of the white preparation confirmed the presence of: Ca, S, Cl.

9

CARVED, WATER GILDED AND PAINTED TABERNACLE FRAME DECORATED WITH SGRAFITTO

Italy (probably Tuscany), probably c.1500
Given by Tito Gagliardi of Florence
6867-1860 (Furniture and Woodwork Collection)

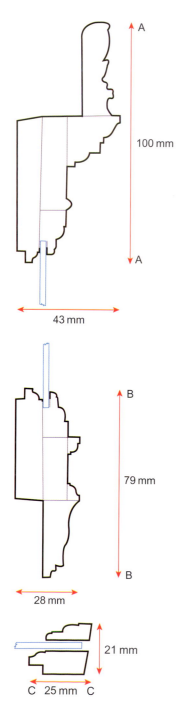

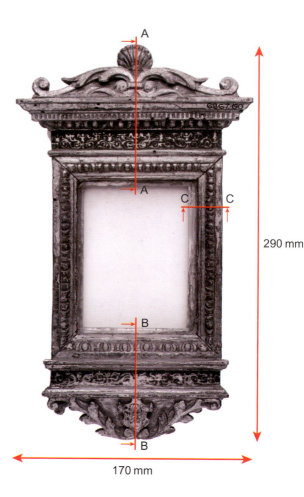

Dimensions (mm)

H: 290; W: 170; D: 43 (overall maximum)
Sight size: H: 105; W: 78
Rebate: W: 5; D: 4
Object accommodation size: H: 116; W: 88
Slot: H: 123; W: 4

Ornament

The sight edge is bordered by a plain moulding followed by an ovolo enriched with egg-and-dart and fillet. The entablature and predella friezes are

decorated with a sgrafitto scrolling leaf pattern. An egg-and-dart and dentil cornice supports a pediment in the form of scrolling volutes and cauliculi surmounted by a shell. The antependium is also formed of scrolling volutes and cauliculi flanking a central cartouche bearing painted arms.

Structure

The frame is made from lime or poplar and is made up of a back and a front frame. The back frame is made from a vertically grained board with a rebate for the framed object. The pediment is made from one piece applied to the front face of the cornice of the entablature. The cornice is made of one piece that is applied on to another piece, the lower half of which forms the entablature frieze and the astragal architrave moulding below. On the back edges, the astragal ends at the join with the back frame but would originally have continued over the outer edge of the back frame, as evidenced by the outline of bare wood. The egg-and-dart sight moulding is mitred. The predella frieze is made of one piece and the antependium another. The mouldings at the top and bottom of the predella frieze are applied and are missing at the back edges. Small pins and glue hold the elements of this frame together. There is a slot on the right side of the frame into which a piece of glass has been inserted. At the back of the frame there is a rebate to hold another object. On the back there is damage from wood-boring beetle.

Decorative Finish

There is one original decorative scheme of water gilding with blue sgrafitto work on the entablature and predella friezes. The cartouche is painted with a coat of arms, now largely worn away; however, two lions supporting a shield can be seen. The gilding has no apparent coating. The gold leaf is thick and has been burnished. The gold is applied over a red/orange bole over a thin white ground that has a light grey hue.

The gilding is quite worn in areas, showing the white ground below. The gilding on the sight edge moulding under the glass is well preserved in some areas.

The sgrafitto work on the entablature and predella friezes would originally have been a brighter blue but now appears darker. An example of the brighter blue can be seen on the predella frieze on the bottom right. The original blue paint has the appearance of egg tempera.

A sample of the blue paint was analysed and showed the presence of azurite and probably charcoal.[1] Gas chromatography–mass spectroscopy (GC-MS) analysis was used to identify the presence of egg in the blue paint. Egg tempera was commonly used on painted wooden objects of the period. Animal glue was also found in the sample but this may have come from the ground layer below.

Analysis of a sample of the gilding found that the bole contained a red earth, such as terra rossa, and the ground layer contained a mixture of chalk and gypsum. The bole colour is very similar to that found on Frame 19 (10-1890).

Hanging Device

There is an early ring hook attached to another, smaller ring fixed to the wood with a bent nail.

Observations and Conclusions

The 5 mm depth of the rebate suggests that this small frame may have contained a mirror or painting, possibly an image of the Virgin and Child, and may have been used as an object for private devotion. Frame 6 (A.45-1926) is another example of a small devotional frame.

The glass may be original and may have been used to protect the object behind. It contains air bubbles and small amounts of debris, and on its surface the raised lines suggest that it could be blown or spun glass. However, if the glass is not original, the slot may have been used to accommodate a sliding cover to conceal, reveal and protect the framed object.

Comparable Frames

Tabernacle frame, Italian, mid-sixteenth century, has a very similar pediment and antependium. See Newbery, T., Bisacca, G. and Kanter, L. *Italian Renaissance frames*. Exhibition Catalogue. New York: Metropolitan Museum, 1990. p. 50, Figure 20.

Reference

1. Analysis carried out by Dr Brian Singer, Northumbria University.

RESULTS OF ANALYSIS
SAMPLE 1

Blue sgrafitto over the gilding (taken from the entablature frieze on the back edge, just below the egg-and-dart cornice moulding).

POLARISED LIGHT MICROSCOPY

Polarised light microscopy indicated that the red bole consisted of a red earth such as terra rossa. The ground layer contained colourless particles which had a refractive index (n) of less than 1.66, were anisotropic with fairly low birefringence and included rods with parallel extinction. These were identified as gypsum. It also contained some colourless particles with n < 1.66, showing high birefringence and a rhombic shape, which were identified as chalk. The blue pigment in the paint showed anisotropic blue particles with bright polarisation colours identified as azurite and also some opaque black particles which were probably charcoal.

GC-MS ANALYSIS

An attempt was made to separate the blue paint layer but some ground was unavoidably included. This mixture was derivatised by acid hydrolysis and then treatment with propan-1-ol and dry hydrochloric acid followed by treatment with pentafluoropropanoic acid anhydride. This procedure gives an opportunity to analyse the amino acids derived from proteins present as their propyl ester/*N*-pentafluoropropanoyl (NPFP) derivatives and also fatty acids derived from any lipids, and oils and resin acids derived from any resins present as their propyl esters.[1] Peaks for the fatty acids were hardly present, only a trace of palmitate

was clearly visible (Figure 9.1), indicating that the sample contained few lipids. The first 23 minutes of the chromatogram (see Figure 10.2, in analysis report for Frame 10, 1079-1884) contains the eluted amino acids. The peaks are large, indicating that protein is present. The profile of the amino acids calculated from their relative abundance (Figure 9.2) matches that of animal glue quite well, but the peaks for serine and aspartic acid seem a little high for glue and the peaks for alanine, proline and hydroxyproline seem a little low. This suggests that a little egg or casein may be mixed in with the animal glue. Perhaps the egg is in the blue paint layer on top of the gesso ground.

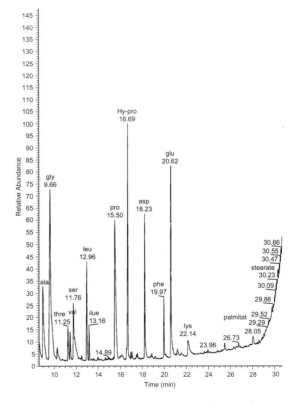

Figure 9.1   GC-MS chromatogram for sample 6867-1860, blue paint.

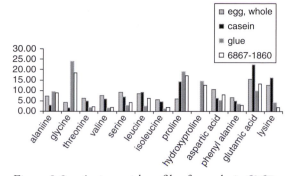

Figure 9.2   Amino acid profile of sample 1, 6867-1860, blue paint compared with standards.

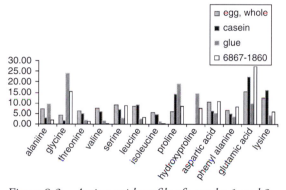

Figure 9.3   Amino acid profile of samples 1 and 3, 6867-1860, blue paint compared with standards, repeat run.

Another sample was taken from sample 1 and from sample 3 which had the same blue paint, this time taking extra care to include as little of the ground as possible, and the procedure was repeated. Again the amino acid profile (Figure 9.3) indicated animal glue, since there is still a sizeable peak for hydroxyproline but perhaps also some egg in a larger proportion than in the first run. However, the sample size was small and there is some ambiguity in the results, the large glutamic acid peak for example. It might be advantageous to sample just the blue layer in situ rather than trying to separate layers on very small samples, then the sample could be analysed again.

SAMPLE 2

Original gilding (taken from egg-and-dart cornice moulding, right back edge)

POLARISED LIGHT MICROSCOPY

Polarised light microscopy of sample 2 from 6867-1860 indicated that the red bole consisted of a red earth such as terra rossa. The ground layer contained colourless particles which had n < 1.66, were anisotropic with fairly low birefringence and included rods with parallel extinction. These were identified as gypsum. It also contained some colourless particles with n < 1.66, showing high birefringence and a rhombic shape, which were identified as chalk.

CONCLUSION

Object 6867-1860 has a white ground consisting of a mixture of chalk and gypsum, a red bole below the gold which consists of a red clay such as terra rossa, and at the point where sample 1 was taken a blue paint containing azurite and probably charcoal.

Reference

1. Singer, B. and McGuigan, R. The simultaneous analysis of proteins, lipids, and diterpenoid resins found in cultural objects. *Annali di Chemica*, 97, 2007. pp. 405–416.

10

CARVED TABERNACLE FRAME WITH PASTIGLIA RELIEF, WATER GILDED WITH SOME AREAS ORIGINALLY PAINTED BLUE

Italy (Veneto), 1500–1525
Bought in London (George Donaldson) for £60
1079-1884 (Furniture and Woodwork Collection)

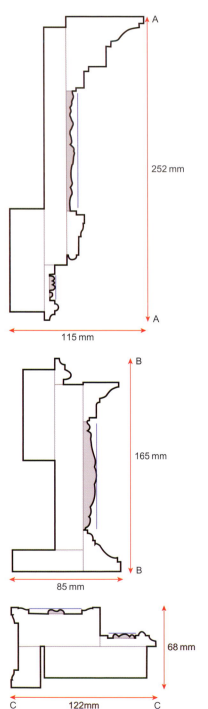

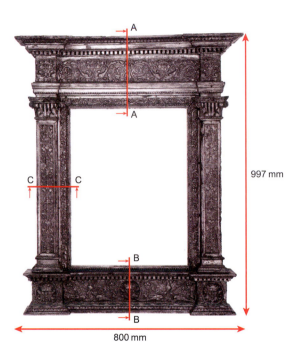

Dimensions (mm)
H: 987–997; W: 800; D: 138 (overall maximum)
Sight size: H: 577; W: 428
Rebate: W: 7; D: 25
Object accommodation size: H: 592; W: 443

Ornament

A cavetto followed by beads borders the sight edge followed, at top and sides, by an undulate band. The pilasters, decorated with foliate candelabra, and composite capitals support the entablature. Dolphins and scrolling foliage and rosettes decorate the entablature frieze. The architrave is largely plain with a band of pearls. The cornice is carved

with dentils and leaf-and-tongue mouldings. These mouldings are repeated in the predella. The predella frieze is decorated with a pair of dolphins supporting an eagle on either side of a central woodwose mask that is echoed in each pedestal.

Structure

The frame is made from poplar (back frame), softwood (front frame) and pear (mouldings and applied detail).[1] Looking at the back the vertical members of the back frame are half lap jointed over the horizontal members. The vertical members run from the top of the front frame and end on the top of the base piece of the predella. The vertical on the right projects above the top of the frame. The verticals sit within the applied back edge pieces of the front frame. The insides of the back frame form the depth of the sight edge rebate.

At the front of the frame, the entablature is made up of one piece of softwood applied on to the back frame. This can be seen at the rear of the frame between the verticals of the back frame. The imposts, with vertical grain, are applied. The rear of the back edge of each impost is made of a vertically grained piece applied on to the outside edge of the back frame. The cornice and architrave mouldings have carved fronts and plain outside returns and are mitred and applied. The low relief frieze decoration on the front surfaces is cast and applied pastiglia.

The pilasters sit between the bottom of the entablature and the top of the predella. The front piece is the full width of the pilaster. At either side, the rear part of the back edge of the pilaster is made of a piece applied on to the outside edge of the back frame. The cyma and fillet mouldings running vertically are carved from the solid wood but the horizontal mouldings are mitred and applied. The carved capitals are made of a front piece and a side piece. The front piece laps the sides and these are applied on to the pilasters into a shallow rebate. The moulding

that forms the bases of the pilasters is mitred and applied. The low relief pilaster decoration is pastiglia.

The predella is made up of one piece of softwood with the vertical grain pedestals applied. At either side, the rear part of the back edge of the pedestals is made of a piece of wood with vertical grain applied on to the outside edge of the back frame. The top and bottom mouldings, with carved fronts and plain outside returns, are mitred and applied. There is a base piece to the predella behind the bottom applied moulding. The low relief frieze decoration on the front surfaces is pastiglia.

The sight cavetto moulding and carved pearls, with the undulate band of scrolling relief (top and sides only), are mitred and applied. The scrolling relief ornament is pastiglia.

There is severe damage caused by wood-boring beetle, with various associated losses.

Later Additions and Alterations

The following are later mouldings:

- On the cornice (from left to right): the left back edge return, left inside return, right inside return, the upper part of the cornice carved with leaves above the impost on the right and the right back edge return.

- On the architrave: the right back edge return.

- On the pilasters: the cyma and fillet applied mouldings on the left back edge at the top, on the right back edge, top and bottom, and at the rear near the bottom an 86 mm section.

- On the right pedestal: the leaf and dentil moulding on the front inside and outside return; on the predella, the whole of the bottom moulding. Behind the cornice moulding at the imposts and back edge returns there are pieces of thin, modern veneer glued in. On top of the capitals there are wooden inserts (5–6 mm high) with the grain direction running horizontally.

- The bottom edge sight moulding has been cut back, the undulate band of pastiglia ornament and flat is missing, and only the cavetto and beads remain. The cyma and flat moulding on the pilasters have some mitre joins with a straight edge through the finish.

Decorative Finish

There is one original gilded and painted scheme and several areas of overgilding and overpainting. As well as these, there are many areas of a later retouching in bronze paint, now oxidised to a dull brown. A transparent shiny coating, which has the appearance of methacrylate, has been applied over the gilded surface. This was probably applied to consolidate the friable wood and flaking early gilded finish.

The areas of overgilding are water gilding on an orange bole, on a thin, white ground and are associated with the later replacement wood parts. This later gilding overlaps on to the adjacent earlier gilded scheme. This has an irregular dark spotting, probably a deteriorated toning layer.

There is a dark blue–black overpaint in the following areas: in between the dentils, in between the fluting on the capitals, on the background of the masks, on the returns of the entablature and predella frieze and the recessed panels on the back edges of the pilasters.

The original gilding is water gilding on red bole on a thin, white ground. The background of the relief on the entablature and predella frieze and pilasters is decorated with very small point punch work. The relief decoration is pastiglia.

Where there are losses of the overpaint, the brighter blue of an earlier painted finish can be seen on the capitals, dentils and on the background of the masks. Below the overpaint on the recessed panels on the back edges of the pilasters, there is

an earlier, orange–red layer very similar to the bole colour, though no gold leaf was observed.

Two samples of the pastiglia decorative relief from the mask on right pedestal were taken for analysis. It was concluded that the cast decoration was calcium sulphate, and contained hardly any binder made of protein, with perhaps just a tiny trace of animal glue.[2]

Hanging Device

No hanging device was observed.

Observations and Conclusions

The frame, which probably contained a painting, shows evidence of being at least partially dismantled, possibly to alter its dimensions or to carry out structural repairs. These include quite extensive replacements to the carving on the mouldings, carried out to repair damage and loss of wood caused by wood-boring beetle. As the whole of the bottom moulding was replaced, it cannot be certain that this is a replica of the lost original. Some alteration of ornament or scale may have occurred.

There are also several other alterations indicating dismantling and subsequent reassembly. The straight edges through the finish at the mitres on the pilaster mouldings indicate either that they have been cut after the gilding was applied or that the edges may have been 'tidied' before being reassembled. There is no indication that the height of the pilaster frieze has been altered. Even though the candelabra decoration has been foreshortened at the base where vases or burners would usually be, it is believed that this was done at the time of manufacture. There are no sharp cut edges to indicate it has been cut through at a later date, for example to shorten the height. Although cracks have formed at the edges of the cast work, the finish and cast work slope up at all edges by the adjacent mouldings. This indicates that it sits in its original place of application.

Other additions and alterations could indicate that the frame's size has been altered. The additional pieces of wood above the capitals were perhaps added to fill gaps after reassembly. Alternatively, they may have been put in when the sight edge moulding was reduced to alter the height of the frame, probably to fit a later painting. The pieces of wood for the rear part of the back edges of the imposts, pilasters and pedestals were possibly originally made from one piece but have been cut into separate pieces. To enable these pieces to be cut, the back frame would have been separated from the front and side parts and then the pieces would have been reapplied to the back frame. There are pieces of thin, modern veneer glued in behind the cornice moulding at the imposts and the back edge returns.

Comparable Frames

Mitchell draws comparisons with the wings on Bellini's triptych with original frame by Jacopo da Faenza, *Altarpiece of Virgin and Child with Saints*. S.Maria Gloriosa dei Frari, Venice. See Mitchell, P. Italian picture frames, 1500–1825: a brief survey. *Journal of the Furniture History Society*, 20, 1984. p. 19, Plate 11C.

Tabernacle frame, Italian, sixteenth century, with similar features. See Lessing, J. *Vorbilder-Hefte aus dem KGL. Kunstgewerbe-Museen Rahmen: Italien und Deutschland XVI Jahdhunder.* Berlin: Verlag Von Ernst Wasmuth, 1888. Plate 2.[3]

Tabernacle frame, Venetian, about 1500, probably for a painting of the Virgin and Child, displayed around *Doge Leonardo Loredan* by Giovanni Bellini 1501–1504, 90.5 × 86.5 cm. This has similar decorative features and general form but no predella and the bottom moulding is black with black showing below. See Penny, N. *Frames*. National Gallery Pocket Guides. London: National Gallery, 1997. p. 33, No. 25.

Tabernacle frame, Venetian, similar in type but with much smaller frame pilasters, which is probably a much later frame for *The Blood of the Redeemer* (between 1460 and 1465) by Giovanni Bellini (active 1459, died 1516), 340 × 470 mm, on display at The National Gallery, London.[4]

Tabernacle frame, Venetian, first quarter of the sixteenth century (Padova, Musei Civici) with similar overall appearance. The carved capitals and cast work on the predella frieze appear identical and the cast work on the column frieze is very similar. See Sabatelli, F. *La Cornice italiana dal Rinascimento al Neoclassico.* Milan: Electa, 1992. pp. 94–95.

Similar dolphin and eagle motifs to those seen in the cast work on this frame can be seen on a wedding chest, possibly Venetian, fifteenth or early sixteenth century, fir wood, gilded pastiglia and tempera with iron handles. H: 600; W: 1720; D: 560. Museo Stefano Bardini, Florence, Inv. No. 1220. See Ajmar-Wollheim, M. and Dennis, F. *At home in Renaissance Italy.* London: V&A Publications, 2006. pp. 61 and 360.

Previous Citations

This frame is referred to in Mitchell, P. Italian picture frames, *1500–1825: a brief survey. Journal of the Furniture History Society*, 20, 1984. p. 19, Plate 11C. Mitchell describes the frame as Venetian late sixteenth century and suggests that it was used for a small secular devotional picture.

References

1. Adam Bowett, personal communication, March 2008.
2. Analyses carried out by Dr Brian W. Singer, Northumbria University.
3. Thanks to Mr Plaut for this reference.
4. Thanks to Meghan Callahan for this reference.

RESULTS OF ANALYSIS

The sample was taken from the cast work on the edge of a damaged area of cast work on the bottom right pedestal.

POLARISED LIGHT MICROSCOPY

Polarised light microscopy indicated that was most of the material present gypsum. The colourless particles had a refractive index (n) of less than 1.66, were anisotropic with fairly low birefringence and included rods with parallel extinction. Some colourless particles were seen with n < 1.66, showing high birefringence and a rhombic shape, which were identified as chalk.

INFRARED ANALYSIS

Infrared analysis of the sample (Figure 10.1) showed peaks due to gypsum (cf. Figure 19.2 in Frame 19, 10-1890). There seems to be very little medium or chalk in this sample. A tiny peak at the wavelength of 1738 cm^{-1} is probably due to the ester carbonyl peak in a lipid. Hence some lipid is visible in the infrared.

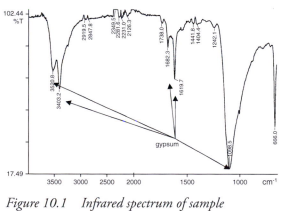

Figure 10.1   Infrared spectrum of sample 1079-1884.

GC-MS ANALYSIS

Peaks for the fatty acids were present and larger (Figure 10.2) than in the sample taken from

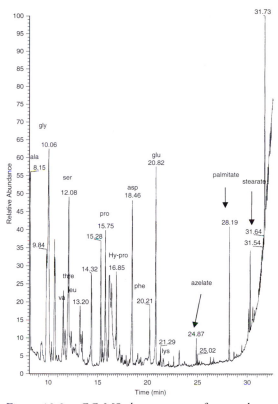

Figure 10.2   GC-MS chromatogram for sample 1079-1884.

Frame 19, 10-1890 (see Figure 19.3 in analysis report for Frame 19, 10-1890), indicating that the sample contained lipids. The azelate to palmitate ratio by percentage area (Table 10.1) is 0.18, confirming the absence of a drying oil.[1] The palmitate to stearate ratio is 1.61, which is within the correct range for egg.[1-3]

The first 23 minutes of the chromatogram (Figure 10.2) contains the eluted amino acids. The peaks are large, indicating that protein is present. The profile of the amino acids calculated from their relative abundance (Figure 10.4) matches that of animal glue quite well, but the peaks for serine and aspartic acid seem a little high for glue, and the peaks for alanine, proline and hydroxyproline seem a little low so a little egg may be mixed in with the animal glue. Perhaps the egg is in the paint layer on top of the gesso.

103

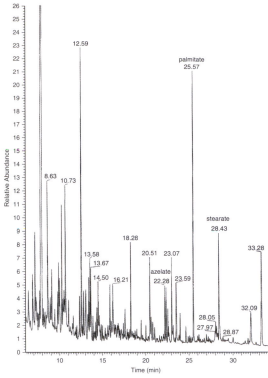

Figure 10.3   GC-MS chromatogram for sample 1079-1884 cast decoration only.

Table 10.1   Retention times and area % for fatty acid esters in sample 1079-1884

RT	Identity	Area (%)
24.87	Dipropyl azelate	10.21
28.19	Propyl palmitate	55.49
30.25	Propyl stearate	34.30

A second sample containing only the cast decoration and no white ground bole or gold leaf was also derivatised and run on GC-MS in the same way, but only a slight trace of a few amino acids were found (Figure 10.3), indicating that hardly any proteinaceous binder was present in the cast decoration layer itself. The amino acid profile (Figure 10.5) seems to be lacking in the more volatile components and skewed towards the less volatile amino acid derivatives, perhaps owing to evaporation of this tiny amount of amino acid

during the derivatisation procedure. The presence of proline and hydroxyproline suggests that there was a trace of animal glue in the sample. A small amount of azelic, palmitic and stearic acid were also found, which may indicate the inclusion of a trace of drying oil and animal fats.

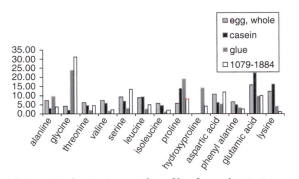

Figure 10.4   Amino acid profile of sample 1079-1884 compared with standards.

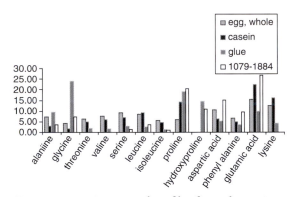

Figure 10.5   Amino acid profile of sample 1079-1884 cast decoration only compared with standards.

Conclusion

1079-1884 consists mainly of gypsum, with a trace of clay.

There was animal glue, and perhaps a trace of egg in the first sample run, but this may have been in the bole layer, white ground layer, size layer or paint layer, so another sample was run on just the cast decoration without the white ground, bole and gold. In the event, despite the fact that the sample was large only a minute trace of a few amino acids was found, suggesting that the cast decoration was just gypsum, formed probably from plaster of Paris, and contains hardly any binder made of protein, perhaps just a tiny trace of animal glue. There is the possibility that a gum binder is present since this possibility was not investigated. Some fatty acids were found and these may be due to a trace of animal fats with a trace of a drying oil.

References

1. Mills, J. S. and White, R. *The organic chemistry of museum objects*. 2nd ed. Oxford: Butterworth-Heinemann, 1994. pp. 170–172.

2. Schilling, M. R. and Khanjian, H. P. Gas chromatographic determination of the fatty acid and glycerol content of drying oils. Part 1. *ICOM Committee for conservation, 11th triennial meeting*, Edinburgh, 1996, Pre-prints, Volume 1. London: James and James, 1996. p. 220. (They quote Mills, J. S. The gas chromatographic examination of paint media. Part 1. Fatty acid composition and identification of dried oil films. *Studies in conservation*, 11, 1966. pp. 92–107.)

3. Ibid., p. 222.

11

TABERNACLE FRAME PAINTED WITH TROMPE L'OEIL DECORATION

Italy (probably Tuscany), about 1530
Bought, presumably from William
Blundell Spence
7820-1861 (Furniture and Woodwork Collection)

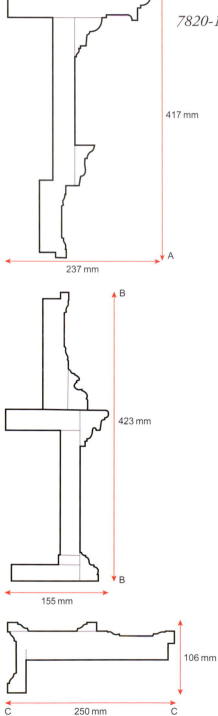

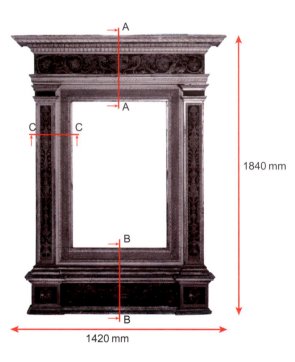

Dimensions (mm)

H: 1840; W: 1420; D: 245 (overall maximum)
Sight size: H: 980; W: 630
Rebate: W: 10; D: 22
Object accommodation size: H: 1000; W: 650

Ornament

The decoration is painted in trompe l'oeil to give the illusion of carving. The painted decorative elements are as follows: the sight edge is painted with guilloche, bordered either side with painted leaf-and-tongue cyma mouldings terminating with roundels at each corner. The pilasters, painted with candelabra, also bordered with leaf-and-tongue painted

cyma mouldings, support an entablature. The architrave is decorated with painted fluted tongues inset with eggs and the frieze comprises scrolling foliage with birds eating seeds sprouting from large flower heads. Two dolphin heads flowing from the foliage flank a tazza, overflowing with fruit and leaves. The cornice is decorated with a succession of painted leaf, dentil, egg-and-dart ovolo, Vitruvian scroll and acanthus-leaf cyma mouldings. The entablature frieze decoration is echoed in the predella frieze and the pedestals are decorated with a painted shield bearing arms showing a smiling sun face above a diagonal band, with three roses on stems.

Structure

The frame is made of lime or poplar. The predella is built separately from the rest of the frame. The upper part of the frame at the back is constructed of two wide vertical members which half lap the horizontal members at the top and bottom.

This frame, with a rebate cut out, forms the sight moulding, the surrounding frieze and the pilasters at the front. A length of applied wood forms the full width of the entablature and can be seen at the back between the tops of the vertical members of the back frame. The back edge of the frame, including the back cyma and fillet mouldings of the pilasters, is made from one length of wood.

At the top, a length of wood caps the frame and forms the overhanging element of the cornice. It is decorated with painted acanthus and Vitruvian scroll. This has been fixed on from the top with later screws. There are also numerous holes at the top, probably from original wrought nails. Some of these holes have gouged marks indicating that the wrought nails were prised out. A modern screw has been put in one of these holes.

The rest of the cornice, i.e. the mouldings painted with egg-and-dart and dentils and the architrave, is made up of applied mouldings mitred at the corners. The pilaster capitals are mitred and 'housed', as can been seen, from the back. The cyma and fillet mouldings on the pilasters at the top, bottom and outer edge are applied. The pilaster plinth

mouldings are rebated into the wood of the pilaster. The same section moulding continues across the front of the frame.

The structure described above sits on the predella, which is constructed like a box, open at the back. Looking from the back it can be seen that the two side pieces of the 'box' sit between the top and bottom. The front of the predella is contained within these four sides. The bottom member of the predella is nailed on to the sides, through the bottom, with wrought nails. The predella front is made from three pieces. There is a join across the length, one-third in from the left at the back (a crack though the paint can be seen at the front), and there is a narrow strip of wood at the bottom. Filler has been applied, probably associated with these joints. At the front of the predella, two pieces of vertically grained wood are applied to build up the thickness for the pedestals. The top and bottom mouldings are mitred and applied. These are held with wrought nails, the points of which can be seen from the back, protruding through the inside of the predella box.

There is now a gap between the main frame and the predella: at the bottom later addition metal straps tie the two together. Later metal hanging straps at the top hold the top of the frame on to the main frame.

There is damage associated with wood-boring beetle and extensive wood loss from the top of the cornice and the top of the left capital. On the predella, the bottom right back edge moulding is missing.

Labels and Inscriptions

There is a paper label pasted on the back of entablature, handwritten in ink: 'Al sig Guliemo Spence Firenze'.

An inscription on the back of the predella, written in ink on the wood, reads: 'Tutto questo Altare Fú dipinto da Bartolomeo Neroni Senese/detto Maestro Riccio' (All of this altarpiece was painted by Bartolomeo Neroni, the Sienese, [known as] doctor, Master Riccio).

Decorative Finish

There is one original decorative scheme, consisting of trompe l'oeil painting and water gilding. The mouldings are plain; the impression of carving is painted in grisaille. The background on the entablature and predella frieze, capitals, pilasters and pedestals is painted blue. The water gilding has been applied to selected areas such as the fillets on the mouldings. The gilding is applied on a red–brown bole applied on to a thin white ground. There are losses and some flaking of finish, particularly in the predella area, and some white surface accretions.

Samples of paint were analysed using polarised light microscopy.[1] Results from a sample of the blue paint showed the presence of coarse blue particles of azurite. The layer also contained charcoal, chalk, red ochre and some clay, which was possibly part of the natural red ochre. A sample of beige paint contained litharge and lead monoxide. The ground layer contained gypsum.

The sample of the bole was found to contain a red earth such as terra rossa. The white ground contained mainly gypsum with some particles of chalk.

Hanging Device

There are four later metal straps screwed on at the back. These have holes for wall fixings. There are also two later hook eyes fixed to the back of the frame.

Observations and Conclusions

The inscription, if original, indicates that the frame once contained a painted altarpiece. Frame 5 (5786:2-1859) is also decorated with trompe l'oeil decoration.

12

CARVED AND POLYCHROMED TABERNACLE FRAME WITH DOLPHIN PEDIMENT AND CHERUB ANTEPENDIUM

Northern France, 1500–1550 (or possibly c.1850)
Bought in London (George Donaldson) for £20
649-1890 (Furniture and Woodwork Collection)
Museum No. 649-1890

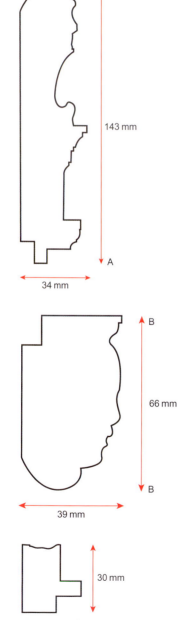

Dimensions (mm)
H: 363; W: 232; D: 40 (overall maximum)
Sight size: H: 155; W: 183
Rebate: W: 11; D: 7
Object accommodation size: H: 173; W: 205

Ornament

Informal Corinthian pilasters enriched with floral candelabra support an entablature with a plain cavetto and carved leaf-and-dart architrave. Imposts are decorated with a single lozenge and a dentil and simple leaf cornice. The arched pediment

Ca vieille Sculpture provient
de l'abbaye de Saint florent

649-1890

has its tympanum fully occupied by a scallop shell. Two leaping dolphins with large balls set between their curling lips surmount the pediment, which is terminated by flower-capped acroteria. The antependium consists of a central cherub head with wings spanning the width of the frame and wing tips supporting floral corbels.

The frieze bears the inscription on a simulated ribbon 'Prospice Superbe' (Contemplate [this], O proud one/in your pride). At the centre of the inscription there appears to be a shield bearing a coat of arms, now illegible.

Structure

The frame is made from two pieces of quarter-sawn oak joined at the centre. The lighter sapwood can be seen at the back top centre. The rebate at the back is later. It is thought that the frame originally had an integral carved panel, now missing. Saw marks are visible on the bottom sight edge. At the inner sides, the remains of the carved panel now form the plain flat sight edge and there is evidence of the remains of the panel which has been cut away.

Fixing holes indicate missing finials at the top left and right.

Inscription

An inscription on the back, 'Cette vieille sculpture provient de l'Abbaye de Saint Florent' (This old carving comes from the Abbey of Saint Florent), gives a clue as to its provenance but is not conclusive.

Decorative Finish

The current painted and gilded scheme appears to be largely original. It is now quite damaged and worn, and the original colour has darkened. It would originally have appeared very colourful and much brighter. Deep pink, and different shades of blue and white can be seen on close inspection.

The cherub's wings have traces of oil gilding, and the face might have been silver as the dulled surface has the appearance of tarnished silver leaf.

Three samples from the painted areas were analysed.[1] The pink, seen for example on the pilasters and inside each impost, was identified as vermilion mixed with two white pigments: lead white, and zinc white and a trace of gypsum. The pale grey blue, seen for example on the leaf-and-dart architrave, contained charcoal and ground glass, probably smalt. The dark blue, found in the recessed areas behind the winged cherub head, was identified as azurite.

Hanging Device

There is no evidence of an early hanging device. Various holes on the back are from recent hanging fittings.

Observations and Conclusions

The motto 'Prospice Superbe' on the front indicates that it may have had an integral panel painting or relief carving of a skull, as a *memento mori*, which would accord with a position in a religious house. The dolphin is a symbol of Christ. It may have been made for the private room of a superior cleric.[2]

The carving on the columns is simply executed without much detail. It has been suggested that the proportions are indicative of a provincial frame, possibly made by a local or amateur carver, perhaps even a member of the abbey from which this may have come.[3] It is not uncommon for older fashions to be employed for a longer time in the provinces than in more fashionable centres.

It has also been observed that the carver had a poor understanding of ornament, particularly the lack of fine detail on the candelabrum decoration on the pilasters, and that the ornament is more nineteenth century in character. It is suggested that the manufacture from a joined panel of wood also points to a nineteenth century date, since Renaissance frame were normally constructed in parts corresponding to the architectural components.[4]

The pigments identified have been in use since antiquity with the exception of zinc white, which has been used as a pigment since the late eighteenth century. Its use on this frame could indicate that the frame may date after this period. It is also possible, however, that the zinc white was used during retouching of worn areas.

The date of this piece remains uncertain. Further research and comparison with other frames or framed reliefs of this type may help to draw more definite conclusions.

References

1. Analyses carried out by Dr Brian W. Singer, Northumbria University.
2. Lynn Roberts, personal communication, February 2008.
3. Lynn Roberts, personal communication, February 2008.
4. Michael Gregory, personal communication, February 2008.

RESULTS OF ANALYSIS

SAMPLE 1

Grey/blue (taken from leaf-and-dart architrave). Polarised light microscopy (PLM) revealed opaque black particles which are probably charcoal. Three types of colourless (white) particles were seen. Some had a refractive index (n) of less than 1.66, were isotropic and showed high relief and chonchoidal fractures. These were identified as ground glass. Also present were highly birefringent particles of low relief, n < 1.66, which were identified as chalk. Thirdly, there was a trace of gypsum present.

SAMPLE 2

Pink (taken from inside return of right impost). PLM revealed red particles, with n > 1.66, which were seen to show orange red polarisation colours. These were identified as vermilion. These were mixed with two white pigments of high refractive index, lead white, which showed highly birefringent hexagonal plates, and zinc white, which showed low birefringence. A trace of gypsum was also seen.

SAMPLE 3

Blue (taken from recessed area behind cherub's head). Greenish blue, pleochroic particles were seen which were anisotropic and had n > 1.66. These were identified as azurite. Lead white was also present.

CASSETTA AND TONDO FRAMES

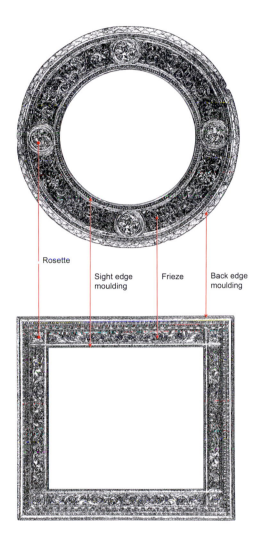

Rosette

Sight edge moulding

Frieze

Back edge moulding

Tondo Frame

Tondo (pl. tondi): a circular frame with sight and back edge mouldings separated by a frieze. The mouldings are derived from the tabernacle entablature in circular form.[1]

Cassetta Frame

Cassetta (pl. cassette): a square or rectangular frame comprising a simple lap jointed back frame. The mouldings are derived from the tabernacle entablature, with sight and back edge mouldings separated by a frieze.

Reference

1. Cecchi, C. and Blamoutier, N. Les cadres ronds de la Renaissance Florentine. *Revue de L'Art*, 76, 1987. pp. 21–24.

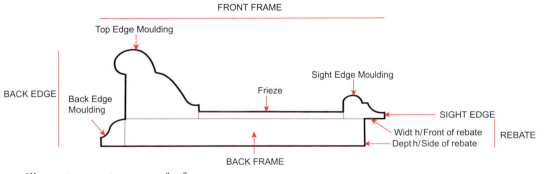

FRONT FRAME

Top Edge Moulding

Sight Edge Moulding

Frieze

BACK EDGE

Back Edge Moulding

SIGHT EDGE

Widt h/Front of rebate

Dept h/Side of rebate

REBATE

BACK FRAME

Illustration naming parts of a frame.

13

CARVED AND WATER GILDED ARCHITECTURAL CASSETTA FRAME ORIGINALLY PAINTED WITH A BLUE BACKGROUND

Italy (probably Siena), 1500–1525
Bought for £45
7816-1862 (Furniture and Woodwork Collection)

Dimensions (mm)
H: 1410; W: 1500; D: 96 (overall maximum)
Sight size: H: 984; W: 1065
Rebate: W: 15 (top), 19 (other sides); D: 30
Object accommodation size: H: 1018; W: 1103

Ornament

A leaf-and-tongue cyma-reversa moulding borders the sight edge and a leaf-and-tongue cyma-reversa surrounds the frieze on all sides and the corners, which are decorated with rosettes. Each frieze is decorated with carved scrolling leaves sprouting from a central mask flanked by two winged dragons. The frieze and corners are bordered by a bead-and-reel acanthus-leaf cyma-reversa moulding. The top edge is enriched with eggs. A leaf-and-tongue moulding decorates the back edge moulding.

1500 mm

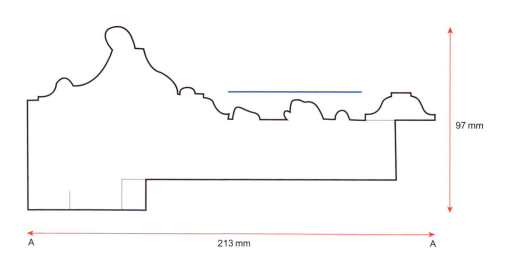

97 mm

213 mm

Structure

The frame is made from poplar or lime. The back frame was probably originally keyed dovetail-half lapped or half lapped on all corners, although the details cannot be seen as the ends of the joints are covered. Mitred and applied mouldings surround the frieze, the back edge and the sight edge. The sight edge moulding and back frame form the sight edge rebate. The top edge moulding is probably also applied. The carved frieze on all four sides is applied. The corner rosettes are also applied.

Later Additions and Alterations

The frame's size has been altered. The frame has been dismantled into component parts with the cuts made at different points on the frame to make the alterations less obvious at the front and in particular to keep the symmetry along the length of the frieze ornament.

Evidence that this frame has been altered can be seen at the back. The joints at the top left and bottom right appear to remain largely as originally constructed. However, at the top right and bottom left there are newer mitre joints with tapered keys. Here the remains of the old joint can be seen. The later added wood is of a lighter colour and has been butt joined on to the older wood of the back frame. On these corners, at the sight moulding, the additional wood has been butt jointed on to the older wood and mitred at the corner. On the outside moulding, additional wood has been scarf joined and mitred at the corner on the two outer pieces, and the inner narrow pieces are butt joined. There are also alterations to the width of the rebate. At the top and bottom the rebate has been enlarged by cutting into the width of the back frame and then, later, it was reduced here by the addition of strips of wood (at the top, width 10–12 mm, and the bottom, width 6 mm). The inside edge of the edge back frame could have also have been cut, as looking at the old joints, the wood of the back frame is wider.

At the front, on the corners with the original joints (top right and bottom left), the acanthus-leaf cyma-recta mouldings retain their carved corner leaf motif. Those that have been altered (top left and bottom right) have lost the carved corner-leaf motif and the carving does not meet well, the ornament having been cut back. The later and additional sections of mouldings (top of the left side and bottom of the right side) have been well carved but a different hand can be recognised, for example the eggs are different.

The masks have remained centred on the carved friezes at the front, indicating that the frieze panels must have been lifted off during the alteration and cut in different places to the other parts of the frame so as not to disrupt the symmetry of the carved frieze. At the ends of the top and bottom carved frieze, the end parts of the scrolling stems for the flowers have been cut through. On the ends of the side friezes, the tight scrolls with flower heads appear to be additions.

Both the bottom corner rosettes look much the same, with three rings of petals and six petals on the outer ring. The rosette at the top right is different. It has two rings of petals and five on the outer ring. The outer petals are more undulating than those at the bottom. The top left rosette is carved differently again and is probably a later repair.

Decorative Finish

There are at least two decorative schemes. The gilding on the carved areas on earlier parts is largely original.

The earliest scheme is painted and gilded. The background of the frieze was blue. Analysis of paint samples, taken from the left frieze near the bottom and the bottom frieze on the left, indicated the presence of natural azurite, with traces of malachite, applied over a red bole on the calcium sulphate ground.[1] The original water gilding was applied over a red bole on a thin white calcium sulphate ground.

Samples from the outside concave moulding and back edge of the frame did not provide clear evidence of the original finish. The outside concave moulding may originally have been painted red, as suggested by traces of vermilion at the base of the paint sample. A loss in the centre of the cross-section, however, is filled with orpiment that was used in one phase of repainting. Traces of vermilion and orpiment are also present at the base of the sample taken from the back edge of the frame. It is unclear to which phase of finish these are related.

The most recent scheme is also painted and gilded. There is later gilding, on added parts and some areas of later repair, carried out with toned water gilding on a red bole and white ground. The background of the carved frieze and rosettes has a heavily applied overpaint that now appears dark blue–black in colour. This blue–black appearance is due to the presence of a dark, pigmented varnish or mordant over a thick layer of orpiment, with dark iron-rich inclusions and a few particles of vermilion. A few particles of gold leaf are also incorporated in this layer, although these loose fragments may originate from adjacent areas of gilding. The thick orpiment layer may have been applied in imitation of gold and represents a phase of redecoration over the original azurite blue.

The gilding is in a much smoother condition on the later-added pieces, without the fine craquelure of natural age. This can be seen, for example, on the flat by the sight moulding on the right side near the bottom and diagonally opposite.

Hanging Device

There are modern hanging fittings on the top and bottom of both sides and various recent holes where hanging fittings have been fitted and removed.

Observations and Conclusions

This frame was probably made for a painting. Earlier photographs of this frame show it in a taller and narrower shape in portrait orientation.[2] The frame's present dimensions are H: 1410 mm × W: 1500 mm. The dimensions given for the frame in Guggenheim are H: 1520 mm × W: 1300 mm.[3] If the frame is rotated by 90 degrees, the differences in dimensions are not so great. The masks at the sides faced each other, but those at the top and bottom were both in an upright position, not facing each other as they are now. This is further confirmation that this was previously a portrait format frame. It appears that the pieces that are now the top and bottom of the frame were originally the sides, and the pieces that are now the sides were the top and bottom. The frame would have been dismantled to alter its dimensions. The bottom frieze panel has been turned 180 degrees so that the bottom ornament reflects that at the top. Probably the longer sides of the frame have had each end of the frieze trimmed away resulting in loss of part of the scrolling stem of the flower head. The shorter sides have probably had pieces added to the frieze at either end with the addition of a carved flower head. The slightly different rosettes at the corners seen today can also be seen in the Guggenheim and Odom pictures of the frame. Rosettes are often carved and applied separately

and can easily be lost and subsequently replaced. They can also be moved from corner to corner.

This frame has been on loan to the National Gallery since 1938.[4] At the date of writing it framed NG 1450, Sebastiano del Piombo's *Madonna and Child with Saints Joseph, John the Baptist, and a Donor* (c.1519–1520), H: 978 mm × W: 1067 mm. Before this it framed NG 270, Titian's *Noli me Tangere* (1510–1515?), H: 1105 mm × W: 919 mm.[5] If the pictorial orientation of the paintings is ignored, the difference in the overall size of each painting is relatively small.

Titian's *Noli me Tangere* can be seen in this frame in portrait orientation in a photograph probably dating from the Second World War. The frame's proportions appear similar to that as seen in Guggenheim and Odom. This photograph was on display in an exhibition entitled *Not One Picture Shall Leave This Island: The National Gallery in World War II* (December 1995 to February 1996).[6] The National Gallery annual report 1938–1959 states that Titian's *Noli me Tangere* was reframed in the 1950s in a frame 'entirely constructed by Arthur Lucas when the picture was cleaned in the 1950s'. At this time the V&A frame was put on Sebastiano del Piombo's *Holy Family*.[6]

To fit the frame to the Titian, the frame would have had to be 38 mm longer on the long sides, bringing the frame to 1538 mm (28 mm greater than the Guggenheim dimensions) and 59 mm shorter on the short sides, bringing the frame to 1351 mm. This is 51 mm greater than the dimensions in Guggenheim before the additions to these sides. The rebate width has been altered in the past, which would add 16 mm to the object/painting accommodation size. The rebate width would have been enlarged to accommodate a painting larger that would not fit the previous rebate.

Further study would be required to confirm exactly how and when the frame has been altered.

The areas of damage carving and gilding could have been repaired and toned and the background of the frieze overpainted at the time that these alterations were done. Indeed, a dark toning layer extends over adjacent areas.

Comparable Frames

Cassetta frame, Tuscany (Siena), first half of the sixteenth century, similar form and carved frieze but with protruding heads. See Sabatelli, F. *La Cornice italiana dal Rinascimento al Neoclassico.* Milan: Electa, 1992. pp. 120–121. This frame is attributed to Antonio Barili in Bock, E. *Florentinische und venezianische Bilderrahmen aus der Zeit der Gotik und Renaissance.* Munich: F. Bruckmann, 1902. p. 70.

Cassetta, Florentine, c.1870, similar carved frieze but with protruding heads, Österreichisches Museum, Vienna. See Grimm, C. *Alte Bilderrahmen: Epochen, Typen, Material.* Munich: Callwey, 1979. p. 172, Figure 403.

Mitchell relates the general form of Frame 13 (7816-1862) to a cassetta frame, northern Italian, c.1500, Plate 12A, altered for Giovanni Bellini's *Madonna & Child* at the Kimbell Art Museum, Texas. See Mitchell, P. Italian picture frames, 1500–1825: a brief survey. *Journal of the Furniture History Society*, 20, 1984. p. 19, Plate 12C.

Frame 14 (76-1892) has a similar carved frieze to this cassetta.

Tondo frame, c.1506–1508, with similar carving but with protruding heads at cardinal compass points, attributed to Marco and Francesco del Tasso for *The Holy Family with the Infant St John the Baptist (Doni Tondo)* by Michelangelo. The Uffizi, Florence. See Fossi, G. *The Uffizi. The Official Guide.* Prato: Giunti, 2005. p. 115. Mitchell describes this Uffizi frame as being carved by Antonio Barile, c.1504; see Mitchell, P. Italian picture frames, 1500–1825: a brief survey. *Journal of the Furniture History Society*, 20, 1984. p. 26.

Previous Citations

This frame was photographed before it was altered and published as Tuscan, first half of sixteenth century by Guggenheim, M. *Le cornici italiane dalla metà del secolo XV o allo scorcio del XVI; con breve testo riassuntivo intorno alla storia ed all'importanza delle cornice.* Milan: U.Hoepli, 1897. Plate 80.

This frame was photographed before it was altered and published in Odom, W. M. *A history of Italian furniture from the fourteenth to the early nineteenth centuries.* Volume I: Gothic and Renaissance furniture. New York: Archive Press, 1967. p. 215, Figure 202.

Mitchell, P. Italian picture frames, 1500–1825: a brief survey. *Journal of the Furniture History Society*, 20, 1984. p. 19, Plate 12C. Mitchell describes the frame as northern Italian, early sixteenth century.

Penny, N. *Frames*. National Gallery Pocket Guides. London: National Gallery, 1997. p. 35, No. 27, described as c.1510, Italian (Siena) and tentatively attributed to the workshop of Antonio Barile.

References

1. Cross-section and SEM/EDX analyses of paint samples were carried out by Dr Helen Howard, Scientific Department, The National Gallery, London.
2. Guggenheim, M. *Le cornici italiane dalla metà del secolo XV o allo scorcio del XVI; con breve testo riassuntivo intorno alla storia ed all'importanza delle cornice.* Milan: U.Hoepli, 1897. Plate 80; Odom, W. M. *A history of Italian furniture from the fourteenth to the early nineteenth centuries.* Volume I: Gothic and Renaissance furniture. New York: Archive Press, 1967. p. 215, Figure 202; Paul Levi survey records at The National Gallery, with thanks to Peter Schade.
3. Guggenheim, loc. cit.
4. From Furniture and Woodwork Collection records.
5. National Gallery, London database of paintings.
6. From The National Gallery, London records, with thanks to Isabella Kocum.

RESULTS OF ANALYSIS
SAMPLE 1/1
LOCATION

Frieze, left side, above second curled tendril from bottom: island of possible original blue paint beneath dark overpaint.

PAINT CROSS-SECTION IN INCIDENT LIGHT

UV LIGHT

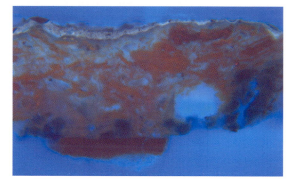

- trace gold leaf and surface accretion
- mordant/varnish
- orpiment with dark, iron-rich inclusions and particles of vermilion

Earliest/original decoration
- natural azurite
- red bole
- trace calcium sulphate.

SEM/EDX

- SEM/EDX analysis of the red bole confirmed the presence of: Fe, Si, Al, K, S, Ti, (As)
- SEM/EDX analysis of the blue pigment particles confirmed the presence of: Cu, O, (As)
- SEM/EDX analysis of the yellow paint layer confirmed the presence of: As, S, (Cu)
- SEM/EDX analysis of the dark orange/brown particles at the top of the yellow layer confirmed the presence of: As, S, O
- SEM/EDX analysis of dark shiny iron-rich particles in the yellow paint layer confirmed the presence of: Fe, S, As, (Cu)
- SEM/EDX analysis of red inclusions in the yellow paint layer confirmed the presence of: Hg, S, (As, Fe, Cu).

SAMPLE 1/2
LOCATION

Frieze, lower edge, right side, left of first main foliate ornament: island of possible original blue paint beneath dark overpaint.

PAINT CROSS-SECTION IN INCIDENT LIGHT

UV LIGHT

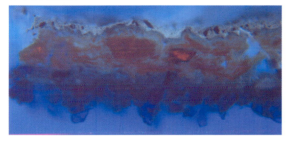

- mordant/varnish, incorporating fragments of gold leaf
- orpiment with dark, iron-rich inclusions and particles of vermilion

Earliest/original decoration
- natural azurite.

SAMPLE 1/3
LOCATION

Frieze, left side, above second curled tendril from bottom: original gilding.

PAINT CROSS-SECTION IN INCIDENT LIGHT

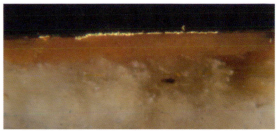

UV LIGHT

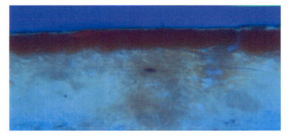

- organic layer on the surface earliest/original decoration
- gold leaf
- red bole
- calcium sulphate preparation.

SAMPLE 1/4
LOCATION
Outer edge of frame, left side: possible original painted finish.

PAINT CROSS-SECTION IN INCIDENT LIGHT

UV LIGHT

- particles of umber incorporated in organic layer on surface
- thick layer of chalk with silica and yellow earth
- tiny particles of vermilion and orpiment at the base of the sample.

SEM/EDX
- SEM/EDX analysis of particles on the surface of the sample confirmed the presence of: Fe, Mn, Ca, Si, Al, P K, Cl
- SEM/EDX analysis of the bulk of the central portion of the sample confirmed the presence of: Ca, Si, (Fe, trace S)
- SEM/EDX analysis of the tiny red particles at the base of the sample confirmed the presence of: Hg, S, Ca, Si, Al
- SEM/EDX analysis of yellow particles at the base of the sample confirmed the presence of: Ca, As, S, (Fe).

SAMPLE 1/5
LOCATION
Outermost cove (concave) moulding, lower left side: possible original painted finish.

PAINT CROSS-SECTION IN INCIDENT LIGHT

UV LIGHT

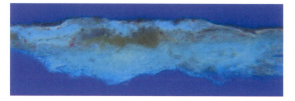

- surface accretion
- chalk layer incorporating particles of earth pigment, vermilion and some orpiment combined with lead white
- particles of vermilion. In the centre of this layer is a zone of orpiment combined with lead white
- calcium sulphate.

SEM/EDX
- SEM/EDX analysis of yellow particles in the centre of the sample confirmed the presence of: As, S, Pb
- SEM/EDX analysis of red particles over the calcium sulphate preparation confirmed the presence of: Hg, S (Si, Ca)
- SEM/EDX analysis of preparatory layer confirmed the presence of: Ca, S
- SEM/EDX analysis of the layer over the red paint layer confirmed the presence of: Ca.

14

CARVED AND WATER GILDED TONDO FRAME ORIGINALLY PAINTED WITH A BLUE BACKGROUND

*Italy (Tuscany), 1510–1540s, said to have
come from the Casa Strozzi, Florence
Bought in Florence (Stefano Bardini) for £208 2s 6d
76-1892 (Furniture and Woodwork Collection)*

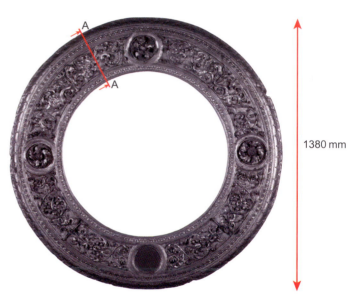

1380 mm

Dimensions (mm)
Diameter: 1380; D: 50 (overall maximum)
Sight size: Diameter: 850
Rebate: W: 23; D: 34
Object accommodation size: Diameter 890
These dimensions do not include the added sight
edge slip moulding in the rebate.

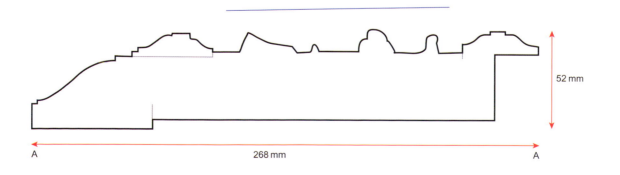

52 mm

A   268 mm   A

Ornament

The frieze is decorated with a carved relief of scrolling and intertwined leaves and grotesque monsters. At the top quarters there are dragons flanking a trident, and at the bottom quarters, the grotesques have the heads of bearded men flanking a cross. The frieze is divided at the four cardinal points by roundels with rosettes. The frieze is bordered by plain cyma-reversa and leaf-and-dart cyma-reversa mouldings divided by a flat. The back edge cyma reversa moulding is decorated with a fish-scale pattern. A plain modern slip is inserted in the rebate at the original sight edge.

Structure

The frame is made from poplar and walnut. At the back, the frame is made of six pieces of poplar. These appear to be butt jointed. The outer edge moulding is made of eight lengths of walnut that are applied to the main frame with cut nails, with the heads in recessed niches. At the front, the carved walnut frieze is inset and the rosettes are applied. One rosette is missing. The sight edge moulding is applied in sections. There are carved wood losses and wood-boring beetle damage. The plain gilded sight edge slip is a recent addition and is not included in the profile drawing.

Decorative Finish

The earliest decorative scheme consists of water gilding with blue painted areas behind the rosettes. There are small areas of repair to the gilding and the background to the rosettes has been overpainted. The early gilding is water gilding in a pale colour gold that is decorated with varied punch work carried out with a squared grouping of small points. There are also some irregular punch marks. The gilding is applied on a brown–red bole on a thin, white ground. There are repairs to this gilding using similar materials. These can be identified by the false cracks cut through the gold leaf to imitate original craquelure. There are many losses that have been toned out and some obvious recent losses. A heavy build-up of dust and dirt has dulled the gilded finish.

Behind the carved rosettes, beneath the overpaint, there is an earlier green–blue paint that appears to have been applied directly over the gold leaf. A paint sample from this area was examined using polarised light microscopy and analysed by SEM/EDX.[1] The results indicate that the blue pigment is azurite and that the overpaint is Naples yellow, an eighteenth century pigment. No underlying gold leaf was present in the sample.

Early gilding from the carved frieze was also sampled. Analysis indicated that the ground consists of calcium sulphate combined with a little yellow earth pigment. Over this, a red bole was applied for the water gilding.

Hanging Device

To the left of the stencilled National Gallery painting number, on the back, there is a paler mark with nail holes which could be evidence of where a crossover wrought iron hook was once attached.

Observations and Conclusions

This frame is thought to have been made to contain a painting. This frame was on loan to the National Gallery, London, from 1938 to 2009. It framed a Virgin and Child tondo attributed to the Workshop of Botticelli (NG 275), which was purchased by the National Gallery in 1855. It replaced the frame, probably original, in which the picture arrived at the Gallery. At the time of writing, the Gallery was restoring this original frame so as to reunite it with the painting. The frame was subsequently returned to the V&A.

The gilded areas would have originally appeared like solid gold. The rosettes would have been further embellished with the original azurite background. The background to the rosettes was painted yellow at a later date. Possibly the blue had darkened and was painted yellow to blend more with the surrounding gilded areas. This, in turn, has now darkened with age.

Comparable Frames

Tondo frame c.1506–1508, with similar carving but with protruding heads at cardinal compass points, attributed to Marco and Francesco del Tasso for *The Holy Family with the Infant St John the Baptist (Doni Tondo)* by Michelangelo. The Uffizi, Florence.[2]

A comparison between the Doni Tondo frame and Frame 14 (76-1892) was made in An echo of Michelangelo. *National Gallery News*, December 1994.

Mitchell compares Frame 14 (76-1892) to the Doni Tondo frame above, which he describes as being carved by Antonio Barile, c.1504. Mitchell, P. Italian picture frames, 1500–1825: a brief survey. *Furniture History: Journal of the Furniture History Society*, 20, 1984. p. 26, Ref. 12.

Tondo frame, Tuscan, 1520–1540, with carved frieze but with protruding heads at cardinal compass points. Museo Horne Florence. See Sabatelli, F. *La Cornice italiana dal rinascimento al neoclassico*. Milan: Electa, 1992. pp. 108–109.

Cassetta frame 13 (7816-1862) has a similar carved frieze.

Cassetta frame, Florentine, c.1870, with a similar carved frieze. Österreichisches Museum Vienna. See Grimm, C. *Alte Bilderrahmen: Epochen, Typen, Material*. Munich: Callwey, 1979. p. 172, Figure 403.

Cassetta frame, Tuscan (Siena), first half of the sixteenth century, with similar carved frieze heads, in Sabatelli, F. *La Cornice italiana dal rinascimento al neoclassico*. Milan: Electa, 1992. pp. 120–121. This frame is attributed to Antonio Barili in Bock, E. *Florentinische und venezianische Bilderrahmen aus der Zeit der Gotik und Renaissance*. Munich: F. Bruckmann, 1902. p. 70.

Cassetta frame, Lombardy, late sixteenth century, with similar carved frieze with extended corners. Newbery, T., Bisacca, G. and Kanter, L. *Italian Renaissance frames*. Exhibition Catalogue. New York: Metropolitan Museum, 1990. p. 75, Figure 48.

Previous Citations

This frame is referred to as Tuscan, end of fifteenth century, in Guggenheim, M. *Le cornici italiane dalla metà del secolo XV allo scorcio del XVI; con breve testo riassuntivo intorno alla storia ed all'importanza delle cornice*. Milan: U.Hoepli, 1897. Plate 37.

Both of the following publications quote M. Davies (National Gallery Catalogues. *The earlier Italian schools*. London: National Gallery, 195. pp. 85–88), who, perhaps assuming that the frame was original to the painting, attributes it to Giuliano da San Gallo (architect, 1443–1516): Peintres et menuisiers au debut de la Renaissance en Italie. *Revue de l'Art*, No. 37: 9-28. p. 17; Sabatelli, F. *La Cornice italiana dal rinascimento al neoclassico*. Milan: Electa, 1992. p. 43. The name Giuliano da San Gallo is written on the back of the painting and it is possible that this was done because, after the painting was complete, it was destined to go to San Gallo's workshop to be framed. However, since the V&A frame is not original to the painting, the inscription is not relevant to the authorship of this frame.

15

CARVED, WATER GILDED AND PAINTED CASSETTA FRAME WITH EXTENDED CORNERS

Probably northern Italy, 1550–1600
Bought in London (Tito Gagliardi) for £40
415-1882 (Furniture and Woodwork Collection)

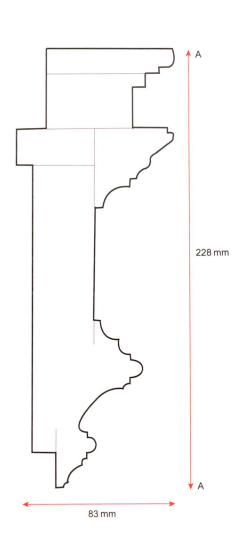

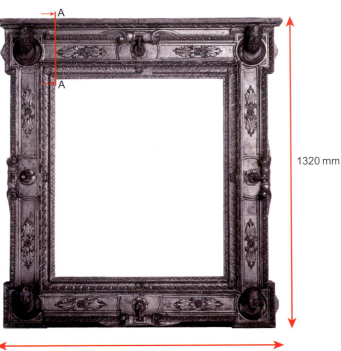

Dimensions (mm)
H: 1320; W: 1220 D: 164 (overall maximum)
Sight size: H: 855; W: 730
Rebate: W: 18; D: 14

Ornament

The sight edge is a succession of leaves, pearl, raking fluted tongue-and-dart with scallop shells at each corner, and bead-and-reel mouldings. The frieze is decorated at the centre of each of the four sides with an inverted flower with a protruding

stem (the stem is missing on the left side). At either side of these flowers there are rosettes set between leaf-enriched lozenges. The top edge moulding is enriched with a fluted tongue-and-dart moulding with bifurcated scrolls at the centres. The frame is surmounted by a twisted ribbon moulding. The extended corners each contain a projecting head, three male and one female.

Structure

The frame is made from walnut and lime or poplar – the back frame is thought to be walnut. The back frame is made of two, vertical members that are half lapped over the two, horizontal members. On the back edges, there are strips of wood that increase the width of the frame. It can be seen from the back that these comprise one long strip on each side, at the top and bottom of which are two short pieces. Of these short pieces, the outer piece forms the width of the extended corners. On the bottom of the back frame, at left and right, the ends of the half lap joints show. There are tool marks from a handsaw and plane.

At the front, the parts of the corners level with the surface of the frieze are made of separate pieces and the joins can be seen across the frieze. The carved wood appears to be lime or poplar. The sight and top edge mouldings are mitred and applied. The bifurcated scrolls at the centres of the top edge moulding are inserted. The circular and squared framework at the corners and the centres are applied separately. The heads and inverted flowers are carved separately and were applied after the rest of the frame was gilded and the punch work was carried out. The leaf enriched lozenges were applied before gilding. The diamond-shaped pieces on the back edges of the

extended corners are applied. The one at the bottom left is missing.

The back edges of the left and right sides are not fully gilded. Only 10 mm towards the face is gilded and the rest is bare wood. The gilded finish ends abruptly here and curves up where it meets the bare wood. The same can be seen at the back edge of the bottom where the wood has remains of glue and several holes from wrought nails. The back edge of the bottom bifurcated centre scroll is flat, unlike those at the sides, which are rounded at the backs. Between the extended corners at the bottom of the frame, the wood is bare.

There are small carving losses and several areas of severe wood-boring beetle damage.

Later Additions

A strip of wood has been screwed across the back at the top and over another additional strip of wood. A further, later piece caps the top of the frame which is not gilded. To the back of this capping piece, at left and right, the ends of the half laps of the original back frame can be seen, the capping piece having been cut around them. At the top back of the back frame, either side of the centre, are two small pieces of new wood held with modern nails. These run behind the additional strip of wood at the back. The capping piece has been cut to fit around the ends of these. The back of the capping pieces has been slightly hollowed out near the centre. There is a cornice missing from the very top and there are also probably pieces missing from the back edges at the sides and from the bottom.

Label

There is a paper label at the back, with several losses and scratches, that reads: 'Sig [?] Geo[rge?] R [?] … Firenze'.

Decorative Finish

The present finish is water gilded and painted. The gilding appears to be original, with a glue size coating. The background of the frieze and the recesses of some of the mouldings are decorated with punch work. The gold is applied over an orange bole and a thin, white ground. The four heads have been overpainted in pale naturalistic tones with coloured drapery. The hair, beards, details of eyebrows and eyes are painted black and the lips are red. The heads are coated with a varnish that has darkened.

Where there are losses of the overpaint on the heads, the original scheme can be seen. Pink was observed on the faces, and red and fragments of gold on the hair and a deeper red on the drapery around the figures' necks.

Samples were taken of the earlier scheme and analysed by polarised light microscopy (PLM).[1] Sample of the deep pink over a white ground from the face at the top right hand corner showed the presence of a red lake on an alumina base along with an orange–red resinous material, possibly dragon's blood. A small amount of vermilion, yellow lead chromate and traces of lead white and a little chalk, clay and gypsum were also present. The combination of these colours would make up a pink colour. A sample from the hair from the top right hand figure showed the presence of iron oxide and a sample from the drapery of the same figure showed the presence of red lake on an alumina base and vermilion mixed with lead white. A gypsum ground layer was found in all samples taken from the painted areas.

Hanging Device

On the back of the frame at top centre there are three marks indicating where wrought metal crossover hanging loops have been fixed. On the lower mark is the remains of a crossover metal loop that is held with three cut nails. On the back of the frame there are two brass mirror plate fittings at the top and one at each side near the bottom.

Observations and Conclusions

The fact that other, similar style frames contain paintings suggests that this frame may have contained a painting.

The gilded and painted areas of the original scheme have the same calcium sulphate ground. It would seem that the figures' faces were originally coloured light pink. Both the hair and robes were once different shades of red, although further examination would be required to determine the exact appearance of these areas. It is not clear whether part of the hair was gilded.

All pigments are consistent with those found on other sixteenth century frames, apart from the small amount of yellow lead chromate used since the late eighteenth century, which possibly came from the overpaint, if not the frame maybe later.

The gilded finish on the back edges of the sides and bottom of the frame stops abruptly and, at the edge of the gilded finish, the surface curls up indicating that the gilded finish once continued up over another raised part of the frame, now missing. The remaining back edge is bare; on the bottom of this are the remains of glue and nail holes. At the bottom, the piece of bare wood between the corners at the back of the centre scroll is flat. This indicates that there was another piece running the length between the corners, inserted behind the centre scroll, placed over the bare wood and nailed on to the wood of the back edge. It is possible that the piece here may have been a twisted ribbon carving like that seen at the top of the frame. A very similar Italian Renaissance frame with the addition of pediment and predella is illustrated in Lessing.[2]

At the top there is a later added bare piece of wood. Originally there was an overhanging cornice as seen on an image in Guggenheim, M. *Le cornici Italiane dalla metà del secolo XV allo scorcio del XVI; con breve testo riassuntivo intorno alla storia ed all'importanza delle cornice*, Milan: U.Hoepli, 1897. Plate 83. This image shows the frame with an overhanging fillet with cyma-recta leaf moulding and with a fluted tongue-and-dart moulding like that seen on the outer moulding that borders the frieze on the rest of the frame. The picture also shows what could be plain narrow pieces on the sides between the extended corners.

Comparable Frames

Cassetta frame, second half of sixteenth century, Louvre Museum, Paris, with many similarities overall. See Sabatelli, F. *La Cornice Italiana dal Rinascimento al Neoclassico*. Milan: Electa, 1992. p. 45, Figure 50. See also Figure 51, showing a copy in the style of this frame made in the first quarter of the twentieth century, commissioned by Galleria Sangiorgi, Rome.

Cassetta frame, Italian, Emilia, first half of the sixteenth century, Adolf von Beckerath, Berlin, with similar bifurcated central scrolls, inverted flowers and extended corners with protruding heads. See Guggenheim, M. *Le cornici Italiane dalla metà del secolo XVo allo scorcio del XVI; con breve testo riassuntivo intorno alla storia ed all'importanza delle cornice*, Milan: U.Hoepli, 1897. Plate 84.

Cassetta frame, Italian, Florence, c.1870, with protruding heads, Österreichisches Museum Vienna. See Grimm, C. *Alte Bilderrahmen: Epochen, Typen, Material*. Munich: Callwey, 1979. p. 17, Figure 403.

Cassetta frame, Italian, Tuscany (Siena), first half of the sixteenth century, showing use of protruding heads, in Sabatelli, F. *La cornice Italiana dal Rinascimento al Neoclassico*. Milan: Electa, 1992. pp. 120–121. See also this same frame attributed to Antonio Barili in Bock, E. *Florentinische und Venezianische Bilderrahmen aus der Zeit der Gotik und Renaissance*. Munich: F. Bruckmann, 1902. p. 70.

Cassetta frame, Italian, Lombardy, late sixteenth century, with extended corners. See Newbery, T., Bisacca, G. and Kanter, L. I*talian Renaissance frames*. Exhibition Catalogue. New York: Metropolitan Museum, 1990. p. 75, Figure 48.

Tondo frame, Italian, Tuscany, 1520–1540, with similar protruding heads, Museo Horne, Florence. See Sabatelli, F. *La Cornice Italiana dal Rinascimento al Neoclassico*. Milan: Electa, 1992. pp. 108–109.

Tondo frame c.1506–1508, with similar protruding heads with circular moulding, attributed to Marco and Francesco del Tasso for *The Holy Family with the Infant St John the Baptist (Doni Tondo)* by Michelangelo. The Uffizi, Florence.

Previous Citations

This frame is referred to as Emilian, first half of the sixteenth century, in Guggenheim, M. *Le cornici Italiane dalla metà del secolo XV allo scorcio del XVI; con breve testo riassuntivo intorno alla storia ed all'importanza delle cornice*. Milan: U.Hoepli, 1897. Plate 83.

References

1. Analysis carried out by Dr Brian W Singer, Northumbria University.
2. Lessing, J. *Vorbilder-Hefte aus dem KGL. Kunstgewerbe-Museen Rahmen: Italien und Deutschland XVI Jahr hundert*, Volume 1. Berlin: Verlag Von Ernst Wasmuth, 1888. Plate 5. Thanks to Mr Plaut for this reference.

RESULTS OF ANALYSIS

All samples were taken from the original scheme from areas of damage on the top right male head.

SAMPLES 1 AND 3

Pink in face: Polarised light microscopy (PLM) revealed the presence of a few particles of a red lake on an alumina base along with much orange–red resinous material, which could be dragon's blood or possibly just a resinous varnish layer. Also present was a trace of lead white and a little chalk, clay and gypsum. One vermilion particle was found together with some yellow rods identified as lead chromate.

SAMPLE 2

Red on drapery: PLM revealed the presence of many particles of a red lake on an alumina base and also one or two red particles, with a refractive index (n) greater than 1.66, which were seen to show orange–red polarisation colours. These were identified as vermilion. These were mixed with a white pigment of high refractive index identified as lead white. There was a trace of gypsum present.

SAMPLE 4

Red on hair: under low magnification under an optical microscope a red and a white layer could be seen. PLM suggested that the white layer was gypsum and the red layer contained isotropic orange–red particles identified as iron oxide.

16

CASSETTA FRAME WITH PASTIGLIA RELIEF, WATER GILDED WITH SOME AREAS ORIGINALLY PAINTED BLUE

Italy (Veneto) 1500–1550
Bought in Florence (Stefano Bardini) for £57
11-1890 (Furniture and Woodwork Collection)

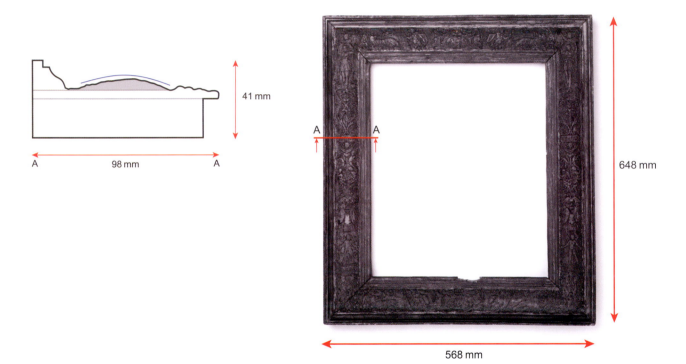

Dimensions (mm)
H: 648; W: 568 D: 40 (overall maximum)
Sight size: H: 450; W: 370
Rebate: W: 8; D: 18
Object accommodation size: H: 470; W: 390

Ornament
The cushion frieze is decorated in pastiglia with intricate grotesque ornament. The sides are decorated, from the top down, with masks, swags, standing female figures, cornucopia, dolphin heads, trophies, winged putti standing on a plinth marked with SPQR and winged caryatids. The top and bottom are decorated with lions and male half figures each holding a spear and shield, centred on a cartouche containing a reclining nude female with a spear.

Structure
The frame is made up of a softwood back frame and a front frame. The back frame is roughly finished with lost knots and is half lap jointed. At the back, the vertical members are lapped over

the horizontal members. The front frame includes the sight edge moulding and is mitred. The outer moulding is mitred and applied. There is wood-boring beetle damage and wood loss to the bottom sight edge at the centre.

Inscription

At the top, 'RM' is inscribed in black on the back.

Decorative Finish

The cushion frieze ornament is pastiglia. On the left and right, the lengths of relief decoration are cast from the same mould. Each length runs from the top to the bottom edge of the frieze and covers the mitres. The diagonal cracks through the cast work at the corners have appeared as a result of movement in mitre joints in the wood below. The top and bottom lengths are placed between the side lengths and are cast from a different mould. At the top corners, a rectangular piece of relief decoration with masks and drapery has been set into the cast work.

There is one painted and gilded finish. The inner and outer mouldings are water gilded on an orange–red bole on a thick white ground. Fragments of blue paint are visible on the outer moulding. On the cast work, there are very small fragments of mordant gilding that is cupping. The surface has a grey–white appearance and is quite degraded and very dirty.

Samples of the cast work and the blue paint were analysed.[1] Both samples were taken from an area of damage on the bottom right hand corner. Polarised light microscopy (PLM) of the cast work indicated that mainly gypsum was present. Infrared analysis also showed gypsum to be present, with very little medium. GC-MS analysis indicated the presence of animal glue and a small amount of egg. The egg may have been mixed in with the animal glue, or may have been in the adjacent painted layers. There was also a trace of drying oil and a trace of another source of palmitic acid in the glue, perhaps fats. PLM identified the blue as smalt with small amounts of gypsum and chalk.

Hanging Device

At the back top centre there are several holes. Two of these are drilled diagonally and emerge at the top edge. These were possibly used for a cord or ribbon hanging. The three holes at the top left and right and bottom centre are from modern mirror plate fixings.

Observations and Conclusions

The frame is thought to have contained a painting. With the amount of wear and damage present, it is difficult to say what the frame's original appearance would have been. The combination of oil and water gilding, blue paint and the intricate raised decoration suggest that it would have had a highly decorative finish.

The combination of gilding, blue paint and cast work can be seen on pastiglia decorated caskets; see for example a pastiglia box (W.23-1953) with scenes from Roman history, Ferrara or Venice, 1500–1550, which has water gilding on red bole and blue azurite paint on the bottom moulding of the casket.[2,3]

Comparable Frames

Cassetta frame, Venetian, end of the fifteenth century, with pastiglia decoration and similar profiles (Antonio Marcato, Venice). See Guggenheim, M. *Le cornici italiane dalla metà del secolo XV allo scorcio del XVI; con breve testo riassuntivo intorno alla storia ed all'importanza delle cornice.* Milan: U.Hoepli, 1897. Plate No. 32 (left hand side).

Two cassetta frames, Venetian, sixteenth century, with similar profiles and cast ornament. See Newbery, T., Bisacca, G. and Kanter, L. *Italian Renaissance frames.* Exhibition Catalogue. New York: Metropolitan Museum, 1990. p. 91, Figures 67 and 68.

Cassetta frame, central Italy, end of fifteenth or early sixteenth century, with similar general profile and cast pastiglia ornament, 400 mm × 480 mm × 100 mm. See Sabatelli, F. *La Cornice italiana dal rinascimento al neoclassico.* Milan: Electa, 1992. pp. 112–113.

Two cassetta frames, sixteenth century, gilt wood with pastiglia decoration and with similar profiles. Nos 17 and 18 in Lodi, R. and Montanari, A. *Repertorio della cornice Europea: Italia, Francia, Spagna, Paesi Bassi: dal secolo XV al secolo XX.* Modena: Galleria Roberto Lodi, 2003. pp. 12-13.

Previous Citation

This frame is referred to as Venetian, first half of sixteenth century, in Guggenheim, M. *Le cornici italiane dalla metà del secolo XV allo scorcio del XVI; con breve testo riassuntivo intorno alla storia ed all'importanza delle cornice.* Milan: U.Hoepli, 1897. Plate 74.

References

1. Analysis carried out by Dr Brian W Singer, Northumbria University.
2. Ajmar-Wollheim, M. and Dennis, F. *At home in Renaissance Italy.* London: V&A Publications, 2006. p. 108, Figure 7.3.
3. Unpublished Report 06-46-LB casket W.23-1953 by Dr Lucia Burgio, V&A Science Section, Conservation Department.

RESULTS OF ANALYSIS
POLARISED LIGHT MICROSCOPY

PLM of sample 2 (taken from the cast work from the edge of damage to cast ornament across mitre, bottom right hand corner) indicated gypsum as most of the material present. The colourless particles had a refractive index (n) of less than 1.66, were anisotropic with fairly low birefringence and included rods with parallel extinction. These were identified as gypsum. Occasional colourless particles were seen, with n < 1.66, showing low birefringence and an irregular shape, which could be clay.

PLM of sample 1 of the blue (taken from the bottom right hand corner) showed the presence of isotropic blue glass-like particles, n < 1.66, showing red with the Chelsea filter and identified as smalt. Gypsum and chalk were also present.

INFRARED ANALYSIS

Infrared analysis of sample 11-1890 (Figure 16.1) showed peaks due to gypsum (see Figure 2 in Frame 19, 10-1890). There seems to be very little medium or clay in this sample; it is mainly gypsum.

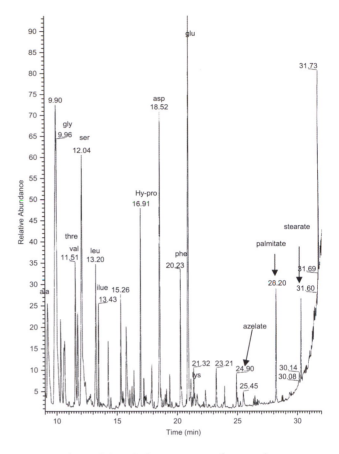

Figure 16.2   GC-MS chromatogram for sample 11-1890.

GC-MS ANALYSIS

Peaks for the fatty acids were present and larger (Figure 16.2) than those found in the sample taken from Frame 19, 10-1890 (see Figure 19.3 in analysis report for that frame), indicating that the sample contained lipids. The azelate to palmitate ratio by percentage area (Table 16.1) is 0.32, confirming the absence of a drying oil.[2] The palmitate to stearate ratio is 2.47, which is within the correct range for egg.[1–3]

The first 23 minutes of the chromatogram (Figure 16.2) contains the eluted amino acids. The peaks are large, indicating that protein is present. The profile of the amino acids calculated from their relative abundance (Figure 16.4) matches that of

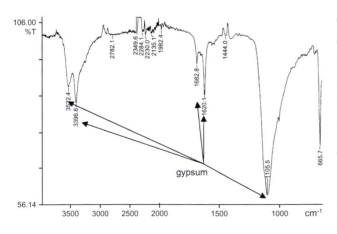

Figure 16.1   Infrared spectrum of sample 11-1890.

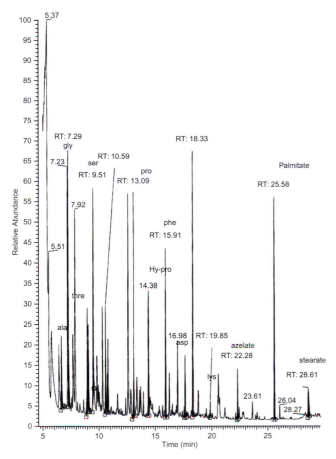

Figure 16.3 *GC-MS chromatogram for sample 11-1890: repeat run, cast material only.*

Table 16.1 *Retention times and area % for fatty acid esters in sample 11-1890*

RT	Identity	Area (%)
24.90	Dipropyl azelate	1.31
28.20	Propyl palmitate	4.56
30.26	Propyl stearate	3.28

animal glue quite well, but the peaks for serine, glutamic acid and aspartic acid seem a little high for glue and the peaks for proline and hydroxyproline seem a little low, so a little egg may be mixed in with the animal glue. Perhaps the egg is in the paint layer on top of the gesso.

Hence a second sample was run containing only the cast raised decoration and no white ground, bole or gold. The chromatogram (Figure 16.3) showed an amino acid profile which matched that of the first sample fairly well (Figure 16.5). There is slightly less glycine present but more proline and hydroxyproline, indicating a slightly higher proportion of animal glue.

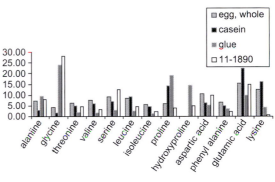

Figure 16.4 *Amino acid profile of sample 11-1890 compared with standards.*

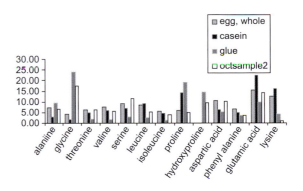

Figure 16.5 *Amino acid profile of the second sample from 11-1890, containing the raised cast material only, compared with standards.*

Conclusion

Sample 11-1890 consists mainly of gypsum, with a trace of clay in animal glue. A small amount of egg is present, perhaps mixed with the glue. There is also a trace of drying oil and a trace of another source of palmitic acid, perhaps fats in the glue.

References

1. Mills, J. S. and White, R. *The organic chemistry of museum objects*. 2nd ed. Oxford: Butterworth-Heinemann, 1994. pp. 170–172.

2. Schilling, M. R. and Khanjian, H. P. Gas chromatographic determination of the fatty acid and glycerol content of drying oils, Part 1. *ICOM Committee for Conservation, 11th Triennial Meeting*, Edinburgh, 1996, Pre-prints, Volume 1. London: James and James, 1996. p. 220. (They quote J. S. Mills, The gas chromatographic examination of paint media, Part 1, Fatty acid composition and identification of dried oil films. *Studies in Conservation*, 11, 1966. pp. 92–107.)

3. Ibid., p. 222.

MIRROR FRAMES

17

PAINTED AND WATER GILDED CARTA PESTA MIRROR FRAME WITH FEMALE FIGURE

Italy (Siena), c.1475–1500, workshop of
Neroccio de'Landi (1447–1500)
Bought in Florence (Bardini) for £28 13s 3d
850-1884 (Sculpture Collection)

457 mm

400 mm

Dimensions (mm)

H: 457; W: 400; D: 44 (overall maximum)
Object accommodation size: D: 107 (approximate: the bottom of the frame is missing)

Ornament

Two putti, whose bodies emerge from foliage, border the edge of the frame. At the centre is a female figure with long flowing hair wearing a necklace with a pendant. Below the figure, held either side by each of the putti, is a small circular space that once would have contained a circular mirror, now missing.

Structure

The whole object is made out of carta pesta. It has been suggested that this mirror frame is a cast from a mould taken from a model (possibly by Neroccio de' Landi), probably of clay and perhaps reproduced several times.[1] The bottom of the frame is missing and may have terminated with an ornament below.

Decorative Finish

The gilded areas are original water gilding over a dark red bole on a thin, white ground applied over canvas applied on top of the carta pesta. Much of the gold leaf has worn away showing the dark red bole below and there are many small losses to the gilded finish. The flesh of the figure is painted naturalistically with pink cheeks and red lips. Several losses reveal the white ground below. There are traces of brown paint on the hair, with a darker colour painted in the recesses to give depth. The hair has been very finely painted with individual hairs expanding on to the blue background. The hair is very abraded, possibly from old cleaning treatments, and much of the brown has worn away. There are deposits of dirt in the recesses of the painted areas and old coatings of an unknown nature.

The necklace is red, probably intended to represent coral. Small losses to this red paint reveal a pale blue paint below. The background to the female figure and the area behind the figure are very dark blue with a darkened coating making the original blue appear almost black. The recesses between the head and arms of the putti are also painted blue, now with a dark appearance.[2] Analysis of the blue paint showed it to be azurite, which would have originally been much brighter.[3]

The frame was conserved in 2007, when a brittle, dark coating and dirt deposits were removed from the gilded areas. Cleaning of the female figure and background was not undertaken.

Hanging Device

There are two small holes at the top to which a modern piece of wire is currently attached. This is probably the location of the original hanging device.

Observations and Conclusions

The mirror housed within the frame could have been made of either metal or glass. Glass mirrors were extremely expensive to manufacture and polished steel or pewter was used as an alternative.[4] It has been suggested that such mirrors were appropriate for a bed chamber and were possibly gifts, exchanged as part of betrothal or wedding rituals from the groom to bride and hung on the wall to commemorate the event. The function of the idealised woman depicted on the mirror frame may be linked to the contemporary understanding of the face as a mirror of the soul. Outer signs of beauty were often related to the goodness of the immortal soul. In this context, women confronted with such a mirror were expected to compare their own reflection with the idealised image above and perhaps to meditate on their own inner beauty and, led by the comparison with the woman depicted, to improve themselves, both inside and out.[5]

The hair was originally painted brown. What can be seen today is the pale white ground with the paint layer having worn away and this gives more the impression of blonde hair rather than brown. On the bead necklace it is possible that the red is overpaint and that the beads were originally painted pale blue, possibly in imitation of lapis lazuli. Further investigation and tests would be required to establish this. The coating on the blue background was probably applied at a later date in an attempt to revive the azurite blue, but this has darkened over time. The blue would have been brighter than we see today. The putti would have originally appeared more like solid gold.

Comparable Objects

Mirror frame, Tuscan, c.1480, stucco, with similar features such as the putti figures. See Newbery, T., Bisacca, G. and Kanter, L. *Italian Renaissance frames*. Exhibition Catalogue. New York: Metropolitan Museum, 1990. p. 79.

Comparisons have been drawn with other works by Neroccio to suggest that this frame may be linked to him. The female figure has been compared to Mary Magdalene in Neroccio's painting of a Madonna and Child from the Metropolitan Museum of Art in New York and the *Portrait of a Lady* by Neroccio in the National Gallery of Art in Washington, DC. It has also been noted that the iconography of putti emerging from acanthus leaves was applied later by Neroccio on the Virgin's chair in an altarpiece of 1496.[5]

References

1. Collections Information Services (CIS) entry, V&A internal database, 2008.

2. Based on authors' examination and observations noted during conservation by Victor Borges, Senior Sculpture Conservator, Conservation Department, V&A, September 2007.

3. Analysis carried out by Lucia Burgio, Object Analysis Scientist, Conservation Department, V&A.

4. See Sandra Cavallo, Health, beauty and hygiene, in Ajmar-Wollheim, M. and Dennis, F. *At home in Renaissance Italy.* London: V&A Publications, 2006. pp. 174–187; Pope-Hennessy, J. A carta pesta mirror frame. *The Burlington Magazine*, 92, 1950. No. 571, pp. 288–291.

5. Collections Information Services (CIS) entry, V&A internal database, 2008.

18

PAINTED AND WATER GILDED STUCCO DECORATED MIRROR FRAME IN THE FORM OF A RING

Italy (Florence), c.1470–1480
Bought in Florence (vendor not recorded) for £2
5887-1859 (Sculpture Collection)

635 mm

508 mm

Dimensions (mm)
H: 635; W: 508; D: 45 (overall maximum)
Object accommodation size: 123

Ornament

The outer frame is formed in the shape of a ring set with a diamond that surrounds a wide figurated frieze.[1] At the base, reclining on rocks, are figures reminiscent of Venus and Mars with attendant putti. The figures are similar to those in Sandro Botticelli's *Venus and Mars* at The National Gallery, London. Above, to the left, a putto rides a goose and to the right are two putti, one of whom leads the other who rides a dragon. The background consists of a landscape and sky. At the top, supporting a shield (charge effaced), three putti stand on a moulding that borders a circular space that once contained a mirror, now missing.

Structure

The outer frame in the form of a ring is apparently made from one piece of an unidentified wood that is largely covered by paint and gilding. The leaf motif below the set diamond and the figurative relief are stucco. At the back there are three pieces of wood, approximately 7 mm thick, on which the outer wooden frame and stucco relief were applied.

Decorative Finish

The ring and leaf motif on the outer frame, the hair of the figures, the wings on the putti and the shield of the stucco work all have the same original water gilding over a deep red bole on a thin,

white ground. The gilding is quite worn, showing much of the bole below. The rosy cheeks, pink lips and the whites of eyes of the figures are painted naturalistically. The putti wear different coloured beaded necklaces, some coral red, some dark red and some a blue–black. The rocks and landscape are green–grey and the sky is painted dark blue. A brighter blue can be seen in some areas. All the painted areas appear to have been painted over the gilded surface. The dark areas on the surface of the diamond at the top have the appearance of tarnished silver leaf that has been applied over red bole. The back of the frame has a circular border painted in pale cream. The rest of the back is coated with mottled red tones, possibly painted to imitate porphyry.

Hanging Device

None observed.

Observations and Conclusions

The mirror housed within the frame could have been made of either glass or metal. Glass mirrors were extremely expensive to manufacture and polished steel or pewter was used as an alternative.[2] The frame largely retains its original finish with no areas of repair or retouching to the gilding. There are some paint losses and retouches to the figures. Originally, the gilded areas would have appeared more like solid gold and the ring would have appeared more jewel-like. Silver leaf at the top, possibly burnished, would have appeared bright in imitation of a diamond. Further analysis is required to confirm the presence of silver.

References

1. The diamond ring was one of Piero de Medici's imprese also adopted by later family members, and was also used by the Rucellai families. See Ames-Lewis, F., Early Medicean devices. *Journal of the Warburg and Cortauld Institutes*, 42, 1979. pp. 122–143.
2. Sandra Cavallo, Health, beauty and hygiene, In Ajmar-Wollheim, M. and Dennis, F. *At home in Reraissance Italy.* London: V&A Publications, 2006. pp. 174–187; Pope-Hennessy, J. A carta pesta mirror frame. *The Burlington Magazine* 92 (571). pp. 288–291.

19

TONDO FRAME WITH PASTIGLIA RELIEF, WATER GILDED AND DECORATED WITH PUNCH WORK

Italy (Tuscany), 1500–1550
Purchased in Florence (Stefano Bardini) for £12
10-1890 (Furniture and Woodwork Collection)

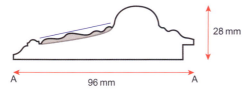

Dimensions (mm)
Diameter: 311–320; D: 33 (overall maximum)
Sight size: 122
Rebate: W: 6; D: 8
Object accommodation size: 135

Ornament
A cyma-reversa moulding borders the sight edge, followed by a torus moulding decorated in pastiglia with an imbrecated leaf pattern. The frieze is also decorated in pastiglia, with scrolling leaves punctuated by palmettes on a punched background. The outer edge consists of an astragal and cyma reversa.

Structure
The frame is made from poplar or lime. The grooves on the reverse of the main frame are

evidence that it is turned from one piece of wood and include the profiles of the outer and sight edge moulding and the sloping frieze.

The frame has warped and is now elliptical, as a result of differential shrinkage of the wood along and across the grain. There is damage from wood-boring beetle. At the bottom of the frame, there is a wooden repair that can be clearly seen when looking at the back of the frame. This is also visible in the execution of concomitant repairs to the gilded finish at the front.

Decorative Finish
The relief decoration on the sloping frieze is made out of pastiglia. The cast work for the

172

frieze decoration is applied in seven lengths, with joins through the middle of each palmette, except for one join, between 3 and 4 o'clock, where the design repeat is truncated and the palmette has been omitted.

It was not possible to see the substructure of the torus moulding – it may be integral with the turned structure with the cast ornament wrapped over it, or the whole torus may have been cast. Two distinct joins can be seen on the cast leaf work on the torus, although there may be more joins concealed by the gilded finish.

The cast work has a coarser texture than the white ground layer applied on top. This can be seen where there is an area of damage. There are shrinkage cracks in the cast work, oriented across the wood grain, that continue through the gilded finish.

A sample of the cast work was analysed.[1] The results indicate that the bulk of the cast work consists mainly of gypsum in animal glue. Traces of chalk were also present, but may be a result of later repairs.

There is one original gilded scheme of water gilding, applied on a red–orange bole, over a white ground, over the cast work. There is punch work on the background to the relief ornament of the leaf motifs.

There are small areas of repair carried out in water gilding with a similar coloured bole to the original. These can be easily identified by the marks from the tool that has been used for the punch work, which differs from the original. This is apparent on an area of the background of the frieze at 1 o'clock. There are also repairs to the gilding around the sight edge and where a wooden repair has been carried out on the bottom edge of the frame. There are several areas of discoloured retouches.

Hanging Device

The top of the frame can be determined by the presence of a lighter mark showing the position of the old hanging device, probably a wrought metal strap and hook, and the remains of two cut nails.

Observations and Conclusions

The frame probably held a mirror, but how it was fixed in place is unclear. The wear and craquelure of the original gilded finish are good examples of the natural wear that would be expected on a piece of this age. This frame illustrates how later areas of repair to the gilded finish, although well executed, can be recognised through the use of a different punch tool.

Comparable Frames

Tondo frame, Tuscany, fifteenth century, diameter 310 mm, with pastiglia, decoration similar decorative motif palmettes (private collection, Capri). See Lodi, R. and Montanari, A. *Repertorio della cornice Europea: Italia, Francia, Spagna, Paesi Bassi: Dal Secolo XV al Secolo XX.* Modena: Galleria Roberto Lodi, 2003. p. 9, Figure 11.

A tondo frame with relief scrolling ornament on the frieze, holding a convex mirror with reflected scene or a convex painted surface, can be seen in the painting *Allegory of Prudence* by Giovanni Bellini, Venice, c.1490, oil on panel (Galerie dell'Acamemia, Venice). See Ajmar-Wollheim, M. and Dennis, F. *At home in Renaissance Italy.* London: V&A Publications, 2006. p. 189, Figure 13.18.

Reference

1. Analysis carried out by Dr Brian W Singer, Northumbria University.

RESULTS OF ANALYSIS
POLARISED LIGHT MICROSCOPY

Polarised light microscopy of sample 10-1890 (taken from area of damage to the cast work) indicated gypsum as most of the material present. The colourless particles had a refractive index (n) of less than 1.66, were anisotropic with fairly low birefringence and included rods with parallel extinction. Occasional colourless particles were seen with n < 1.66, showing high birefringence and a rhombic shape, which could be chalk.

INFRARED ANALYSIS

Infrared analysis of the sample 10-1890 (Figure 19.1) showed peaks due to gypsum (cf. Figure 19.2). There seems to be very little medium or chalk in this sample; it is mainly gypsum.

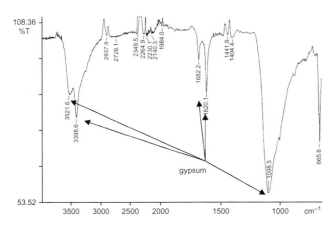

Figure 19.1   Infrared spectrum of sample 10-1890.

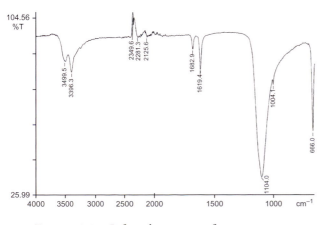

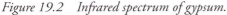

Figure 19.2   Infrared spectrum of gypsum.

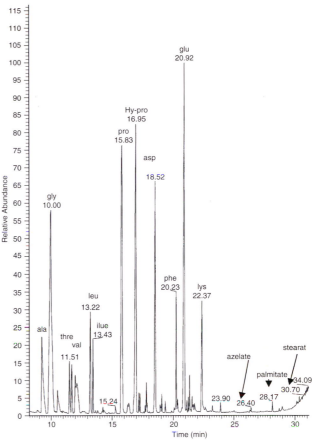

Figure 19.3   GC-MS chromatogram for sample 10-1890.

GC-MS ANALYSIS

Peaks for the fatty acids were present but small (Figure 19.3), indicating that the sample contained few lipids. The azelate to palmitate ratio by percentage area (Table 19.1) is 0.1, confirming the absence of a drying oil.[1] The palmitate to stearate ratio is 2.02, which is within the correct range for egg,[1-3] but it could also represent a small amount of fats associated with glue.

Table 19.1   Retention times and area % for fatty acid esters in sample 10-1890

RT	Identity	Area (%)
24.99	Dipropyl azelate	6.36
28.17	Propyl palmitate	62.62
30.26	Propyl stearate	31.02

20

CARVED AND PARTIALLY WATER GILDED WALNUT TONDO

Italy (Ferrara), 1502–1519; with the emblem of
Alfonso d'Este, Third Duke of Ferrara (1486–1534)
Bought, with a gilt-bronze relief (7694:A-1861),
from the Managers of the Guarantee Fund for purchasing the
Collection of Monsieur Soulages of Toulouse for £150
7694-1861 (Furniture and Woodwork Collection)

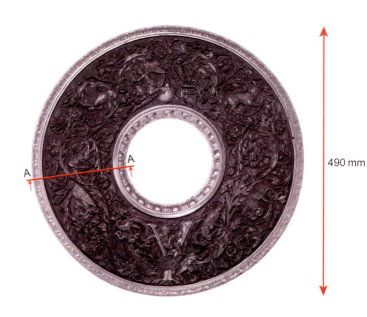

490 mm

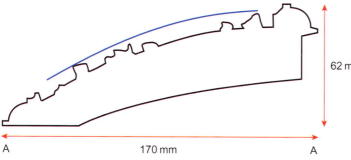

62 mm

A   170 mm   A

Dimensions (mm)

Diameter: 490; D: 62 (overall maximum).
Sight size: H: 150
Rebate: W: 8; D: 22
Object accommodation size: 166

Ornament

An egg-and-dart ovolo borders the sight edge. The main frieze of the frame is decorated with scrolling acanthus leaves, interspersed with allegorical figures and animals holding gilded letters, which read bonum (good) on the left side and malum (evil) on the right. At the bottom is a large gilded letter Y, the Pythagorean symbol for the choice between a life of virtue or vice. At the top left is an angel, representing eternal salvation, and on the right is a skeleton, symbolising death and damnation.

The 'good' emblems on the left include an eagle holding a hare in its claws (possibly symbolising military prowess), a unicorn (chastity) and a lion (fortitude). The 'bad' emblems on the right include a satyr (pride), a hog (gluttony), a porcupine (ferocity), a monkey (lust) and a wolf (cruelty). At the top, between the skeleton and the angel, is a gilt flaming grenade, the personal emblem of Alfonso d'Este, Third Duke of Ferrara (1486–1534). The outer edge consists of a leaf-and-dart ovolo moulding.[1]

Structure

The frame is made of one piece of turned and carved walnut. The frieze has been intricately carved in relief with deep undercutting and the background surfaces are punched. Turning marks can be seen on the edges of the gilded borders and on the back of the frame. The back is concave, with a flat outer rim.

The front has suffered from wood-boring beetle, with the hog's and porcupine's snouts partly eaten away, while the monkey's cheek and upper lip have been repaired with filler. An old split runs across the dished surface of the back, roughly behind the monkey.

Decorative Finish

The frame is partially gilded. There are two decorative schemes. The later gilding is oil gilding on a yellow mordant over a white ground and is found on the egg-and-dart sight edge, leaf-and-dart outer edge, lettering and flaming grenade. An earlier water gilded scheme on red bole over a thin white ground is visible on the outer leaf-and-dart ovolo moulding below the later oil gilded scheme.

Hanging Device

At the top there is pale area in the shape of an inverted V where a hanging device, possibly a wrought metal crossover strap with a loop at the top, was held with nails.

Observations and Conclusions

The earlier water gilded scheme would have appeared much brighter than today, resulting in a different balance of the ornament. It is possible that some elements such as the lettering were highlighted through burnishing. It is not possible to establish fully this possibility as the original surface is largely concealed by the present oil gilded scheme.

This frame probably held a mirror. The frame was acquired by the museum with a gilt-bronze relief of the Madonna and Child with Angels. It has not been concluded, however, whether this was the original object for this frame and it has been suggested that the back of this relief possibly served as a mirror.[1]

Previous Citation

This frame is referred to as Tuscan, first half of the sixteenth century, in Guggenheim, M. *Le cornici Italiane dalla metà del secolo XV allo scorcio del XVI; con breve testo riassuntivo intorno alla storia ed all'importanza delle cornice.* Milan: U.Hoepli, 1897. Plate 65.

Reference

1. Wilk, C. *Western furniture in The Victoria & Albert Museum 1350 to the present day.* London: Philip Wilson, 1996. Entry written by James Yorke, p. 32.

21

CARVED AND ORIGINALLY WATER GILDED FRAME THOUGHT TO HAVE BEEN A RESTELLO

Northern Italy, 1500–1550
Bought for £1 10s
7150-1860 (Furniture and Woodwork Collection)

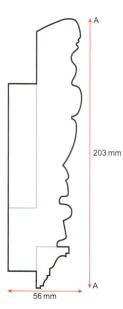

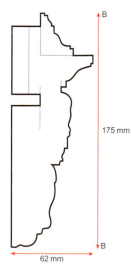

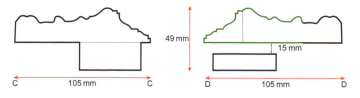

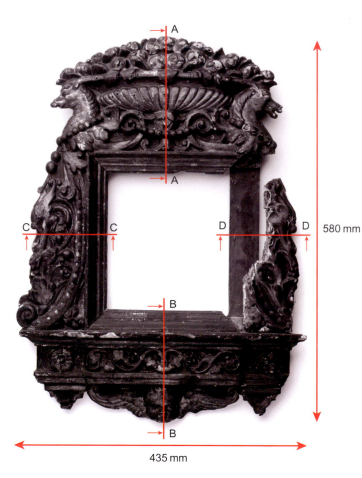

Dimensions (mm)
H: 580; W: 435; D: 66 (overall maximum)
Sight size: H: 208; W: 173
Rebate W: 8; D: 22
Object accommodation size: H: 228; W: 193
Slot H: 229; W: 15

186

Ornament

The sight edge is bordered by a double cyma and fillet moulding. The top is formed by a large gadrooned tazza overflowing with fruits and leaves, flanked by two hippocamp heads with beads and scrolling foliage around their necks. More beads are suspended from volutes below the tazza. An elongated scroll runs down the sides, terminating in a volute resting on the predella. Above the volute, there is more scrolling foliage with fruits, with a downward facing winged grotesque eating the fruit. A winged cherub head can be seen on the other lower side of the elongated scroll. The predella frieze is decorated with an undulate band of leaves and fruits, possibly grapes. The pedestals at either side of the frieze are decorated with a single patera. An antependium carved with a winged cherub head is set between two corbels.

Structure

The frame is made up of a softwood back frame which forms the structural support, to which lime or poplar pieces for the carved front frame are attached, held with cut nails driven in from the back.

The back frame is made of two vertical members that are joined with the horizontal members by a pegged T-bridle joint. The tongue of the joint is on the verticals. The inside of the back frame forms the depth of the rebate. The rebate width at the top, bottom and left corners has been slightly enlarged by cutting parts of the joints away. The cut-away area has darkened, indicating that this happened some time ago.

The vertical members of the back frame extend in length beyond the joints. The gap between the vertical members at the top is filled with a rectangular piece of softwood. At the bottom, the gap between the vertical members is filled by a softwood piece that is rectangular at the top and sits

behind the applied wood of the predella frieze. This piece is shaped at the bottom and forms the carved antependium at the front. At the sides near the bottom, the depth has been built up with two roughly rectangular pieces of wood. There is a later nail in each.

At the front of the frame, the top is made from one piece of wood. The sides are butt joined between the top and the predella. The depth of the right side is thinner than that on the left and creates a slot between it and the back frame for a sliding panel that would have concealed protected and revealed a painted panel or mirror fitted behind. The sight moulding on the left side appears to be formed out of the wood used for the side vertical member. At the top and bottom, the sight moulding is applied and on the right side, there would have been an applied sight moulding which is now missing.

The main part of the predella is applied to the back frame. The predella cornice mouldings are mitred and applied at the front and on the returns. The lower predella moulding is applied, with a fillet of wood behind it, on to the back frame. The returns are housed into the outside edges of the back frame. It is unclear whether the mouldings on the pedestals are made from the same piece of wood as the predella.

The corbels at the bottom of the frame are held with cut nails driven through the centre of each from the bottom. On the underside of the predella cornice moulding at the centre, there is a square hole from a cut nail.

The frame has been extensively attacked by wood-boring beetle, with flight holes up to approximately 2 mm in diameter. The larval tunnels extensively undermine the structure and there is considerable wood loss. The top half of the right side is lost, showing the severity of the internal damage.

Later Additions

A fabric-covered, chamfered, softwood board has been inserted into the rebate. This was removed for photography.

Inscriptions

On the bottom horizontal member at the back of the frame there is an armorial shield that is abraded. Below the shield an inscription reads 'DVS CASIMIRUS'. Other worn writing is visible, largely in lower case Roman script, 'verd litac Abox' and below, 'v…decea sa…'.

Decorative Finish

There are two decorative schemes. The more recent scheme is gilded and possibly silvered, applied on a red bole, on thin white ground. The beads and the carved fruit on the sides and on the predella and some of the leaves in the tazza appear almost black. These are thought to be silvered because bright silver was visible below the black on beads and fruits on the sides. If it is silver the silver leaf has tarnished and blackened through oxidation. The dark colour on the beads and fruits on the sides, however, could also have been the result of the darkening of a coating, perhaps once translucent and tinted with colour. The rest of the carved relief is decorated with burnished water gilding. In general, the entire surface of the gilding has been coated with a glue size, which is now dark and opaque, because of a build-up of trapped dust in the surface of the size. On some areas of the gilding, however, the coating appears to be deliberately darker, as if pigmented. This can be seen on the tips of the leaves on the hippocamps' necks.

On the background to the carved relief, a similar dark colour to that seen on the silvered areas was observed over a red bole on a white ground. It is not clear whether this dark surface also once contained silver. Samples were taken from the

Digital reconstruction giving an impression of the original carving and decorative scheme.

background for pigment identification but the results were inconclusive.[1] The white ground layer beneath is gypsum.

On the carved relief, at areas of loss of the later finish, there is an original scheme of water gilding on an orange–red bole, on a thin white ground.

The back of the frame is decorated with red paint randomly applied over yellow paint on a very thin white ground. This effect was possibly created by dabbing on paint with a sponge or rag. Similar paint effects have been found on the backs of some Italian cassone (for example painted and gilded cassone, c.1430, V&A, 8974-1863).

Hanging Device and Fittings

There are several holes at the back top centre. Two of these are drilled diagonally and emerge at the top edge. These were possibly used for a cord or ribbon hanging. The other holes, at the top left and right and bottom centre, are from more recent hanging fittings.

On the front, on the bottom predella moulding, there are remnants of two wire hooks. These may have been added for a picture label. Alternatively, they may be earlier hooks for hanging items associated with restelli, such as grooming devices or personal ornaments.[2]

Observations and Conclusions

The shape of the frame and remnants of hooks lead to the conclusion that this frame is likely to have been a restello. This was a piece of furniture invented in the fifteenth century that typically consisted of a wall mirror set into a wooden frame. It was often richly decorated with painting and gilding, with hooks from which articles for the toilette were hung. These could be '… hairbrushes, combs, code (horse tail switches to clean combs), scriminali (styli or needles of bone, glass or silver

for parting the hair), azebellino (a small fur to hold in the hand), profume golavorado da pomo colla sua catenella (a perfume ball on a chain), paternostri (rosaries), spugnette (sponges), bottigliette di profumi (perfume bottles), vasetti di pomette (glass jars of pomade)'.[2]

The carved relief was originally water gilded. No gilding was observed on the background under the dark colour, but the red and white ground could be part of the original scheme. It is not clear whether the background to the carved relief was originally painted or silvered. A digitally reconstructed image of this frame, shows its right side replaced, and gives an impression of how the frame may have looked today if it were originally gilded overall.

Comparable Frames

All the frames below have columns on the sides near the sight edge.

Restello frame, Italian, c.1500–1550, carved poplar, painted and gilded, with similar scrolling leaves and hippocamps at each side (H: 985; W: 1050; D: 160), Museo Stefano Bardini, Florence, Invn. 990. See Ajmar-Wollheim, M. and Dennis, F. *At home in Renaissance Italy.* London: V&A Publications, 2006. Catalogue entry p. 360, p. 188, Figure 13.16.

The Museo Stefano Bardini frame, photographed with a pediment not seen in the Ajmar-Wollheim and Dennis image, features in Guggenheim, M. *Le cornici Italiane dalla metà del secolo XV o allo scorcio del XVI; con breve testo riassuntivo intorno alla storia ed all'importanza delle cornice.* Milan: U.Hoepli, 1897. Plate 71.

Restello frame, Venetian, c.1520–1530, very similar to the Museo Stefano Bardini frame, with a small gadrooned tazza at the top, hippocamps on the sides and grotesque dolphins on the predella. See *Schöne Rahmen aus den Bestanden der Berliner Gemäldegalerie.* Exhibition Catalogue. Berlin:

Gemäldegalerie Staatliche Museen zu Berlin, 2002. p. 55.

Restello frame, Bologna, sixteenth century. See Pedrini, A. *Il mobilio; gli ambienti e le decorazioni del Rinascimento in Italia, secoli XV e XVI.* 2nd ed. Genova: Stringa, 1969. Figure 402.

Restello frame, Venetian, early sixteenth century. See Newbery, T. *Frames in the Robert Lehman Collection.* Princeton: Metropolitan Museum of Art in association with Princeton University Press, 2007. pp. 96–97; Newbery, T., Bisacca, G. and Kanter, L. *Italian Renaissance frames.* Exhibition Catalogue. New York: Metropolitan Museum, 1990. p. 48.

Restello frame, Venetian, first half of the sixteenth century, with grotesques at the sides with heads of bearded men. See Guggenheim, M. *Le cornici Italiane dalla metà del secolo XV o allo scorcio del XVI; con breve testo riassuntivo intorno alla storia ed all'importanza delle cornice.* Milan: U.Hoepli, 1897. Plate 55b.

Restello frame, Italian, sixteenth century, with winged hippocamp. See Lessing, J. *Vorbilder-Hefte aus dem KGL. Kunstgewerbe-Museen Rahmen: Italien und Deutschland XVI Jahr hundert.* Berlin: Verlag Von Ernst Wasmuth, 1888. Tafel No. 1.

A drawing depicting hippocamps whose form is echoed in the carved hippocamps on Frame 21 (7150-1860). See *Neptune*, c.1504, by Leonardo Da Vinci (1452–1519). The Royal Collection (UK).

References

1. Analysis carried out by Dr Brian W Singer, Northumbria University.
2. Jeffries, J. and Romano, D. *Venice reconsidered: the history and civilization of an Italian city-state.* Baltimore: Johns Hopkins University Press, 2000. p. 315.

RESULTS OF ANALYSIS

Samples were taken from a recessed area in the pediment, adjacent to the scroll emerging from the hippocamp's head.

POLARISED LIGHT MICROSCOPY

Low-powered microscopic observation of a fragment revealed a black layer on top of a red layer on top of a white layer. Polarised light microscopy revealed opaque black particles which may be charcoal, or dirt or a corroded silver foil. Also a large amount of an orange–red resinous substance was also found, which was thought to be either a red varnish or dragon's blood. The white ground layer contained gypsum.

GC-MS ANALYSIS

A sample of the red resin was treated with meth prep II reagent and subjected to gas chromatography–mass spectroscopy to determine whether dragon's blood was present. Azelic acid, as its dimethyl ester, was present (Figure 21.1), with an azeate/palmitate ratio of 1.7 indicating a drying oil. The azelate to suberate ratio was 4.3 and the azelate to sebacate ratio was 10, together indicating that the oil had been partially heat bodied. The palmitate to stearate ratio was 2.7, which indicates walnut oil. Also present were the methyl esters of dehydroabietic acid, 7-methoxytetrahydroabietic acid and 7-oxodehydroabietic acid, all of which indicate the presence of coniferous resin, probably pine resin. Hence, the chromatogram showed the presence of pine resin in a heat bodied walnut oil. None of the components found in the reference sample of dragon's blood was found in this sample.

CONCLUSION

The dark finish may be a paint containing charcoal or just dirt or a discoloured, corroded metal foil over a walnut oil/pine resin varnish or adhesive. The white layer beneath is gypsum.

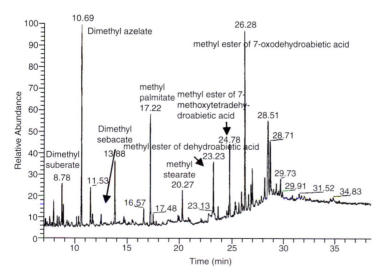

Figure 21.1   Chromatogram of red resinous layer from 7150-1860, sample 4.

SANSOVINO FRAMES

Sansovino frames are named by association with the Florentine architect Jacopo Sansovino (1486–1570), whose work in Venice brought together in the second half of the sixteenth century a group of craftsmen who worked in the Mannerist style. Sansovino frames can be distinguished by their use of interlacing scrolls, volutes, cherub heads, festoons, clasps, caryatides and masks, often exaggerated in scale. Similar motifs may be found in sixteenth century Venetian interiors, for example in the stucco decoration of ceilings in the Palazzo Ducale, Venice, c.1575, by the workshop of Alessandro Vittoria (1525–1608), and in the woodwork of Cristoforo Sorte. Sansovino frames employ not only such motifs but often their characteristic parcel gilding.

Mannerism grew out of a sophisticated and playful distortion of the Classical style, in which elements of the latter – either architectural or (in painting) anatomical – were exaggerated, elongated or broken. For instance, the restrained and proportional scrolls of a Classical aedicule were enlarged, drawn out and applied out of rational context; this can be seen in Frames 22, 24, 25 and 26. Caryatides were combined with these scrolls, as though the boundary between human and architectural were dissolving (see Frames 22, 23 and 24) and grotesque masks appeared on the pediments and aprons of frames (see Frame 26). Outset corners, stepped levels and broken pediments were common (see Frame 22); these features are influenced by the late architectural work of Michelangelo (the Porta Pia and Bibliotreca Laurenziana, Rome) and of Giorgio Vasari (see the engraved frontispiece to his *Lives of the Artists*, 1550 and 1568).

Similar distortions may be seen in contemporary paintings, notably in the elongated anatomy depicted by Parmigianino (1503–1540) and Bronzino (1503–1572). Frame 27, for example, uses as the supporting Adam and Eve elegant, etiolated

Carved, painted and gilded lantern, V&A (7225-1860).

figures that are reminiscent of Parmigianino's *Madonna of the Long Neck* (1534, Uffizi, Florence).

The carved, painted and gilded lantern (V&A, 7225-1860) pictured above is illustrative of the Sansovino style. This features scrolls, caryatides, radial flutes and clasps similar to the Sansovino frames discussed in the following entries.[1]

Reference

1. Thanks to Lynn Roberts for her valuable contribution to this section.

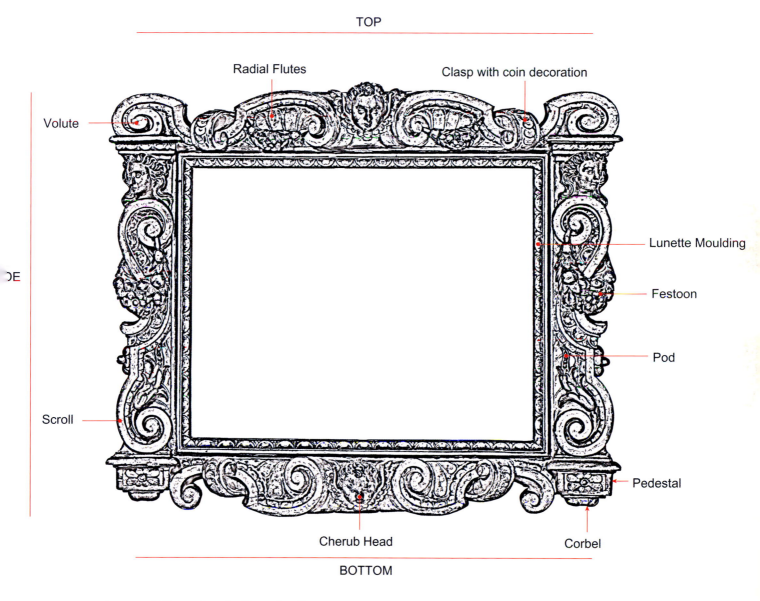

TOP

Radial Flutes

Clasp with coin decoration

Volute

Lunette Moulding

DE

Festoon

Pod

Scroll

Pedestal

Cherub Head

Corbel

BOTTOM

Annotated illustration of a Sansovino frame.

22

BLACK PAINTED AND PARTIALLY WATER AND MORDANT GILDED MANNERIST FRAME

Italy (Tuscany), 1550–1575
Bequeathed by John Meeson Parsons; acquired with a
painting, Adoration of the Magi (535-1870)
535A-1870 (Furniture and Woodwork Collection)

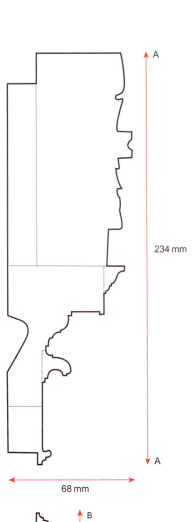

234 mm

68 mm

95 mm

30 mm

33 mm

90 mm

648 mm

502 mm

Dimensions (mm)
H: 648; W: 502; D: 85 (overall maximum)
Sight size: H: 310; W: 352
Rebate: W: 9; D: 13
Object accommodation size: H: 335; W: 272

Ornament

A bead-and-pearl enriched astragal moulding borders the sight edge. A running moulding intersects
the entablature, where it surrounds a panel painted

with a swag, and at the bottom forms outset corners, each decorated with a rosette. The sides are flanked by female herms in profile supporting triglyphs and a broken scrolling pediment with leaf work cresting at the centre. The scrolling antependium is set between corbels.

Structure

The frame is made from a hardwood, possibly poplar. At the back, two narrow vertical members half lap the horizontal members. The one at the top is very broad and extends beyond the joints above the herms' heads. The sight edge bead-and-pearl moulding and rebate are made of one piece of wood inserted into the aperture of the back frame. On the front, the running moulding is mitred and applied all round. The main part of the pediment is made of one piece. The overhanging cornice moulding and the cyma are mitred and applied at the front and sides. The herms on their plinths are each made of once piece. Below the plinths are two fillets of wood. The scrolls inside the triglyphs and the rosettes at the bottom corners are applied. The antependium at the bottom is made from a separate piece. The corbels at the bottom, left and right, are applied. There are losses to the carved detail on the corbels. The central ornament at the base of the frame are incomplete as a result of damage.

Later Additions

The frame has been glazed by The National Gallery, London. There is a spacing bar behind the glass and the frame has been built up at the back with a solid piece of plywood, which was removed for photography. There is a balsa wood fillet applied at the bottom and top rebate and velvet ribbon has been applied to the width of the rebate.

Decorative Finish

The present finish is painted black and partially gilded. It has been suggested that the frame has

been painted black to imitate ebony.[1] There is much overpaint, varnish and bronze and black paint retouching, resulting in an uneven finish. The original finish can be seen in some areas.

The original scheme was also black and partially gilded, with areas of water gilding on an orange–red bole seen on the volutes and the bead-and-reel decoration. Both the paint and water gilding are applied on a white ground. On the black painted areas there is finely drawn, gold line work. This can be seen on the veining on the acanthus leaves in the cresting and on the fluting on the cornice. On the sight edge moulding on the left side, next to the second bead down, a detailed bright gilded leaf pattern can be seen. These may form part of the original scheme. Other details, such as the herms' necklaces, are applied over black and are also mordant gilded. A broad, bold brush stroke is used on the painted swag at the top. These are thought to be overpaint.

The black overpainting varies: in some places black is applied over black; in other areas it is applied over the losses in the earlier finish. These earlier losses appear as shallow recesses in the paint surface. There is also black overpaint on a white ground layer applied over the earlier black. It is not certain that the overpaint and gilding replicate the earlier decorative scheme.

Analysis of a paint sample from the black paint on the chin of the female herm suggested that the earliest black paint layer incorporates a bone black pigment that had been applied over a calcium sulphate ground. The cross-section of this sample shows several successively applied layers of paint and varnish. Later layers of varnish have penetrated into cracks in the underlying paint.[2] A sample of the oil gilding on black paint, which appeared to be earlier, was taken from the plinth of the female herm on the right side. This analysis

found varnish, a dark organic layer, gold, a black paint layer incorporating bone black, a dark paint layer incorporating bone black and a calcium sulphate ground. Published thicknesses for gold leaf in medieval Europe range between 0.25 and 6 μm, while modern leaf typically ranges from 3 to 8 μm.[3] In this case, the gold leaf varied in thickness from approximately 12 to 20 μm. This is exceptionally thick for gold leaf and is more in the range expected for foil made from tin, although SEM/EDX analysis of the metal leaf confirmed that it was gold.

Hanging Device

There is a recessed hole at the back with a lozenge-shaped metal surround that may have been where the frame was attached to a hook on a wall. There is also a cut-out area at the top where a metal fitting was once attached.

Observations and Conclusions

The frame is used to frame a painting. It has been suggested that it was probably originally made for a sacred image.[4] Since 1938, this frame has been on long-term loan to The National Gallery, London, framing *Saint Jerome in a Landscape* by Cima da Conegliano (c.1500–1510).

The repeated overpaint and coatings make it difficult to interpret and distinguish the original and later finishes. Further investigation is required.

Comparable Frames

Designs for similar frames in Vasari's album ff. 52 and 33, Soane Museum, London. See Sabatelli, F. *La Cornice italiana dal Rinascimento al Neoclassico.* Milan: Electa, 1992. p. 48.

Mitchell draws comparisons with Bartolomeo Ammanati's (1511–1592) drawings for frames with similar elements. See also Mitchell, P. and Roberts, L. *A history of European picture frames.* London: Merrell Holberton, 1996. pp. 26–27, Plate 14A.

Previous Citations

Odom, W. M. *A history of Italian furniture from the fourteenth to the early nineteenth centuries.* Volume I: *Gothic and Renaissance furniture.* New York: Archive Press, 1967. p. 344 Figure 341; and Hasluck, P. N. *Manual of traditional woodcarving.* New York: Dover Publications, 1977. p. 309, Figure 609 date this frame to the late sixteenth century.

Mitchell, P. Italian picture frames, 1500–1825: a brief survey. *Journal of the Furniture History Society*, 20, 1984. p. 20, Plate 14b, describes this frame as Tuscan, c.1550. See also Mitchell, P. and Roberts, L. *A history of European picture frames.* London: Merrell Holberton, 1996. pp. 26–27.

Penny, N. *Frames.* National Gallery Pocket Guides. London: National Gallery, 1997. pp. 34–35, No. 26, dates this frame to c.1560.

References

1. Penny, N. Frames. National Gallery Pocket Guides. London: National Gallery, 1997. p. 34.

2. Cross-section and SEM/EDX analyses of paint samples were carried out by carried by Dr Helen Howard, Scientific Department, The National Gallery, London.

3. Nadolny, J. and Lins, A. Some observations on northern European metalbeaters and metal leaf in the Late Middle Ages. Basic properties of gold leaf. In R. Rushfield, M. Ballard, eds. and D. Bigelow, ed. *The materials, technology and art of conservation: studies in honor of Lawrence J. Majewski on the occasion of his 80th Birthday, February 10, 1999 Gilded wood conservation and history.* New York. Madison, CT: Conservation Center, Institute of Fine Arts, New York University: Sound View Press, 1999, 1991. pp. 134–. pp. 19–160; .

4. Penny, op cit., pp. 34–35, No. 26.

RESULTS OF ANALYSIS
SAMPLE 2/1
LOCATION
Female herm on left side, chin: black paint.

PAINT CROSS-SECTION IN
INCIDENT LIGHT

UV LIGHT

INCIDENT LIGHT

- varnish
- dark organic layer on surface
- black paint layer incorporating bone black
- dark paint layer incorporating bone black
- calcium sulphate.

SEM/EDX
- SEM/EDX analysis of the lower of the two black paint layers confirmed the presence of: Ca, S, Cl, P, Si, K, Al, Mg
- SEM/EDX analysis of the upper black paint layer confirmed the presence of: Ca, S, Cl, P, Si, K, Fe
- SEM/EDX analysis of a particle within the area below the black paint layer which appears 'spotty' in UV confirmed the presence of: Ca, S, (As, Si, P, Cl, K, Ti)
- SEM/EDX analysis of the substrate confirmed the presence of: Ca, S.

SAMPLE 2/2

LOCATION

Plinth of female herm on right side: possible original gilded decoration over black paint.

PAINT CROSS-SECTION IN INCIDENT LIGHT

UV LIGHT

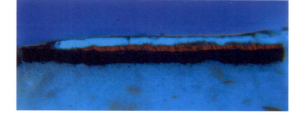

INCIDENT LIGHT

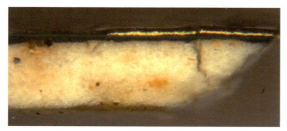

- varnish
- dark organic layer on surface
- gold
- black paint layer incorporating bone black
- dark paint layer incorporating bone black
- calcium sulphate.

SEM/EDX

- SEM/EDX analysis of the black paint layer confirmed the presence of: Ca, S, Cl, P, Si, K, Fe
- SEM/EDX analysis of the substrate confirmed the presence of: Ca, S
- SEM/EDX analysis of the metal leaf confirmed the presence of: Au.

23

CARVED WALNUT AND PARTIALLY WATER AND MORDANT GILDED SANSOVINO FRAME

Italy (Venice), 1550–1600
Bought for £16 4s 6d
682-1883 (Furniture and Woodwork Collection)

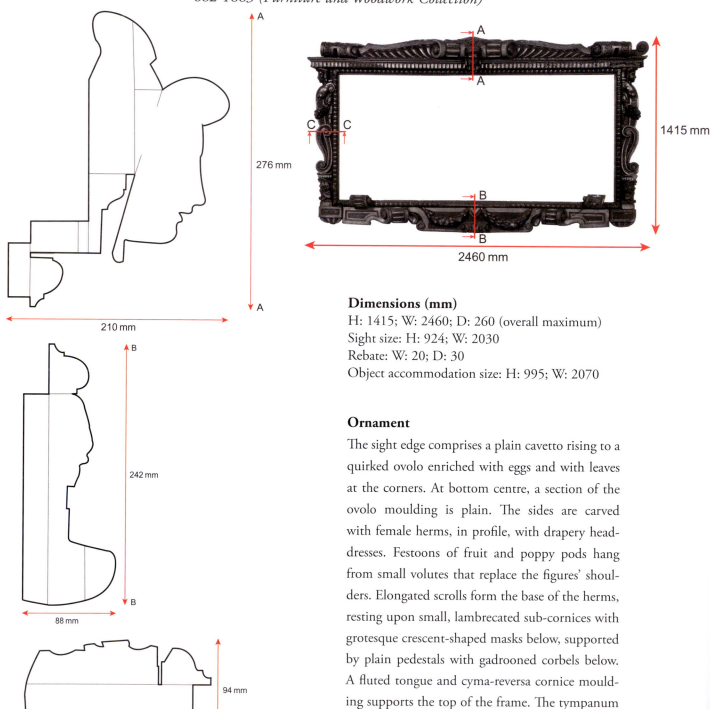

Dimensions (mm)

H: 1415; W: 2460; D: 260 (overall maximum)
Sight size: H: 924; W: 2030
Rebate: W: 20; D: 30
Object accommodation size: H: 995; W: 2070

Ornament

The sight edge comprises a plain cavetto rising to a quirked ovolo enriched with eggs and with leaves at the corners. At bottom centre, a section of the ovolo moulding is plain. The sides are carved with female herms, in profile, with drapery head-dresses. Festoons of fruit and poppy pods hang from small volutes that replace the figures' shoulders. Elongated scrolls form the base of the herms, resting upon small, lambrecated sub-cornices with grotesque crescent-shaped masks below, supported by plain pedestals with gadrooned corbels below. A fluted tongue and cyma-reversa cornice moulding supports the top of the frame. The tympanum is radially fluted. A central projecting mask, with

a drapery headdress, is set between heavy bifurcated fluted volutes with spreading leaf work above. At either end are bifurcated clasps enriched with coins and upturning volutes, one of which is missing on the left side. The residual predella has scrolling strap work with two large clasps placed over the sight moulding and two large festoons above a small bifurcated clasp at the centre.

Structure

The frame is made of walnut and softwood. The carved wood at the front of the frame is walnut. There are no interlocking joints: the frame parts are butt joined and nailed together. There are several small wrought nail heads on the back. At the top of each side, there is a large, roughly circular, facet-headed nail. There are various later screws, cast iron metal straps and pieces of wood that support the structure at the back.

The sides of the frame are butt joined between the top and bottom. The sight moulding is separate and is mitred. The depth of the sides is made up of three pieces. The back of the front piece and the sight moulding are level which each other. The middle piece is softwood and this partly sits behind the sight moulding and forms the sight edge rebate. The back piece is softwood.

On the top, the depth of the cornice is made up of three pieces. The carved fluted tongue and cyma moulding is mitred and applied on to the middle piece. The middle piece at each end rests on top of the front pieces of the sides. The back of the top middle piece and the back of the side front pieces are level with each other. The back piece is made of roughly cut softwood and its back is level with the backs of the sides' middle pieces.

Above the carved cornice moulding sits a length of wood that forms the majority of the rest of the carving. This is supported at the back by various blocks of wood, some screwed on with modern

screws. The volute at the right end is made of a separate piece; the left one is missing. Extra pieces are applied at the front to add depth for the front two-thirds of the protruding volutes and clasps. The mask at the centre is carved from a separate inset piece.

At the bottom, the depth is made up of two pieces. Extra pieces are applied over the sight moulding for the two large protruding clasps. The back piece is made of softwood and is level with the backs of the sides.

Later Additions

At the top front, on the left, a repair has been carried out to a section of the fluted tongue cornice. The new wood is evident by the lack of gilding in the flutes and it is butt and scarf jointed on to the original wood. The original fluting at the left has been cut through along the top of the fluting

below the cyma, probably when this repair was carried out. At the back of the frame a later tongue and groove panel with lengths of wood applied top, bottom, left and right has been fitted into the rebate. The photograph of the front was digitally manipulated to remove this.

Decorative Finish

The gilded areas are original and consist of both water and mordant gilding. The water gilding has bright gold on a red–orange bole, over a thin, white ground and is applied to the eggs, the edges of the voluted scrolls and the fruit in the festoons. Gilded details on each herm and the central mask are finely executed on the eyebrows, lips, chins and nipples and these were possibly once brightly burnished. The decorative stripes on the cheeks, neck, chest and breasts of each herm and the forehead and cheeks of the central mask are mordant gilded. No colour was seen in the mordant.

211

The gilded surface has a dark coating and a dirt layer that now partially obscures the brightness and details of the gilding. Originally these would have appeared much brighter. Some areas of the wood have a later varnish.

Hanging Device

At the top of the back there are two large crossover wrought iron hanging loops, held with wrought nails that appear to be original and four later cast iron straps screwed on with holes for wall fixing.

Observations and Conclusions

This very large frame would have contained a painting. The plain area at the centre bottom on the sight edge ovolo moulding may have once had an inscription or plaque with the title of the painting and the name of the artist. Apart from a few later repairs to the structure and accretions of dirt, the decorative finish of this frame remains largely unaltered.

A very large frame such as this was probably carved for an important late sixteenth century painting. If this frame could be matched with a painting, it might be possible to determine the palazzo for which the frame was carved.[1]

Comparable Frames

Sansovino frame (F 20056) from The National Gallery, London, with 'Pavlo Veronese 1528–1588' inscribed on the cartouche at bottom centre.[2]

Sansovino frame with very similar overall character, although fully gilded, framing *Il doge Agostino Barbarigo presentato alla Madonna e al Bambino* by Bellini (Murano, San Pietro Martire). See Sabatelli, F. *La cornice Italiana dal Rinascimento al Neoclassico.* Milan: Electa, 1992. pp. 58–59.

Sansovino frame, Venetian, second half of the sixteenth century (Padova, Musei Civici, 1180 790) has very similar half moon masks on the top. See Sabatelli, F. *La cornice Italiana dal Rinascimento al Neoclassico.* Milan: Electa, 1992. pp. 154–155.

Sansovino frame, Venetian, sixteenth century, smaller but with similar placement of partially gilded decoration. See Sabatelli, F. *La cornice Italiana dal Rinascimento al Neoclassico.* Milan: Electa, 1992. pp. 152–153.

Sansovino frame, Venetian, second half of sixteenth century with similar volutes, masks, swags and radial fluting. See Guggenheim, M. *Le cornii Italiane dalla metà del secolo XVo allo scorcio del XVI; con breve testo riassuntivo intorno alla storia ed all'importanza delle cornice.* Milan: U.Hoepli, 1897. Plate 91 (right hand side).

References

1. Tim Miller, personal communication, February 2008.
2. Thanks to Peter Schade.

24

CARVED, ORIGINALLY WATER GILDED SANSOVINO FRAME

Italy (Venice), 1550–1600
Bought, with two paintings in tempera from an altarpiece
by Vittore Crivelli (765A-1865 St Catherine and
765:1-1865 St Jerome), from the Managers of the
Guarantee Fund for purchasing the Collection of Monsieur
Soulages of Toulouse for £70
765:2-1865 (Furniture and Woodwork Collection)

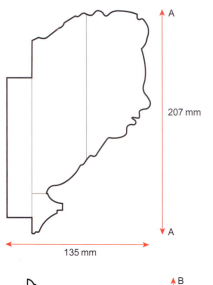

207 mm

135 mm

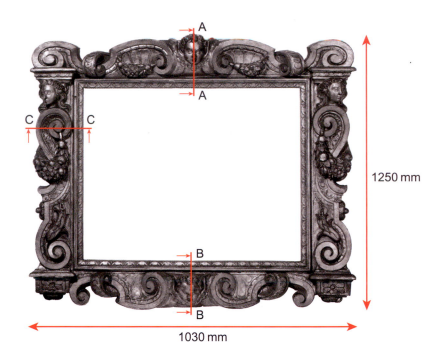

1250 mm

1030 mm

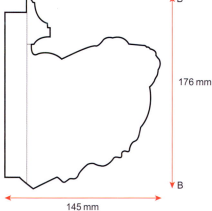

176 mm

145 mm

Dimensions (mm)

H: 1250; W: 1030; D: 160 (overall maximum)
Sight size: H: 668; W: 845
Rebate: W: 15; D: 17
Object accommodation size: H: 695; W: 870

Ornament

A cavetto moulding enriched with lunettes filled with half flowers borders the sight edge. The sides are each carved with a female head with flowing hair, supported by elongated scrolls. Heavy festoons hang from the top volute and a flowering pod springs from the lower volute. The pedestals are enriched with a condensed flower and decorated

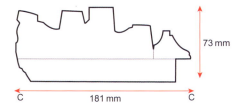

73 mm

181 mm

at the bottom with a floral corbel. The top and bottom are carved with a winged cherub head at the centre and scrolls with radially arranged tongues and strap-work clasps enriched with overlapping coins. Two small festoons are hung from the scrolls at the top.

Structure

The original frame is constructed of a softwood back frame to which a lime carved front frame is applied. The back frame is partially obscured by a later build-up. The back frame's vertical members are joined at the corners with a keyed dovetail half lap joint into the front face of the horizontal members. The ends of the dovetails are visible at the top. On the sides, wood has been added on the outside edges to create width for the carving.

The top and bottom horizontals of the front frame run the full width, with the side members butt joined between. At the top centre, wood has been added for the protruding, carved cherub head.

The cherub head, swags and the female heads are carved in high relief and the female figures have long noses, pointed chins and long wavy hair. The heads of iron nails, which can be seen on the back frame, are used to hold these to the frame. There is a large drilled hole at the top left. The sight mouldings are mitred and applied. There are some losses to the carving, and areas of wood-boring beetle damage, particularly at the bottom back.

Later Additions and Alterations

There is a later softwood build-up, probably nineteenth century. (This is not included in the profile drawing.) The horizontal members of this build-up are butted between the vertical members. The outside edges have been chamfered. Nails have been driven through to hold these pieces to the original frame. On the left, an additional piece of wood has been screwed on. Gummed paper has been applied over the build-up and the original sight edge moulding, probably to hold a later backboard. This build-up is not included in the profile drawings. A later painted pine tongue and groove board that had been inserted into the rebate was removed for photography.

Inscriptions

On the later build-up at the centre, '765-65' is written in pencil and on the left side, near the top, '74' underlined, with '7.' below. To the right of this original back frame, is written '374' underlined and, below, 'N.7'.

Decorative Finish

There are two decorative schemes. The most recent is water gilding on an orange–red bole on a medium white ground. Below this is the original water gilding on red–orange bole on a medium white ground.

Hanging Device

At the top centre of the original frame there are old fixing holes and an indentation, probably from an old wrought iron crossover hanging loop. At the top left and right there are two later iron rings attached with large screws. On the later build-up, there are metal hanging straps that are screwed on and have holes for a wall fixing. On the right, these extend at the top and bottom of the frame and on the left they extend at the side.

Observations and Conclusions

This frame probably contained a secular painting. It was acquired with paintings *St Catharine* (765A-1865) and *St Jerome* (765:1-1865) from an earlier fifteenth century altarpiece by Vittore Crivelli.[1]

The later gilded scheme seems largely to follow the earlier scheme. The later scheme obscures the original sculptural detail, which would have been sharper; the earlier gilding would probably have been burnished and more reflective. No evidence of earlier paint was found on the flesh areas of the figures, nor of the carved relief having had a different coloured background, as is seen on other Sansovino frames.[2]

Comparable Frames

Sansovino frame, Venetian, c.1580–1590. See Newbery, T., Bisacca, G. and Kanter, L. *Italian Renaissance frames.* Exhibition Catalogue. New York: Metropolitan Museum, 1990. p. 69, No. 39.

Sansovino frame, Venetian, second half of the sixteenth century, H: 245; W: 335; D: 70. Although a narrower frame, it has similar volutes and placements of flowers and of top and side festoons, use of female and winged cherub heads and bottom clasps (Verona, Museo di Castelvecchio). See Sabatelli, F. *La cornice Italiana dal Rinascimento al Neoclassico.* Milan: Electa, 1992. pp. 156–157.

Sansovino frame, Venetian, second half of the sixteenth century (Padova Musei Civici), H: 1180; W: 790; D: 180, appears to be very similar to Frame

24 (765:2-1865), having an identical sight moulding, moulding of capital, character of volutes, radial
fluting at bottom, radial flutes at top, and corbels,
top and bottom. See Sabatelli, F. *La cornice Italiana
dal Rinascimento al Neoclassico.* Milan: Electa,
1992. pp. 154–155.

Two Sansovino frames, Venetian, sixteenth century,
stylistically similar in character to Frame 24 (765:2-
1865), both having similar sight edge mouldings
(Padova, Museo Civico and Barozzi Collection,
Venice). The frame from Padova has ash-blue figures and festoons. See Pedrini, A. *Il mobilio; gli
ambienti e le decorazioni del Rinascimento in Italia,
secoli XV e XVI.* 2nd ed. Genova: Stringa, 1969. p.
161, Plates 408 and 409.

Sansovino frame, north Italian, probably Venetian,
c.1590, with similar positioning of scrolling
volutes and clasps. See Penny, N. *Frames.* National
Gallery Pocket Guides. London: National Gallery,
1997. pp. 60–61.

References

1. In the Soulages Collection, the paintings were attributed to Carlo Crivelli.
2. See for example the Sansovino frame at the National
   Gallery, London, north Italian, probably Venetian,
   c.1590, with pink painted mask with green and metal
   spangled recessed background. See Penny, N. *Frames.*
   National Gallery Pocket Guides. London: National
   Gallery, 1997. pp. 60–61.

25

CARVED AND PIERCED WATER GILDED SANSOVINO FRAME

Italy (probably Venice), 1550–1600
Bought with a mirror plate for £10
4215:1-1857 (Furniture and Woodwork Collection)

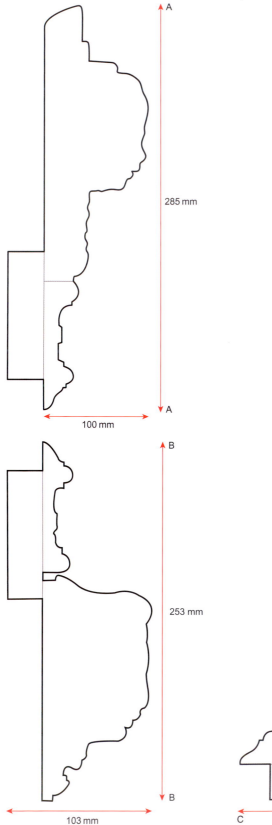

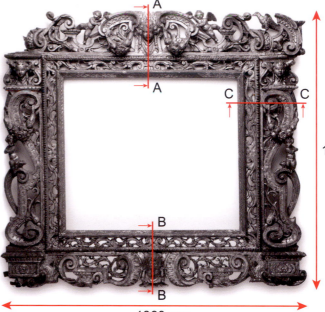

1190 mm

1360 mm

Dimensions (mm)
H: 1190; W: 1360; D: 100 (overall maximum)
Sight size: H: 650; W: 746
Rebate: W: top and left 15, right 20, bottom 17; D: 25
Object accommodation size: H: 685; W: 781

Ornament
The inner frame consists of a cyma-recta sight edge enriched with imbricated leaves, followed by a pierced frieze with an undulate band of scrolling acanthus leaves, bordered by a fluted tongue moulding. Each side of the outer frame consists of an elongated leaf-and-dart enriched scroll. Festoons hang from the top of the scrolls and

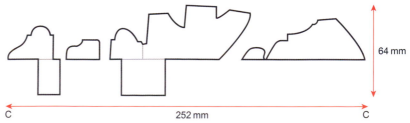

285 mm

100 mm

253 mm

103 mm

64 mm

252 mm

half way up is a putto seated on another scroll, and a winged cherub head, with drapery, supported by scrolls, forms the capital on each side. On the top a central cherub head, also adorned with drapery, is placed between two scrolls, with hanging festoons. These scrolls are held on either side by winged putti. Foliate scrollwork at either end is held with clasps that are surmounted with birds. At the bottom, a central female head, also adorned with drapery, is framed by scrolls, strap work and undulating foliage. At either side, the pedestals are enriched with overlapping coins. The bird and scroll on the top left corner and a scroll on the bottom left corner are missing.

Structure

The frame is made up of a soft, pale hardwood back frame that forms the structural support to which the lime or poplar pieces of the carved front frame are attached.

The back frame is made of two vertical and two horizontal members. The horizontal lengths, which extend beyond the joints, are half lap jointed over the vertical lengths. On each length, in between the ends and the centres, the central portion of the width has been removed to ensure that the back frame does not generally show behind the pierced and carved work at the front. The insides of the back frame are positioned behind the sight edge moulding and form the depth of the sight edge rebate.

At the front, the carved and pierced top, bottom and sides with scrolling strap work, festoons, birds, putti and masks are each carved from one piece. The top and bottom pieces run the full width of the frame. The sides are butt joined between these. An inner frame consists of the sight edge moulding, the pierced and carved undulate frieze and the fluted tongue moulding, which are

carved from single lengths and mitred at the corners. These, and the outer parts of the frame, are attached to the back frame with nails. The outer part of the back frame bridges the join between these and holds them together.

Areas of the back frame that can be seen from the front have been gilded. The back frame can clearly be seen on the top and right side of the frame, outside the fillet surrounding the fluted tongue moulding, behind the pierced work. The top ends of the vertical members of the back frame can be seen behind the pierced work, beside the carved clasps on which the birds sit.

In general, the carving is in relatively shallow relief and undulates little in depth along the scrolls, especially on the sides. The clasps, festoons, putti and masks are higher relief.

Later Additions

There are several areas of replacement carving: the right wing of the putti at the top right and the scroll below the seated putti on the left side, a section of the top sight edge moulding (approximately 290 mm in length towards the centre), has been scarf jointed in. These replacements are identifiable as later repairs because of the predominantly red ground of the gilded finish. The carving is also by a different hand. There is a bird and one scroll missing from the top left corner. At the back there are two thin pieces of wood, on the top and bottom of the left side, which were possibly applied to support repairs to carvings, now missing. There is also a new fillet of wood applied to the top centre on the back frame. A later fabric-covered softwood board had been inserted into the rebate. This was removed for photography.

Decorative Finish

There is one original water gilded scheme on blue–red bole, on a thin white ground, with some areas of later water gilding on a bright red bole on a white ground. The later finish employs little gold leaf and much of the bright red bole is left showing. This gilding is applied on the carved replacements and on areas where original gilding was lost. The frame is covered by a dark brown coating, probably associated with later repairs to the carving and gilding. This coating has shrunk into islands and is cupping and flaking, pulling away the bole and gilding and revealing the white ground. On the back of the frame, there is a thin, white ground covered with dark brown paint that appears to be water based, probably with an animal glue binder. A sample from the original scheme from the central female head at the bottom showed that the ground contained gypsum and the bole contained red and yellow ochre.[1]

Hanging Device

There is no evidence of original fittings. There are later brass mirror plate fittings and various associated holes from later fittings. These are mainly in groups of three from mirror plate fittings.

Observations and Conclusions

The pierced work of the frame would have shown off the colour of the wall behind.[2] The frame has suffered from exposure to damp conditions at some point. There are water marks and some mould marks on the back. The white ground is quite powdery, either from being poorly bound in manufacture or as a result of exposure to damp.

Comparable Frames

Sansovino frame, north Italian, probably Venetian, c.1590, with similar clasps and scrollwork. See Penny, N. *Frames*. National Gallery Pocket Guides. London: National Gallery, 1997. pp. 60–61.

Sansovino frame, Italian, with carved and pierced sight edge and similar carved detail. See Bock, E. *Florentinische und Venezianische Bilderrahmen aus der Zeit der Gotik und Renaissance.* Munich: F. Bruckmann, 1902. p. 139.

Sansovino frame, Italian, sixteenth century, with pierced carving, Bayerische Staatsgemaldes-ammlungen, Munich. See Grimm, C. *Alte Bilderrahmenn: Epochen, Typen, Material.* Munich: Callwey, 1979. p. 77. Figure 120.

Frame with an example of use of a fretted sight moulding. See Mitchell, P. and Roberts, L. *Frameworks.* London: Merrell Holberton Publishers, 1996. p. 63, plate used as frontispiece for Chapter Two.[3]

Previous Citation

This frame is referred to as Venetian, second half of the sixteenth century, in Odom, W. M. *A history of Italian furniture from the fourteenth to the early nineteenth centuries.* Volume I: *Gothic and Renaissance furniture.* New York: Archive Press, 1967. p. 343, Figure 340.

References

1. Samples analysed using polarised light microscopy by Dr Brian Singer, Northumbria University.
2. Lynn Roberts, personal communication, February 2008.
3. Thanks to Lynn Roberts for this reference, February 2008.

RESULTS OF ANALYSIS
SAMPLE 1

Taken from the original scheme from the central female head at the bottom.

The earlier paint was investigated by polarised light microscopy (PLM) and found to contain red and yellow gel-like particles, some of which were birefringent. These were recognised as a mixture of red and yellow ochre. Mixed with the ochre were chalk and opaque black particles thought to be charcoal. The ground was investigated by PLM and found to contain no gypsum.

26

CARVED SANSOVINO FRAME, ORIGINALLY WATER GILDED AND PAINTED BLACK

Probably northern Italy, 1575–1600
Bought, with a portrait of a young lady in Swiss costume
(771:1-1865), from the Managers of the Guarantee Fund
for purchasing the Collection of Monsieur Soulages of Toulouse for £50
771:2-1865 (Furniture and Woodwork Collection)

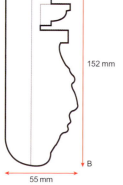

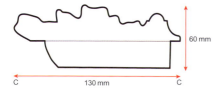

Dimensions (mm)

H: 810; W: 632; D: 95 (overall maximum)
Sight size: H: 430; W: 335
Rebate: W: 10; D: 20
Object accommodation size: H: 445; W: 351

Ornament

At the sight edge is a cavetto enriched with inverted
leaf-and-dart moulding and bead-and-pearl astragal
moulding. The architrave is made up of a cavetto
leaf-and-dart moulding that projects on to the top

of the adjacent capitals. These are also enriched with egg-and-dart and dentils. The capitals support acroteria. The egg-and-dart moulding on the capitals is echoed in the cavetto moulding just below the sight edge at the bottom. All four sides are carved with interlaced strap work scrolls and heavy foliate and fruit festoons. The volutes and scrolls are enriched, from the top, with egg-and-dart, pierced coin, overlapping coin and collared three-lobed flower head and dart decoration. There are central masks placed at the top and bottom, with that at the top set within a broken pediment.

Structure

The frame is made up of a softwood back frame that forms the structural support to which the carved front frame of a hardwood, possibly poplar or lime, is attached.

The back frame extends almost to the outer edges of the front frame with the inner sides forming the depth of the rebate. The outer sides are chamfered. The horizontal members are joined into the verticals with keyed dovetail half lap joints that are on the front face of the back frame. The ends of the dovetails are visible at the sides. A block of wood is applied at the top centre to support the carving on the front frame. The depth of the front frame at the top is made up of two thicknesses of wood, while the sides and bottom are each made of one piece. The top and bottom horizontals of the front frame run the full width of the frame. The sides, with scrolling strap work and festoons, are butt joined between.

At the top the carving, comprising mask, broken pediment, strap work, festoons and acroteria, is carried out in the upper layer. The top sight edge moulding architrave moulding are made from one applied piece, mitred at the sight edge. Above, the leaf-and-dart architrave is mitred to join the leaf-and-dart moulding on the projecting capital with plain returns, which is made from an inserted block of wood. The sides are butt joined between the top and bottom. The side sight mouldings are integral with the sides and are mitred at the corners. On the bottom, of the sight edge the egg-and-dart moulding is applied, with an inserted piece with plain sides forming a projection to this moulding. Where one festoon is missing, it is clear that egg-and-dart and insertion both were originally pegged in position – one peg remains intact, the other is mostly lost. There are several other losses to the carving: on the left of the frame, the acroterion and a section of the egg-and-dart moulding from the bottom are missing, and strap work is missing from the bottom centre.

There are areas of wood-boring beetle damage, particularly at the back near the sight edge.

Label

At the back bottom centre there is a remnant of paper with four nails, possibly from an old label.

Decorative Finish

Two decorative schemes are evident. The most recent scheme is water gilding with a glue size coating, on a pale orange–yellow bole on a medium white ground. This scheme is cracked and is flaking, resulting in many losses, revealing the crispness and depth of the original sculptural detail.

Where there are losses, the original black painted and water gilded decorative scheme can be seen. The masks are painted black and the ornament on the mouldings alternate between black and gold. The black paint and the gilding, on an orange–red bole (similar to Venetian red), is applied to the same ground. Brush strokes depicting veins in leaves are painted in black on the gilded leaves on the swags.

A sample of the black paint and ground was analysed by polarised light microscopy (PLM).[1] The

Digital reconstruction giving an impression of the original carving and decorative scheme.

particles from the black layer were found to contain vegetable charcoal and chalk. The ground layer contains gypsum and clay.

Hanging Device

At the top centre there is an early wrought iron crossover hanging loop held with wrought nails that appear to be original.

Observations and Conclusions

This frame is thought to originally have contained a painting. The frame came into the V&A with a nineteenth century panel painting, *Portrait of a Lady in Costume of c.1530* in the manner of Cranach, Lucas the Elder (771:1-1865).[2]

The frame's original appearance was markedly different from its appearance today. A digitally reconstructed image of this frame, giving an impression of the original scheme, has been created.

Comparable Frame

Sansovino frame, Venetian, second half of the sixteenth century (295 mm × 227 mm × 100 mm), has similarities in form. See Lodi, R. and Montanari, A. *Repertorio della cornice Europea: Italia, Francia, Spagna, Paesi Bassi: dal secolo XV al secolo XX.* Modena: Galleria Roberto Lodi, 2003. p. 118, Figure 217.

Previous Citation

This frame is dated to the late sixteenth century in Odom, W. M. *A history of Italian furniture from the fourteenth to the early nineteenth centuries.* Volume I: *Gothic and Renaissance furniture.* New York: Archive Press, 1967. p. 346, Figure 343.

References

1. Analyses carried out by Dr Brian W. Singer, Northumbria University.
2. Kauffmann, C. M. *Victoria & Albert Museum catalogue of foreign paintings before 1900.* London: Eyre & Spottiswoode, 1973. p. 77. If the painting were found to be a genuine Cranach rather than a nineteenth century painting in the style of Cranach, it would not be out of character for a Netherlandish painting to appear in an Italian frame. Although Cranach did not go to Italy, the popularity of Netherlandish paintings was known and admired in several Italian cities, for example a painting by Jan van Eyck of a woman emerging from a bath was recorded in Italy in the 1450s. Dunkerton, J., Foister, S., Gordon, D. and Penny, N. *Giotto to Dürer: early Renaissance painting in the National Gallery.* London: National Gallery Publications, 1991. p. 198.

RESULTS OF ANALYSIS
SAMPLE 1

Black from earlier finish (taken from top central mask).

The lower ground was investigated by PLM and found to contain gypsum and some highly birefringent rods with a refractive index (n) of less than 1.66, which could be china clay.

The lowest black layer was investigated by PLM and found to contain gypsum and chalk. This sample also contained fairly large black opaque shapes. To determine whether these are silver corrosion products a sample was taken for EDX analysis.

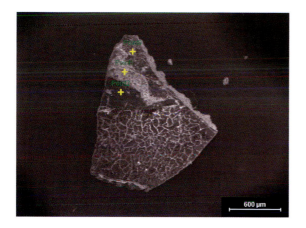

Figure 26.1   Electron micrograph of sample of lower layers separated from 771:2-1865 sample 1, showing sample points taken in the black-looking lower layers.

Three sample points were analysed, all in what appeared to be a black area on this chip containing the lowest layers. At point 0 (Figure 26.2), calcium and sulphur were in evidence, which supports the presence of gypsum. Sodium, potassium, magnesium, chlorine, silicon and aluminium were present, which supports the finding of clay-like minerals in the grounds. A little iron was also present, which also may be in the clay. The peak for carbon is very strong, which indicates that the black colour is probably due to charcoal. The absence of phosphorus indicates that this is a vegetable charcoal rather than bone black.

At point 1 (Figure 26.3), calcium and sulphur were the most abundant two elements in evidence, which confirms that gypsum is the main component at this point. This seems to be a thin layer in between the other two black layers. The peak for carbon is present, which indicates that the black colour is probably due to charcoal. The absence of phosphorus indicates that this is a vegetable charcoal rather than bone black.

At point 2 (Figure 26.4), calcium and sulphur were present, which supports the PLM finding of presence of gypsum being present in the layer. The peak for carbon is very strong, which indicates that the black colour is probably due to charcoal. The absence of phosphorus indicates that this is a vegetable charcoal rather than bone black.

There is no silver present in at any of the three points analysed and hence the black colour is not due to silver corrosion products.

SAMPLE 2

Bole and lower ground, taken from sight edge moulding. The bole layer was investigated by PLM and found to contain some low birefringent hexagonal plates with n < 1.66 and some rods with higher birefringence with n < 1.66. This mixture is typical of china clay. Hence the bole is a white clay.

The lower ground layer was investigated by PLM and found to contain gypsum and chalk.

SAMPLE 4

Dark layer and ground, taken from top central mask.

The dark layer in Sample 4 was investigated by PLM and found to contain charcoal and chalk. The ground layer contained gypsum and some low birefringent hexagonal plates with n < 1.66, which were identified as clay.

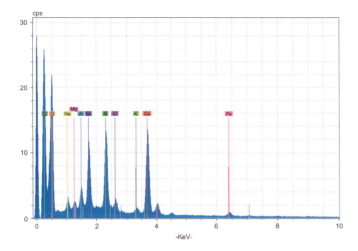

Figure 26.2   Spectrum: X-ray spectrum at sample point 0 on object 771:2-1865 sample 1, lower layers.

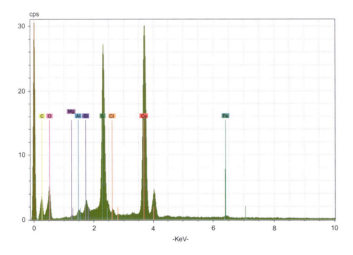

Figure 26.3   Spectrum: X-ray spectrum at sample point 1 on object 771:2-1865 sample 1, lower layers.

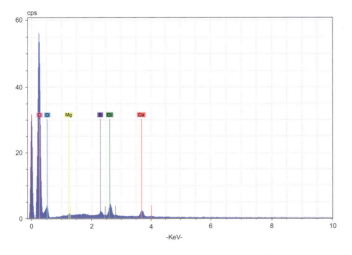

Figure 26.4   Spectrum: X-ray spectrum at sample point 2 on object 771.2-1865 sample 1, lower layers.

27

CARVED OAK MANNERIST FRAME WITH FIGURES OF ADAM AND EVE, ORIGINALLY PAINTED AND GILDED

Probably Flanders (Belgium) or The Netherlands, 1550–1580
Bought for £20
1605-1855 (Furniture and Woodwork Collection)

A

193 mm

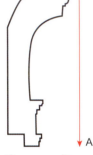

33 mm

A

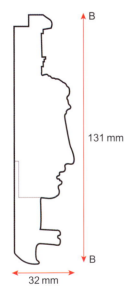

B

131 mm

B

32 mm

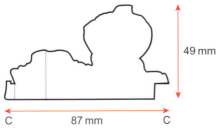

C   87 mm   C

49 mm

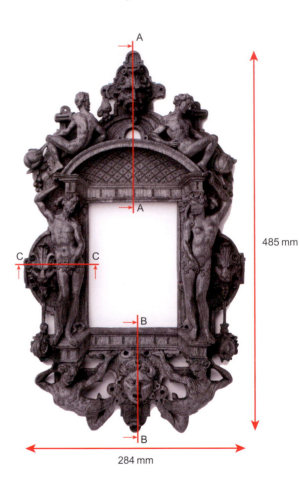

A

A

C   C

B

B

485 mm

284 mm

Dimensions (mm)
H: 485; W: 284; D: 50 (overall maximum)
Sight size: H: 158; W: 110
Rebate: W: 5 (horizontal), 7 (vertical); D: 8
Object accommodation size: H: 167; W: 125

Ornament
Adam and Eve, standing at the aperture of the perspectival aedicule, support with outstretched arms a generalised Doric entablature that carries a segmental arch and coffered vaulting decorated with

lozenges. The serpent appears behind Eve's head, proffering an apple. The same figures of Adam and Eve appear to be above the vault. At the top centre is a male bearded mask, set on a cruciform support hung with fruit at either side. The antependium is formed by a central female mask with a tiny lion's head carved within the hair. The mask is flanked by two diabolical figures with sinister expressions. The figure on the left has spiralling horns and that on the right, pointed ears. Lion masks protrude from either side with drops of fruit hanging from their strapwork support.

Structure

The frame is carved from one piece of vertically grained oak. Also made of oak and joined to the main body of the frame are: the top mask, the fruit drops by the feet of the reclining figures at the top, the outer edges of the lion masks at the sides, the fruit drop on the right below the lion, the protruding arms on each of the figures in the antependium and the pendant moulding below the mask at the base. The grain on the fruit drops at the top and the arms of the antependium figures runs in a different direction. There are joins below the knee and through the calves and drapery of the figures, which are not visible at the back. The male bearded mask at the top has been skilfully applied, lapped at the back and very carefully joined through the intricately carved beard at the front. The outer edges of the lion masks are also well joined to the main body of the frame.

There are small losses to the carving. The fruit is missing from the right side of the cresting at the top and carved semi-circular elements are missing either side of the lions' faces. A fruit drop is missing from behind the head of the reclining figure of Eve, as is a leaf tip adjacent to the fruit by her foot. Several toes are missing from standing figures of Adam and Eve.

Decorative Finish

The frame is now unpainted. Closer inspection shows traces of a white ground, for example, in the recesses of the figures' hair. Various fragments of dark blue over a white ground can be seen, particularly in the coffered ceiling. A small fragment of gold can be seen at the very top point of the frame.

Hanging Device

There is a recessed area cut out behind each of the figures at the base of the frame, at the bottom left and right. These are possibly for supports by which the frame was fixed into a more extensive wooden structure. The frame would probably not have been displayed alone but possibly on a stand with other objects surrounding it.[1] There are two pierced strips of wood adjacent to each of the figures' heads at the top. These could have been grafted on at a later date and were probably added as a means to hang what was then treated as an independent frame. There are two large screw holes above and below a hanging hole through the top mask, and several other later fixing holes.

Observations and Conclusions

The frame may have been made to contain a mirror or painting. It is possible that the piece of wood available to the carver was not quite large enough to incorporate all the carved protruding elements and that the top part and the sides were added separately at the time of manufacture. Alternatively, some of these added parts may be extremely well executed replacements of lost carving. This hypothesis is supported by the fact that the punch work on the background of the piece of wood applied below the female mask on the antependium appears to be slightly different to the punch work directly behind the female mask.

The protruding outer arms on each of the figures in the antependium are possibly replacements.

The modelling suggests that these could have been carved by a different hand. In addition, the carving to the inside of the joins is strangely formed. There is a step at the join in the legs and the rest of the leg is amorphous, with no foot. On the right antependium figure, the carved lines dividing the drapery do not run smoothly through the join and a detail of veining on the bottom part of the drapery is missing. This may suggest later carving of these parts. These are either later additions for missing parts or, alternatively, could be areas where there was damage and loss to the original carving that has been smoothed and partially recarved to disguise the damage. Another suggestion is that these additions could be part of an attempt to make an independent hanging frame from what was previously fixed into a more extensive structure with the antependium figures without legs.

It appears that the whole frame has been stripped of its original finish. The remaining traces of paint are not sufficient to establish how it originally appeared. The fragments of ground, paint and gilding on the coffered niche suggest that the frame may have been painted and gilded. The ceiling of the coffered vault was possibly painted blue with lines and dots picked out in gold to represent a celestial ceiling.[2] The combination of colour and gold together with the intricate nature of the carving would have given the frame a highly decorative appearance.

Comparable Frames

None found; however, the anatomy of the figures may derive ultimately from those of Day, Night, Dusk and Dawn on Michelangelo's tomb of Lorenzo de' Medici in the Sistine Chapel. The coffered vaulting of lozenge shapes loosely recalls that of the vaulted ceiling of The Temple of Venus and Rome in Rome and the ceiling in Santa Maria della Consolazione also in Rome. It also strongly evokes the chapel vault at the Château d'Anet by Philibert De l'Orme (1552). The carver may well have been familiar with Androuet de Cerceau's *Les Plus Excellents Bâtiments de France* (1576–1579), Paris, with prints showing this castle. There are also similarities with figures sculpted by Bartolomeo Ammanati (1511–1592), for example Leda with the swan, in marble, at the Museo Nationale del Bartello, Florence, Italy.

Previous Citation

This frame is described as Italian, sixteenth century, in Hasluck, P. N. *Manual of traditional woodcarving*. New York: Dover Publications, 1977. p. 314, Figure 612. The image shows the leaf tip on the top right and the side semicircular elements intact.

References

1. Olaf Lemke, personal communication, February 2008.
2. Tim Miller, personal communication, February 2008.

PART RENAISSANCE AND RENAISSANCE STYLE FRAMES

Renaissance frames were highly prized and avidly collected in the nineteenth century. This interest prompted a considerable market for genuine Renaissance frames, as well as imitations and deliberate fakes. The following entries represent a selection of frames in the Renaissance style, mainly produced in the nineteenth century. These are included to facilitate their comparison with, and differentiation from, Renaissance frames.

Nineteenth century frames made in the Italian Renaissance style often pay homage to the original but were interpreted through the eye of the maker. The carving is often crisper and more detailed, demonstrating exemplary craft skills. Their style and execution are quite different from the generally soft, more expressive, fluid and relaxed carving form used on original pieces. Frame 36 (W.100-1921) is an example of this nineteenth style of carving that is not in character with the Renaissance period.

Nineteenth century frames could also be made to look original by using recycled old wood, or by artificially ageing new wood and decorative finishes. Frames could also be made by marrying genuine Renaissance parts with new parts. In both cases, some frames may have been made as fakes and passed off as genuine, while others may have been made and sold honestly, for example new frames built up around salvaged parts from damaged Renaissance frames.

Frame 33 (4242:1-1857) is an example of a frame created by combining old and new parts. The older parts on this frame, which display characteristics such as wood-boring beetle damage and worn carving, are easily distinguishable from the new, undamaged pieces that have differently drawn and crisper carving. There has been no attempt to artificially age the new parts. The original parts may simply have been the inspiration to make up a frame, combining them with new carving inspired by the old.

Frame 29 (163:2-1910) is also made of old and newer parts. In this case, newer parts have been finished to blend with older parts. This may be an example of a reconstruction of a frame severely damaged by wood-boring beetle, in which original material was retained and new parts were used to replace losses and damage. The resulting 'new' frame may have been altered to fit the dimensions of the bronze it was acquired with, which itself may have been part of a larger object. Alternatively, the aim may have been to present the whole frame as original with the intention to deceive.

Frame 32 (113-1910) represents a further example of marrying old and new. This frame incorporates a beautiful, salvaged part of a Renaissance object. The frame may have been made in order to show and enable the appreciation of the salvaged element, rather than as a fake.

28

CARVED AND ORIGINALLY PARTIALLY WATER GILDED SANSOVINO FRAME WITH LATER PAINTED AND WATER GILDED SPANDRELS

Sixteenth century Sansovino style frame with nineteenth century spandrels. The frame holds a tin glazed terracotta roundel relief of the Virgin and Child by Andrea della Robbia (1435–1525), 5633:1-1859 Bought from Soulages Collection 5633:2-1859 (Sculpture Collection)

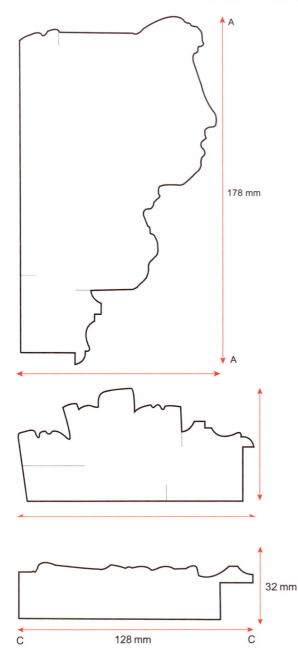

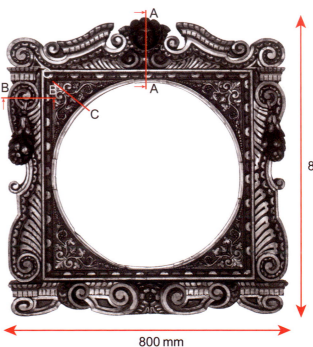

Dimensions (mm)
H: 847; W: 800; D: 95 (overall maximum)
Sight size: Diameter: 530
Rebate: W: 14; D: 18

Ornament

The spandrels are decorated with foliate scrolls, flowers and pea pods, and a`re surrounded by a cavetto moulding carved with a simplified leaf-and-dart. The sight edge of the outer, original frame consists of a cavetto moulding enriched with a

lunette-and-dart pattern. The sides are carved with two scrolls, with ovolo moulding enriched with the same lunette-and-dart as on the cavetto and infilled with radially fluted tongues. The capitals, which support the top of the frame, are decorated with dentils and gadrooning. Set between a broken swan neck pediment, a winged cherub head rests on volutes and scrolls decorated in the same manner as the sides, with lunette-and-dart mouldings, infilled with radially fluted tongues. The base of the frame is enriched with dentils and gadrooning, echoing the capitals. At the centre there is a flower, with scrolls and two guilloche enriched clasps on either side.

Structure

The frame is made of walnut or mahogany, and softwood. The back frame is made of softwood, the horizontal members are half lap jointed over the verticals. At the back corners, keys are inserted diagonally from the inside of the verticals through to the ends of the horizontals. Fixed into the back frame is the cavetto moulding frame with horizontal members set between the verticals at the back and mitred at the front. The spandrels are placed in a rebate in the cavetto frame. The front frame is made of walnut or mahogany. At top centre, wood has been added for the cherub's face. The bottom area of the frame shows signs of wood-boring beetle damage. There are cracks in the sight edge of the spandrels.

Later Additions

The spandrels are believed to be a later addition. The small central volutes on each side at mid-height are replacements.

Labels and Inscriptions

A paper label reading 'ART TREASURE EXHIBITION MUSEUM OF ART' refers to the loan of the object to Manchester City Art Gallery in 1857. There is also a label printed with 'SOULAGES' and (handwritten) '4B7' or '487'.

Decorative Finish

There are two decorative schemes: the present painted and gilded scheme and an earlier water gilded scheme. Areas of paint have been retouched and losses to the gilding have been retouched with bronze paint. A black wax has been applied overall. The spandrels are painted and gilded. The carved foliate scrolls are water gilded and burnished on a Victoria-plum coloured bole over a brick-red bole applied on a white ground. The background is painted a dark blue–green over the gilding, evidence that the spandrels were gilded before the application of the paint. The rectangular outer Sansovino style frame is partially gilded with the same gilding as the spandrels and painted brown. An earlier, probably original scheme of burnished water gilding on an orange–red bole on a white ground was observed beneath this scheme on the outer frame but not on the spandrels. The back is covered with a dark coating and has traces of white paint. Filler has been used between the joins on some parts of the frame.

Hanging Device

There are various holes from previous hanging fittings.

Observations and Conclusions

The spandrels are believed to be nineteenth century additions made after the manufacture of the main frame and probably put in to accommodate the tin-glazed terracotta relief it now frames. The use of burnished gold on the plum-coloured bole over a brick-red bole of the most recent gilded scheme is associated with nineteenth century English gilding. The fact that there is an earlier gilded finish beneath on the main frame but not

on the spandrels suggests that the spandrels were added later. The older main frame, in the style of a sixteenth century Sansovino frame, was probably overgilded when the spandrels were gilded. Further research would be required to establish the exact date of the main frame.

Comparable Frames

Frame for a miniature *Portrait of an Unknown Woman* by Isaac Oliver, painted c.1596–1600 (P.12-1971), has an almost identical design but with a naturalistic rose at the top centre, instead of a cherub head. See Evans, M. *The painted world from illumination to abstraction.* London: V&A Publications, 2005. p. 49.

Sansovino frame, English, c.1880, for *Portrait of Conte Fortunato,* by Martinengo Cesaresco, partially gilded with general similar use of ornament, National Gallery, London (NG 299). See Penny, N. *The sixteenth-century Italian paintings*, Volume I. National Gallery Catalogue. London: National Gallery, 2004. p. 176.

Sansovino frame, Venetian, c.1550, with general similarities, particularly the scrolling volutes at the base of the frame for *Portrait of a Venetian Lady* by Paolo Veronese (1528–1588). See Strange, A. and Cremer, L. *Alte Bilderrhamen.* Darmstadt: F. Schneekluth, 1958. p. 35, Plate 18.

Sansovino frame, Venetian, sixteenth century, 770 mm × 980 mm × 150 mm, partially gilded with symmetrically placed ornament, similar bottom edge. See Sabatelli, F. *La cornice Italiana dal Rinascimento al Neoclassico.* Milan: Electa, 1992. pp. 152–153.

Previous Citations

This frame is referred to as Venetian c.1550–1580, in Mitchell, P. Italian picture frames, 1500–1825: a brief survey. *Journal of the Furniture History Society*, 20, 1984. Figure 14C.

This frame is referred to as Italian, end of the sixteenth century, in Grimm, C. *The book of picture frames.* New York: Abaris Books, 1981. pp. 117–118.

Pope-Hennessy, J., assisted by Lightbown, R. *Catalogue of Italian sculpture in the Victoria and Albert Museum*, Volume 1. London: Her Majesty's Stationery Office, 1964. pp. 214–215.

29

CARVED WALNUT AND PARTIALLY GILDED TABERNACLE FRAME

*Post-sixteenth century with some probable
sixteenth century elements*
163:2-1910 (Sculpture Collection)

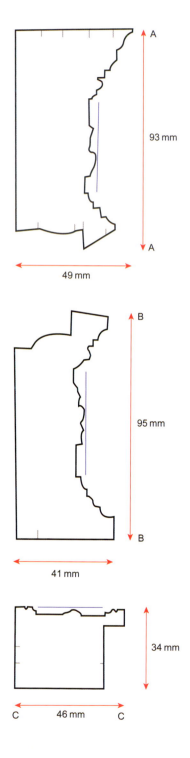

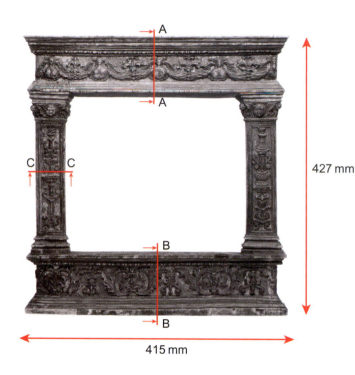

Dimensions (mm)

H: 427; W: 415; D: 50 (maximum overall)
Sight size: H: 235; W: 285
Rebate: W: 9; D: 27
Object accommodation size: H: 252 (near sight edge), 265 (at back of frame); W: 300–305

Ornament

Pilasters, each decorated with candelabrum, with capitals in the form of winged cherub heads, support an entablature with an architrave, frieze and cornice. The base of the entablature and the predella cornice is enriched with bead-and-reel. The entablature frieze is decorated with female busts set between festoons of laurel leaves and the predella frieze is carved with scrolling foliage.

Structure

The frame is made of walnut. Its thickness is built up in layers with pieces also added to the width. The back layer of the frame is made largely from one piece. The grain direction is vertical throughout. The depth of the entablature is made up of five layers. At the top edge towards the right, there is a wooden plug. Pieces are added to outside edges of the back layer. From the back, on the left there is one piece and on the right there are two pieces one above the other. At the front left of the cornice, there is a join in the front layer, above the second bust. The carved frieze decoration on the entablature is not symmetrically placed.

On the capitals, the moulding with the internal return, carved in perspective, is inset at the front and at the sides. The left pilaster is made from three layers. There is a thin light-coloured veneer-like piece between the back two layers. On the front, the outer left of the pilaster is made of an added piece. In comparison, the inside moulding has finer carving. The depth of the right pilaster is made of three layers of wood. Looking at the back, two pieces have been added to the back layer, at the inside and outside edge, which is chamfered. There appears to be a cut through the back, from above the carved area of the capital to the rebate. At the front the carving of the pilaster is made from one piece and has mouldings similar in character to most of the left pilaster.

The depth of the predella is made of two layers. On the bottom left of the centre is the end of a wooden plug. Looking at the back, there are pieces added at each side of the back layer. On the right there is a rectangular piece inserted. On the front of the predella, the frieze carved decoration is not symmetrically placed. At either end of the front layer there is a piece added. At the bottom corner of the frieze on the left, the additional piece is triangular. It is carved with a leaf tip naturalistically curling around the corner from the front on to the back edge. On the right, the added piece is carved as if the front leaf sprouts from the back edge, with the carving partially carried out on to the back edge.

The added parts are in better condition. There is extensive wood-boring beetle damage, on the left side at the back, the front left of the entablature (not the cornice), the whole of the left pilaster (not the outside fifth), the far left of the predella bead and reel and frieze. The left pilaster base has been filled at the back edge and centre of its base. The front layer at the bottom is heavily coated and filled.

Labels

Two paper labels annotated with 'Mr G Salting' (handwritten) and '2527' (printed) refer to the former loan of the framed relief to the museum.

Decorative Finish

The frame is partially gilded. Both the wood and the gilding are coated with a dark thick coating that has been worn away in many places. The background to the entablature, predella frieze and pilasters appear to be mordant gilded, including the added piece on the right end of the predella. The gilding has short vertical cracks and in some places what appear to be small circular punch marks. There are traces of what appears to be a rough textured water gilded finish on red bole on a white ground in the following areas: the right side bead-and-reel returns, the architrave return and the capital return. The front part of the right back edge of the predella has rough textured gilding. There are traces of a rough textured ground on the left capital return and on the side of the pilaster base.

Hanging Device

There are holes from two brass mirror plate fittings at the top of the frame. There are various other holes for other fittings. The bronze relief, now removed, had been held in place with a recent metal framework.

Observations and Conclusions

The frame was acquired with a bronze relief of the Flagellation c.1460 that has been generally attributed to the Sienese artist Vecchietta (1410–1480) (A.163:1-1910). The frame had, until recently, been accepted as probably original to the relief. It was assumed to have been carved to Vecchietta's design owing to the relationship of the architecture of the frame to the recession of the relief. The right hand pilaster was recognised as a replacement by Anthony Radcliffe and Peta Motture during the 1990s, suggesting that the frame may have been modified. The lack of symmetry and varied treatment of the carving led Motture to suspect that the frame was a later concoction, confirmed by examination with

Top of entablature.

the authors in 2008. The relief was then removed from the frame.

The frame's construction and the asymmetry of the carving on the frieze on the entablature and predella are atypical for tabernacle frames. The pieces added to the width of the frame are, for the most part, placed roughly symmetrically. This could indicate an original construction method; however, the condition of the wood of these and other pieces, such as the inset mouldings above the cherub head decorated capitals, the left capital with pilaster and base, appears newer than other parts of the frame where the wood has suffered from wood-boring beetle and wear. There are other parts of the frames that also appear in quite good condition, such the cornice, architrave and much of the mouldings above and below the predella frieze, that are made from the same pieces as the frieze.

In addition, the character of carving is different on the additional pieces. For example, the bead-and-reel carving on the added pieces is more rounded in form, while the bead-and-reel at the front has faceted carving. The carving on the capitals is subtly different from the pilasters, and the candelabrum design on each pilaster is different. Although designs can vary between paired Renaissance pilasters, the subtle differences in the drawing, execution and tools used, as well as the condition of the wood, indicate that the right pilaster, capital and base may be a well-carved copy of the one on the left.

It is possible that the additional pieces were applied to repair insect-damaged areas of a frame. However, the asymmetrical placement of the frieze suggests that the newer pieces were reused from existing carvings cut down from a larger frame or other object. The carving on the added pieces at either end of the predella, with leaves naturalistically curling around the returns, is atypical. The back layer has suffered damage from wood-boring beetle. The rectangular piece at the back right bottom edge could have been added to repair insect-damaged wood, although the damaged wood itself could also be old wood reused, possibly from the same object as the other, similarly damaged parts.

The thin veneer, seen between the layers of the wood at the rebate on the left pilaster, is not generally associated with the Renaissance, but this may be a thinly cut sliver of wood used to fill a gap rather than a piece of precut veneer.

The water gilding is very worn and the mordant gilding has darkened and cracked, indicating that both are naturally aged. The mordant gilding on the background to the entablature and predella frieze and on both the pilasters appears to be of a similar age. The appearance, positioning and materials of the gilding do not help to date the parts of the frame. However, water gilding was not found on the back third of the predella or on the moulding placed beneath the entablature directly above the capitals, perhaps indicating these were applied after the water gilding. The piece inserted on the front left which partly intercepts the predella frieze is not mordant gilded and was therefore applied later than the application of the mordant gilding.

The date of the frame, in its current form, is uncertain, although it was already fitted to the bronze relief by the V&A acquisition date of 1910. Observation suggests that the frame was made up of earlier, possibly fifteenth or sixteenth century carved pieces, such as the entablature, predella and left pilaster, and reused pieces from other frames or perhaps another object.

30

CARVED WALNUT AND PARTIALLY GILDED TABERNACLE FRAME WITH A SIDE SLOT

Italy, 1800–1850, in the style of Tuscany 1500–1550, or
Italy, Tuscany, 1500–1550, with alterations carried out in 1800–1850
Bought from William Blundell Spence for £3
148-1869 (Furniture and Woodwork Collection)

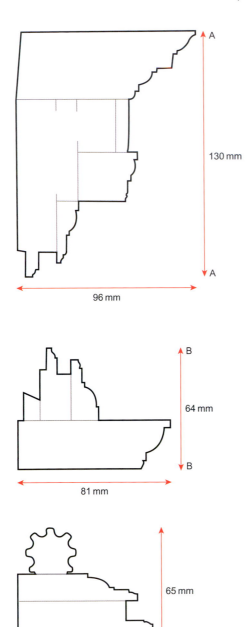

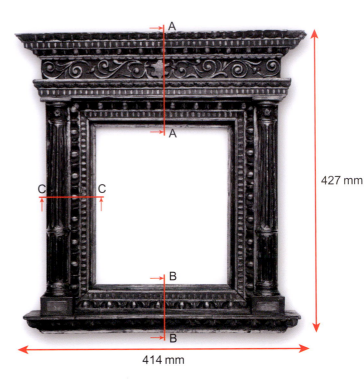

Dimensions (mm)
H: 427; W: 414; D: 108 (overall maximum)
Side slot: H: 260; W: 9
Front sight size: H: 245; W: 210
Front rebate: W: 7; D: 9 (runs into slot on right side)
Object accommodation size: H: 259; W: 224 (not including slot).
Rear sight size: H: 228; W: 191
Rear rebate: W: 10; D: 3.
Rear object accommodation size: H: 248; W: 211

Ornament

The sight edge consists of a fluted fillet followed by an egg-and-dart ovolo moulding. Engaged fluted and stopped fluted columns with Doric capitals support the entablature. The architrave consists of a fluted fillet, giving the impression of dentils, followed by a leaf enriched ovolo and fillet. An undulate band on a punched background decorates the frieze with a hide-shaped cartouche bearing a coat of arms. This has a painted motif, possibly the monogram 'M'. The cornice reflects in reverse the sight edge egg-and-dart ovolo, followed by fluting dentils. It also carries a leaf-and-dart enriched cyma recta which terminates the entablature at the top. The moulding at the base is also enriched with leaf-and-dart.

Structure

The frame is made of walnut, a light-coloured hardwood and softwood. On the rear of the back frame, there are two softwood vertical members at outside left and right, with chamfered outside edges. There is a narrow piece between them at the bottom. These all have inverted chamfers on the inside edges.

The light-coloured hardwood back frame is probably lap jointed with the vertical members over the horizontal member. On the left side (looking from the back) there is a slot for a panel that would slide behind the front sight moulding. There is also a sight moulding behind for the object framed behind the sliding panel. The rebate for the front sight edge moulding at top, bottom and left is made out of the front part of the back frame. The rear sight edge moulding and rebate is cut out of the rear part of the back frame.

The front frame is made from walnut. The cornice is made of one piece that caps the rest of the entablature below and at the back it is shaped to cover the top of the back frame and the applied

vertical chamfered members. The cornice is held by three roughly circular (approximately 10 mm in diameter) facet-headed wrought nails driven in from the top, each set within a gouged counter-sunk hole. On the back of the cornice piece there are several gouge marks and near the end on the right (as seen from the back), there is a wrought nail like those used above. The rest of the entablature is made of one or more pieces that are applied to the back frame, with an applied carved frieze and an inset architrave.

The sides with integral sight mouldings, and the top and bottom sight moundings, are applied to the back frame. The sight mouldings are mitred. The carved design does not meet well at the top mitres, the left corner has two eggs cut through next to each other and on the right there is only half an egg. At the bottom mitres there are no eggs but the carving does seem to meet. Inside the egg-and-dart moulding, the fluting is cut through.

The applied columns are carved from a (probably) turned piece. A quarter of the depth of each column has been cut away at the back before the columns were applied to the side pieces. This was done after carving, as the carving of the fluting continues past the front half of the column – the angles of the fluting could not be carved without great difficulty after application. The fleurons on the capitals are carved separately and applied with glue. The abacus and column base plinths are made of separate pieces glued and inserted. The base of the frame is made from one piece. At the underside of this, near the ends, there are wrought nails each set within a gouged countersunk hole. The nail on the left (looking from the front) is circular headed, while that on the right is rectangular headed. Along the front of the underside of the base towards the front there are remains of glue with a distinct ridged line of glue about 25 mm

from the front. Towards the front at each end there is a hole from the pointed end of a wrought nail. Off centre towards the right is a large, gouged cone-shaped hole that is tapered towards the top. Inside this, at the far end of the hole the lighter coloured wood of the main frame can be seen, as well as some animal glue. There is also a small hole in front of this. A later light brown filler has been used on the back over the upper joints and on the underside of the base piece. There is considerable wood-boring beetle damage to the softwood.

Later Additions
A fabric-covered softwood board has been inserted into the rebate. This was removed for photography.

Inscription
There is a scratched geometrical figure on the back.

Decorative Finish
There are possibly two gilded schemes present. The most recent partially water gilded scheme consists of burnished water gilding on an orange–red bole on a thin, white ground. The gold leaf is clumsily applied, overlapping on to adjacent areas, particularly on the dentils. A dark coating is applied over the wood and the gilding. The gilding on the plinth blocks has a semi-opaque light brown coating. On back edges of the sides there are remains of a white ground, coated with yellow that has scratches down to the wood from being roughly abraded. Some parts of the sides are covered with a brown transparent coating, possibly tinted shellac. There is paint on the cartouche on the entablature frieze. The motif, possibly the monogram 'M' is painted in black, the top half of the background is gilded and the bottom half is grey–white, possibly silver, with traces of red and a dark coating. On the background of the frieze

References

1. Ojetti, U. *Dedalo: Rassegna D'Art*, Vol. Terzo. Milan–Rome: Casa Editrice D'Arte Bestettie Tumminelli, 1921. p. 629.

2. Tim Miller, personal communication, February 2008.

3. For example, a tabernacle frame in the Leman Collection at the Metropolitan Museum of Art made in c.1920 in the sixteenth century style. See Newbery, T. *Frames in the Robert Lehman Collection*. Princeton: Metropolitan Museum of Art in association with Princeton University Press, 2007. pp. 82–83, No. 46. Exhibited in 1990, see Newbery, T., Bisacca, G. and Kanter, L. *Italian Renaissance frames*. Exhibition Catalogue. New York: Metropolitan Museum, 1990. p. 100.

4. Notes from a discussion with Michael Gregory, Olaf Lemke, Thomas Knoell, Lynn Roberts, Peter Schade and Achim Stiegel, February 2008.

31

CARVED WALNUT AND PARTIALLY GILDED TABERNACLE FRAME WITH A SIDE SLOT AND CARVED GROSTESQUES

*Italy, 1800–1850, in the Italian style of
1500–1550 Bought with stone high relief
panel carved with the Virgin and Infant Saviour,
French, c.1540–1550 (88-1865,
Sculpture Collection) for £24
88A-1865 (Furniture and Woodwork Collection)*

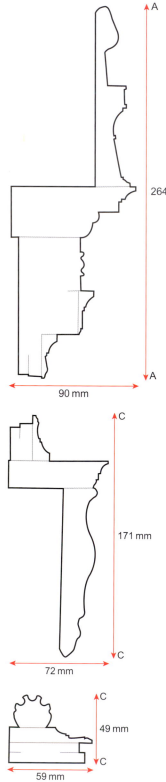

Dimensions (mm)
H: 638; W: 355; D: 90 (maximum overall)
Sight size: H: 188; W: 155
Rebate: W: 14 (left); D: 9
Object accommodation size: H: 195; W: 179

Ornament

The sight edge is enriched with simplified leaf, dentils and tongues. Fluted columns with Doric capitals

support an entablature with a tetraglyth frieze and meteopes filled with patarae. The cornice is made up of egg-and-dart, dentil and tongue mouldings, and the pediment, with a punched background, depicts a pair of outward facing grotesques. The antependium is carved with a pair of downward facing grotesques whose stylised wings are attached to a cartouche depicting golden armorial balls.

Structure

The frame is made of walnut and softwood. The back frame is made of softwood that is half lapped with the horizontal members over the vertical members, except for at the top left (as seen from the back) where the vertical laps the horizontal. In between the back frame and the front frame there is a layer of softwood. On the inner edge this is cut to form a housing between the sight edge and the back frame. At the inner left side (as seen from the back) the recess is deeper and there are gaps on either side of the central piece of wood. At the top inner side there is a later strip of wood held with modern nails. At the bottom the inner layer is level with a strip of wood that has been applied to the back frame; these together form a rebate.

The front frame is made from walnut. The pediment is made from one piece that is very flat and even on the back and is applied on top of the cornice towards the front edge. The head of the left grotesque is a separate applied piece. The cornice is made from one piece that caps the frame below, with various holes on the back. On the top edge of this, at the back, are two rusty, roughly round, facet-headed nails approximately 10 mm in diameter towards each end set within a gouged countersunk hole. The architrave moulding is applied with the return lapping the front. The moulding appears to be the same as that used on the sight edge. The frieze is also applied with carved returns that lap the front frieze.

The sides with integral sight moulding, and top and bottom sight mouldings are mitred and applied on to the softwood layer between these and the back frame. The sight edge moulding carved design does not meet with a separate element at the corners. The applied columns are probably turned and then carved. They have been cut back at the rear before being applied to the sides. There is no carved fluting beyond the front half of the columns. Modern round-headed nails hold the columns at front top and bottom. The columns' chamfered abacus blocks and the column plinth blocks are made of separate pieces.

The base of the frame is made from one piece with various holes on the back. On the bottom edge of this, towards each end, are two rusty, roughly round, facet-headed nails, each set within a gouged countersunk hole. The antependium is made from one piece and, like the pediment, is flat and even on the back.

The back frame and sides, the columns and sight edge have some wood-boring beetle damage. There are several small losses to the carved detail. There are later carved repairs, including the right grotesque's head on the pediment, the top leaf moulding on the left cornice return and the tip of the antependium. The pediment has a glued break along the grain one-third of the way down. Filler has been applied at the sight edge mitres. On the back, a later piece of wood with chamfered edges has been fixed with five nails as a brace to reinforce the repair. On the right side there was probably once a slot that has since been filled with a piece of wood.

Decorative Finish

The front walnut show wood has remnants of partial 'gilding'. The background to the carved relief on the pediment and antependium is decorated with punch work in the wood. There is an unidentified dark brown coating over the show wood.

There are some remnants of early mordant gilding on the flowers on the architrave frieze. In some places, for example the recessed areas of the tetraglyths, the fluting on the cornice and sight moulding and on the columns, the mordant gilding has been deliberately textured, possibly by adding a material such as sand to the mordant.

There is later bronze paint, in some places covering the earlier gilding and in others apparently applied to base wood, for example there appears to be bronze paint in the grain of the wood on the leaf carving on the architrave. In some places, such as the armorial balls on the cartouche on the antependium, it is hard to tell whether these are mordant gilded and retouched with bronze paint, or simply coated in bronze paint. Some of this 'gilding' is seen in the wood grain and covers the nails on the columns.

The back of the back frame has been painted brown. In several areas there is filler or a thick ground layer, for example at the top back of the back frame and by the bottom rebate. The bottom edge of the back frame and the back of the antependium have crude wood graining of dark red–brown over red–yellow. The same red–brown colour can been seen applied in swirling brush strokes on the back of the pediment.

Hanging Device

On the back there are pieces of a twisted hanging cord emerging from two diagonally drilled holes at the top centre of the cornice. There is also wrought metal hook at the back held with modern screws. There are numerous old fixing holes.

Observations and Conclusions

On the back, on each of the inner sides of the frame there is a housing. On the left side (as seen from the back) there was probably a slot, which is now filled. At the inside top, the rebate is very shallow because of the later addition of a strip of wood. If this strip were removed, a housing may be revealed. At the bottom 'rebate', the inner layer looks old but the additional strips of wood on the back frame may be a later repair. Again, there may formerly have been a housing here to retain the framed object that was accessed via a slot, now filled, in the side. Without this, the frame would have to have been built around the object. The asymmetric lap joining of the back frame at the top could also be explained if there was originally a slot on the right side (looking from the front), in which case the lap position would have been reversed from that used on the other corners for practical reasons.

The slot may have been filled when the original framed object was removed. At present it would not be possible to frame an object behind the sight edge moulding because of the housing. To frame an object behind the sight moulding, the wood at the back that forms the part of the housing would need to be removed, which would create a rebate in which an object could be framed, fitted in from the back. Alternatively, a slot could be created in the side, or the frame would have to be dismantled.

It has been suggested the frame is part sixteenth century with alterations to the sight size dimensions and with parts added to appeal to the nineteenth century market. The suggested additional parts are pediment, entablature, columns and antependium.[1]

There are several possible reasons for fills in the mitres. The frame could have been dismantled, perhaps to remove the panel, and then reassembled with the mitres filled after the mitres were cut to reduce the sight size, or simply trimmed in an attempt to improve a poor fitting mitre joint. Trimming and filling, or just filling, may be carried out after mitres have opened through wood shrinkage without dismantling the frame.

Renaissance frames typically have the carved design laid out to meet at the sight moulding mitres to form a complete element of the repeating ornament, or with a corner motif, for example Frame 3 (19-1891). Gilding is carried out after assembly. In this case, the carved design on the sight edge moulding does not meet well at the mitres. There are two possible explanations for this. It may indicate that the mitres have been cut back to alter the sight dimensions, or it could be evidence of lower quality manufacture.

The pediment and antependium are unusually flat and even at the back, whereas some distortion could be expected in older wood. The dark red–brown paint on these appears similar. The character of carving on these components differs from the rest of the frame. The pediment and antependium have higher relief carving in comparison to the shallow carving used of the rest of the frame. The armorial balls painted on the cartouche could have been applied to add a spurious sixteenth century decorative detail. The white ground or filler and brown coating may have been deliberately applied to the back of the frame to conceal alterations.

Attribution to the nineteenth century is based on the smooth, even and relatively fresh carved quality of all the wooden elements and the use of brown toned coating to suggest greater age. It has been suggested that the repetition of fluted and dentil ornament is aesthetically unsatisfactory and would not have occurred in original Renaissance work.[2] The wrought iron hanging hook is unlike other Renaissance hooks observed on frames in this book. It may be a nineteenth century wrought iron hook or a hook that was added at an earlier point. It may have been purposely aged to make the frame appear more authentically of the Renaissance period.

Comparable Frames

Frame 30 (148-1869), similar in form and construction but without pediment and antependium.

Tabernacle frame, c.1920, made in the sixteenth century Tuscan style, H: 360 mm × W: 341 mm, pastiche frame made for a mirror, with very similar general form. Newbery, T. *Frames in the Robert Lehman Collection.* Princeton: Metropolitan Museum of Art in association with Princeton University Press, 2007. pp. 82–83, No. 46.

Tabernacle frame, Italy, early twentieth century, bequest of George Blumenthal in the Metropolitan Museum, with a similar pediment and antependium. Newbery, T. *Frames in the Robert Lehman Collection.* Princeton: Metropolitan Museum of Art in association with Princeton University Press, 2007. p. 82, Figure 46.1.

Italian frame, sixteenth century, carved, with similar form but without pediment and antependium. See Pedrini, A. *Il mobilio; gli ambienti e le decorazioni del Rinascimento in Italia, secoli XV e XVI.* 2nd ed. Genova: Stringa, 1969. p. 158, Figure 401.

Tabernacle frame, first quarter of the sixteenth century (Budapest, Szepmuveszeti Museum) with similar form and stylised grotesques. The bottom edge shows diagonal cracks and smoother carved detail to the right, indicating that the sight size has been enlarged. See Sabatelli, F. *La cornice Italiana dal Rinascimento al Neoclassico.* Milan: Electa, 1992. p. 34, Figure 33.

Tabernacle frame, northern Italian c.1500, and French c.1850 (Wallace Collection, London, F502), 'extensively restored and altered in the nineteenth century'. Some similarities, with pediment and antependium believed to be added. The entablature has triglyphs. See Hughes, P. *The Wallace Collection catalogue of furniture*, Volume 1. Cambridge: Cambridge University Press, 1996. p. 143.

References

1. Notes from a discussion with Michael Gregory, Olaf Lemke, Thomas Knoell, Lynn Roberts, Peter Schade and Achim Stiegel, February 2008.
2. Lynn Roberts, personal communication, February 2008.

32

CARVED AND PARTIALLY WATER GILDED TABERNACLE FRAME WITH PEDIMENT OF TWO RECLINING FIGURES SET WITHIN A SHELL

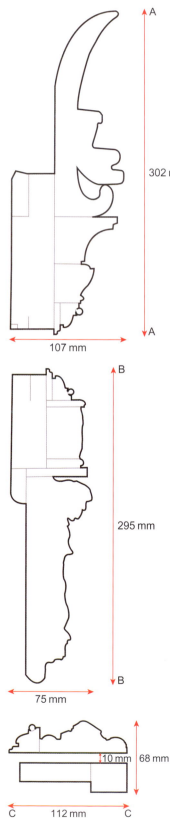

Probably Italy, 1850–1900, in the style of Italy, 1550–1600, the crest possibly c.1550
Salting Bequest
113-1910 (Furniture and Woodwork Collection)

302 mm

107 mm

B

295 mm

75 mm

10 mm
68 mm

112 mm

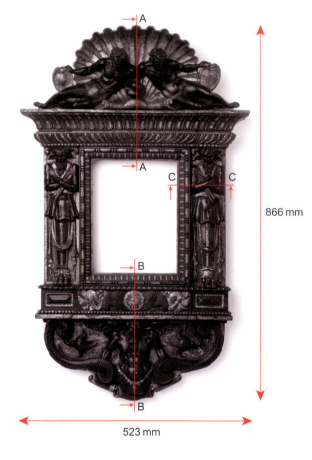

866 mm

523 mm

Dimensions (mm)

H: 866; W: 523; D: 110 (overall maximum)
Sight size: H: 262; W: 195
Rebate: W: 7; D: 25
Object accommodation size: H: 278; W: 215
Slot: H: 272; W: 10

Ornament

The sight edge consists of a succession of fluted tongue and bead-and-reel mouldings.

Two terminal satyrs holding double pipes and rising from a single lion paw support an entablature with a succession of pearl, gadrooning and fluted tongue mouldings. The pediment consists of two male, Michelango-esque, heroic nude male figures that recline, arms entwined, on a large shell with outstretched hands resting on small shields. The predella frieze displays martial symbols: a rosette flanked by shields, swords, cudgels and cornetti. The antependium is carved with a winged triton holding up his elaborate scaled tail terminating in leaves.

Structure

The frame is made of walnut and poplar or lime. The wood on the back of the frame has the appearance of lime or poplar. The back frame is half lapped, with vertical members over the horizontal. In front of this is another layer with a slot at the right side for the sliding cover that would have concealed, revealed and protected the framed object. The top, bottom and left sides of the back frame were constructed to allow the cover to slide into a housing. At the top back and right side, the back part of the housing has been removed, leaving a rebate. There is a large metal plate across a break on the lower part of the frame, fixed on with modern screws. There is an area of repair with filler and canvas at the right hand upper corner.

The front frame is made of walnut. The pediment is made from a separate piece supported at the back. On the cornice, the fluted tongue moulding is made of one piece and laps the cornice returns. The gadroon moulding below is also one piece and laps the returns. The sides are carved and applied. The predella top moulding, the main body of the predella, the carved bottom moulding and fillet are all made of separate pieces. The sight edge moulding is made of three parts, the bead-and-reel

moulding is applied separately, the fluted tongue moulding is separate and applied over the moulding below.

The carving on the main frame is very different from that of the pediment, of two figures reclining in a scallop shell. The head of the male figure on the right in the pediment is loose and a later pin has been inserted to fix it to the body. The tip of the triton's skirt is missing. There is wood-boring beetle damage, particularly at the back.

Decorative Finish
The water gilding on the pediment appears to be original and is applied over a dark red bole over a thin, white ground. Dark bole is common on Bolognese pieces.[1] The gilding on the front frame has a similar bole colour to that on the pediment. Gilded areas are worn, showing the bole, white ground and wood below. The frame is coated in a dark layer, possibly wax.

Hanging Device
There is a housing at the top of the back frame, probably from a recessed support or hanging device. There are several screw holes on the back, probably from hanging fittings.

Observations and Conclusions
The frame may have been designed to hold a mirror or painting.

It has been suggested that the pediment with figures reclining in a scallop shell is original sixteenth century and the rest of the frame is nineteenth century.[2] Thoughts on the intention behind making this frame are divided. It was considered possible that the parts were married together in an attempt to pass the whole object off as sixteenth century, to appeal to a nineteenth century market. Alternatively, the frame could have been made in appreciation of the sixteenth century fragment

with no intention of deception. It was suggested that the pediment may have come from a piece of furniture and the frame was used as a vehicle to display this genuine sixteenth century fragment.

The carving of the subjects of the pediment is of extremely high sculptural quality in comparison to the rest of the frame. The marks of small carving tools can be observed that are not present on the rest of the frame. The carving of the figures is well realised and the tapering of the legs to the feet is both optically clever and very elegant. The figures are not, however, anatomically correct, which can be indicative of genuine sixteenth century work, when a full understanding of anatomy was not fully developed. This can also be seen in the figures on Frame 27 (1605–1855).

The carving on the rest of the frame, particularly of the trophies, although skilful, appears to be from a different hand and appears consistent with nineteenth century practice.[3]

The gilding on the main frame has been carefully executed, using the same colour bole, to imitate that on the pediment. The dark coating applied over the surface may have been intended to unify the old and new parts of the frame. It is possible that some elements of the back frame are also old.

Comparable Frame
Tabernacle frame, Florentine, mid-sixteenth century, Alfredo Barsanti Collection, with a similar cornice. Ojetti, U. *Dedalo: Rassegna D'Arte*, Vol. Terzo. Milan–Rome: Casa Editrice D'Arte Bestettie Tumminelli, 1921. p. 639.

Previous Citation
This frame is dated to the second half of the sixteenth century in Odom, W. M. *A history of Italian furniture from the fourteenth to the early nineteenth centuries*, Volume I: *Gothic and*

Renaissance furniture. New York: Archive Press, 1967. p. 347, Figure 345.

References

1. Thomas Knoell, personal communication, February 2008.
2. Opinions expressed by Michael Gregory, Olaf Lemke, Thomas Knoell, Lynn Roberts, Peter Schade and Achim Stiegel, February 2008.
3. Opinion expressed by Michael Gregory, February 2008.

33

CARVED AND EBONISED TABERNACLE STYLE MIRROR FRAME

Probably Italy, 1800–1850, incorporating some sixteenth century elements
Bought for £12
4242:1-1857 (Furniture and Woodwork Collection)

810 mm

952 mm

Dimensions (mm)

H: 810; W: 952; D: 68 (overall maximum)
Sight size: H: 534; W: 423

Ornament

The sight edge is of plain rectangular section. Four pilasters decorated with candelabrum support an entablature divided into three panels. The central panel is enriched with an undulate band of scrolling foliage emerging from two crescent moon-like faces. The panels on either side are decorated with two fantastical creatures with tails terminating in scrolling leaves, flanking a vase. The base is also divided into three undecorated panels. A wooden tablet is pinned to the front of the frame, which reads 'Metal mirror, carved walnut frame, Italian, About 1500, 4242-1857'.

Structure

The back frame is made of softwood. Looking from the back, there are two vertical members side by side on the left, one on the right and horizontals at top and bottom. At the top, the verticals are lap jointed over the horizontal member. The same probably occurs at the bottom; however, the applied return pieces of the predella conceal the joint. Two vertical pieces secure the metal mirror at the back.

At the front of the frame, the entablature, pilasters and predella parts are applied on to the back frame. The back frame shows between these parts and forms the plain rectangular sight moulding, which is mitred at the corners. The cornice and frieze panels are made from a light-coloured

METAL MIRROR,
CARVED WALNUT FRAME,
ITALIAN; ABOUT 1500.

Detail of entablature.

Detail of pilaster.

wood, possibly lime. The cornice is applied on to the back frame, with separate return pieces mitred and applied at each end. The three entablature frieze panels, with carved relief ornament, are carved out of the solid and are also applied to the back frame. The walnut running mouldings surrounding the three entablature panels are mitred and applied. The capitals, pilaster frieze panels and pilaster bases are made from walnut and are applied separately on to the back frame. The upper parts of the pilaster bases are mitred and

applied on to the back frame. The lower parts are made of one piece. On the pilaster frieze, the relief ornament on the pilaster friezes has been carved separately and applied to the flat background of the frieze panel. The mitred and applied running mouldings surrounding the pilaster frieze panels are made from walnut. Along the bottom, a length of applied light-coloured wood, possibly lime, forms the predella and laps the applied returns. The top predella moulding is mitred and applied to the back frame, with separate returns mitred and applied on to the ends. Running mouldings have been applied on the front of the predella to give the illusion of three separate panels. The running mouldings are held with pins and there are some joins along the length.

The carving on the four pilaster friezes has a different character to the carving on the entablature frieze panels and is worn. Both the carved detail and background panels have extensive damage from wood-boring beetle. The carving and wood of the capitals, entablature frieze and applied running mouldings are in much better condition, with minor wood-boring beetle damage. There are several losses and detached pieces. There are

several areas where wood-boring beetle damage has been filled with black wax.

Decorative Finish

The frame is stained black and has a coating of wax. Uncoated wood can be seen where there is missing running moulding on the right of the central panel in the entablature, and a missing capital on the left. There is no evidence of earlier decorative schemes below.

Hanging Device

There are numerous previous fixing holes. On each side at the bottom there are metal mirror plate fittings.

Observations and Conclusions

The frame holds a heavy metal mirror. The frame appears to be mainly later work, possibly nineteenth century, incorporating four earlier carved pilaster frieze panels, thought to be sixteenth century. The original and later carving can quite clearly be distinguished. The sixteenth century carving on the pilaster friezes is soft and rounded, while the carving of the capitals and the entablature frieze panels is more crisp. Two different carving hands are evident, with the later work copying the sixteenth century work of the pilaster frieze panels. The drawing of each is also very different. For example, on the top right panel of the entablature, the carving of the fantastical creatures with crescent-shaped faces is very crisp compared to the earlier carving of the same fantastical creatures within the bottom half of the candelabrum decoration on the outer pilasters. Here the carving, carried out in walnut, is much softer. The carving technique is also different, with the early carving on the pilaster friezes being applied, whereas the carving of the entablature is carved out of the solid.

Previous Citation

This frame is referred to as Venetian, end of the fifteenth century, in Guggenheim, *M. Le cornici Italiane dalla metà del secolo XVo allo scorcio del XVI; con breve testo riassuntivo intorno alla storia ed all'importanza delle cornice*. Milan: U.Hoepli, 1897. Plate 42.

34

CARVED AND PARTIALLY MORDANT GILDED OVAL FRAME WITH CHERUB HEADS

*Possibly Italian, nineteenth or early twentieth century,
in the style of Italy, 1550–1600 Given by Sannyer Atkin
W.2-1938 (Furniture and Woodwork Collection)*

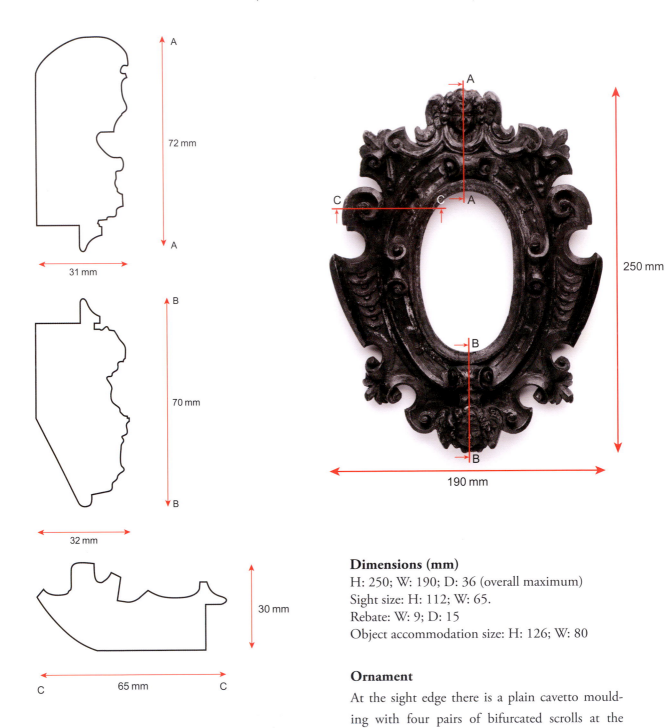

Dimensions (mm)
H: 250; W: 190; D: 36 (overall maximum)
Sight size: H: 112; W: 65.
Rebate: W: 9; D: 15
Object accommodation size: H: 126; W: 80

Ornament
At the sight edge there is a plain cavetto moulding with four pairs of bifurcated scrolls at the

80 A small oval frame, carved with Cherubs, festoons and scrolls in relief, and partly gilt—*Italian, 16th Century*—9¾ in. by 7½ in. ;

cardinal compass points. Flaring scrollwork enriched with overlapping coins forms the prominent sides. Winged cherub heads decorate the top and bottom, with the one at the top resting on drapery.

Structure

The frame is carved out of one piece of lime or poplar. The front has wood-boring beetle flight holes. On the back wood-boring beetle larval channels are exposed. There are traces of canvas on the inside of the rebate.

Decorative Finish

The gilded areas are mordant gilded and are quite worn. There is a thick, dark, brown–black coating applied on the front and back of the wood that overlaps on to the gilded areas.

Hanging Device

At the top, there is a ring held by a metal strap fixed to the back with two screws.

Observations and Conclusions

The original use of the frame is unknown. Oval frames for reliefs and paintings from the Renaissance are not abundant; however, the oval form is commonly found in other Renaissance art forms such as architecture, furniture and drawings.[1] The design of the oval frames in this book has been influenced by the Sansovino style.

The wood-boring beetle flight holes at the front of the frame are common on old objects. Exposed channels on an otherwise flat surface can indicate the reuse of old, damaged wood. In this case, however, the wood has warped and it is possible that it was planed down at the back to flatten the concave curve that resulted from the warping to make it more suitable to hang.

Walnut was commonly used in the sixteenth century as a show wood for partially gilded frames. The use of lime or poplar could be evidence against this frame being sixteenth century. However, other timbers were sometimes also used, either because their texture was preferred or because they were more readily available.[2]

The dark coating may have been applied to the front to give the impression of an aged object, to disguise the lighter wood and give the impression of walnut. The coating may have been applied to the back to tone down the lighter colour of the wood after the back had been planed.

The wear on the gilded areas is not consistent with natural wear and the surface finish appears to have been deliberately distressed.

Traces of canvas observed on the inside of the rebate could have been applied to strengthen the wood. The canvas remnant in the rebate may also be from a painting canvas.

Comparable Frames

Oval Sansovino style frame, Venetian, second half of the sixteenth century, with similar placement of cherub heads at the top and bottom. See Roche, S. *Cadres Français et étrangers XVième siècle au XVIIIième siècle: Allemagne, Angleterre, Espagne, France, Italie, Pays Bas.* Paris: E. Bignou, 1931. Plate 113.[3]

Oval Sansovino style frame, Venetian, sixteenth century, parcel-gilt ($500 \times 400\,\text{mm}$) with similar scrolls. See Lodi, R. and Montanari, A. *Repertorio della cornice Europea: Italia, Francia, Spagna, Paesi Bassi: dal secolo XV al secolo XX.* Modena: Galleria Roberto Lodi, 2003. p. 118.[3]

Illustration of a book cover showing a portrait from the frontispiece of a MS collection of poems by Lucia Albani, c.1580, showing portrait of the author by Giovanni Fortunato Lolmo, in a frame with similar scrolling strap

work, volutes and swags. See Penny, N. *The Sixteenth Century Italian Paintings*, Volume I. National Gallery Catalogues. London: National Gallery, 2004. p. 221, Figure 5.

References

1. See Mitchell, P. and Roberts, L. *Framework.* London: Merrell Holberton, 1996, in which the photograph on p. 65 shows an oval decorative element in the ceiling of the Sala delle Quattro Porte in the Pallazzo Ducale, Venice, decorations c.1575, by the workshop of Alessandro Vittoria (1526–1608). See also Penny, N. *The sixteenth century Italian paintings*, Volume I. London: National Gallery Publications, 2004. p. 221, Figure 5. Other examples of oval frames include: Guggenheim, M. *Le cornici italiane dalla metà del secolo XVo allo scorcio del XVI; con breve testo riassuntivo intorno alla storia ed all'importanza delle cornice.* Milan: U.Hoepli, 1897. Plates 48 and 55; Lessing, J. *Vorbilder-Hefte aus dem KGL. Kunstgewerbe-Museen Rahmen: Italien und Deutschland XVI Jahdhunder.* Berlin: Verlag Von Ernst Wasmuth, 1888. Plate 6; A Dutch oval frame, c.1662, similar in size (210 mm height), in Grimm, C. *The book of picture frames.* New York: Abaris Books, 1981. p. 138, Figure 159.

2. Newbery, T., Bisacca, G. and Kanter, L. *Italian Renaissance frames.* Exhibition Catalogue. New York: Metropolitan Museum, 1990. p. 28.

3. Thanks to Olaf Lemke for this reference.

35

CARVED WALNUT, PARTIALLY MORDANT GILDED OVAL FRAME WITH CARYATIDS

Probably Italy, nineteenth or early twentieth century,
in the style of Italy, 1550–1600
Bequeathed by David Martin Currie
W.100-1921 (Furniture and Woodwork Collection)

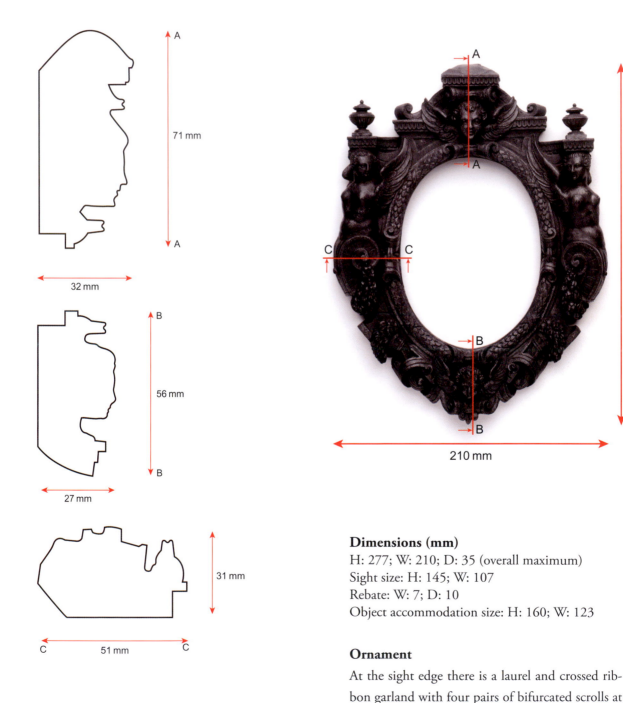

Dimensions (mm)
H: 277; W: 210; D: 35 (overall maximum)
Sight size: H: 145; W: 107
Rebate: W: 7; D: 10
Object accommodation size: H: 160; W: 123

Ornament

At the sight edge there is a laurel and crossed ribbon garland with four pairs of bifurcated scrolls at

W.100-1921

EXHIBITION
ITALIAN A...
54

cardinal compass points. Two winged figures, heads turned to face each other, support a sub-cornice with urn finials. At the top a winged cherub head, surmounted by bifurcated scrolls, supports the base for a now missing finial. The cornice mouldings, arranged in a triple hierarchy, are all enriched with fluted tongues. Scrolling tongue-enriched volutes support the winged figures and from these volutes hang swags of fruit. A pair of cornucopiae is entwined within the strap work and a winged cherub head is supported at the base of the composition by the union of the mirrored strap work.

Structure

The frame has been carved from one piece of walnut. The turned urn finials on square bases have been added separately and are held on to the frame with pegs through their centres. There is a hole at the top centre, probably for a peg for another finial that is now missing.

Labels and Inscription

On the back right there is a printed label: 'EXHIBITION ITALIAN ART'. Pasted over this is another printed label: '54'. On the left, below the museum acquisition number, the following is written in white: 'Gia.Ba …'. The rest is illegible.

Decorative Finish

There is one original partially gilded scheme, with gilding applied directly on to the wood. The very fine gilded lines decorating the caryatids' faces and chests have been delicately applied and do not overlap on to the surrounding areas. A translucent yellow–orange coating can be seen in some areas over the gold leaf. A translucent red can be seen over the gold in the following areas: the triangular recessed areas adjacent to the cresting, the cherub's wings, the crossed ribbon motif over the garland on the sight edge and on the dots at the centre of each tongue within the scrolled volutes below the caryatids. The coloured glazes were applied to emphasise areas of the carved detail. The finish is now quite worn and the gilded areas would originally have been much brighter and more colourful.

Hanging Device
The present metal wire fitting is not original. The holes, however, appear old.

Observations and Conclusions
The original use of this frame is unknown. The design and carving of the frame have a Victorian character. The carving is very crisp and detailed, as if to show off the carving skills required for intricate decoration. In contrast, genuine Renaissance frames have a looser, more expressive carving style.

Comparable Frame
Frame, Venetian, second half of the sixteenth century, Museo Civico, Padova, with an elongated oval form and similar decorative features, such as the caryatids and bifurcated scrolls. See Guggenheim, M. *Le cornici Italiane dalla metà del secolo XVo allo scorcio del XVI; con breve testo riassuntivo intorno alla storia ed all'importanza delle cornice*. Milan: U.Hoepli, 1897. Plate 100. It frames a painting of *The Crucifixion* in Pedrini, A. *Il mobilio; gli ambienti e le decorazioni del Rinascimento in Italia, secoli XV e XVI*. 2nd ed. Genova: Stringa, 1969. p. 160, Plate 406.

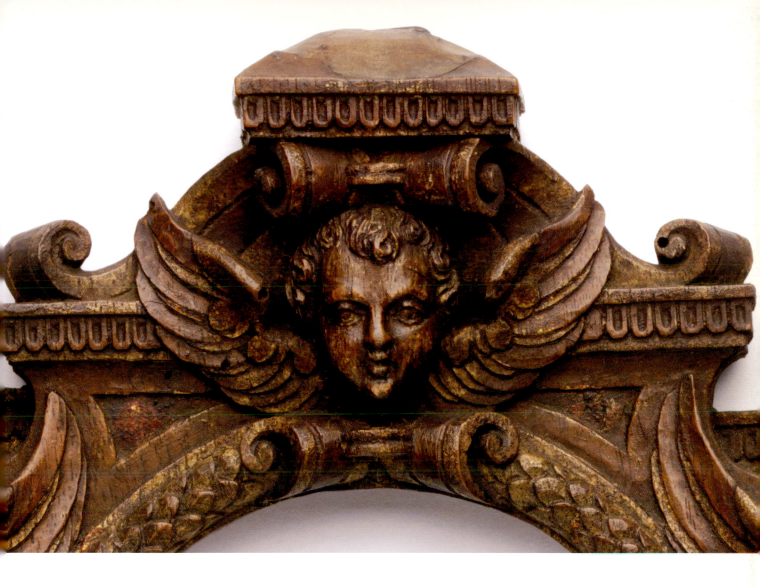

36

CARVED AND PIERCED WALNUT, ORIGINALLY PARTIALLY WATER GILDED OVAL FRAME

Possibly Italy, nineteenth or early twentieth century,
in the style of Italy, 1550–1600
Bequeathed by David Martin Currie
W.102-1921 (Furniture and Woodwork Collection)

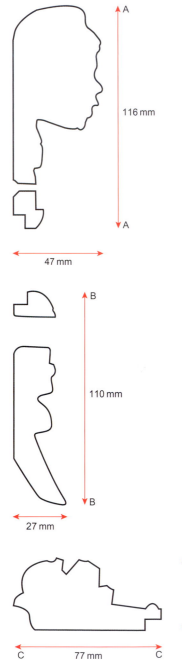

Dimensions (mm)

H: 410; W: 264; D: 50 (overall maximum)
Sight size: H: 172; W: 117
Rebate: W: 8; D: 5
Object accommodation size: H: 187; W: 135

Ornament

The sight edge is decorated with beeds and four pairs of bifurcated scrolls at the cardinal compass points. Two winged figures in profile support scrolling and pierced volutes and a winged cherub

W.102-1921

16

ON LOAN FROM
D. M. Currie, Esq
April 1902 18

110

head at the top centre. Coin enriched scrolls, hung with drapery, form the base of each figure and lead towards a central scallop shell at the base.

Structure

The frame is carved from a single piece of walnut, with an oval aperture. There are pronounced grooves on the back of the frame from a carving gouge.

Labels and Inscription

There are three labels pasted on the back: two of printed numbers, '16' and '110', and the third printed and handwritten 'ON LOAN FROM D.M. Currie, Esq. April 1902, 18'. At the top, the museum acquisition number is written in white.

Decorative Finish

The frame is partially gilded. The walnut has been stained dark and coated. There is one original water gilded scheme, with areas of later mordant gilded repair and bronze paint retouches. The water gilded areas, seen for example on the volutes and on the coin enriched scrolls, are carefully applied and these are probably the remains of the original scheme. The water gilding consists of a thin, translucent coating over the gilding on an orange–red bole on a thin, white ground. The oil gilded areas, seen for example on the recessed areas of the scallop shell and inside the drapery, are thought to be later repairs. The gold leaf of the oil gilding has been imprecisely applied and overlaps on to the adjacent areas.

Hanging Device

No hanging device was observed.

Observations and Conclusions

The intended use of this frame is not known. The wood is in good condition and very clean on the back. There is little fluidity or confidence in the carving style, suggesting that it is of a later date imitating an earlier style, possibly even by an amateur carver.

Comparable Frames

Oval Sansovino style frame, Venetian, sixteenth century, partially gilded (H: 500 mm × W: 400 mm), with similar scrolls and beaded sight edge moulding. See Lodi, R. and Montanari, A. *Repertorio della cornice Europea: Italia, Francia, Spagna, Paesi Bassi: dal secolo XV al secolo XX.* Modena: Galleria Roberto Lodi, 2003. p. 118.

Oval frame with winged female figures for the painting *Self Portrait with a Burning Candle* by Godfrid Schalcken (1643–1706). See Exhibition Catalogue *Schöne Rahmen aus den Bestanden der Berliner Gemäldegalerie.* Berlin: Gemäldegalerie, Staatliche Museen, zu Berlin, 2002. Image on back cover and p. 91.

Frontispiece illustration by Giovanni Fortunato Lolmo of a collection of poems by Lucia Albani, c.1580, showing a portrait of the author within a frame of similar character with scrolling strap work, volutes and drapery. See Penny, N. *The sixteenth century Italian paintings.* National Gallery Catalogues. London: National Gallery, 2004. p. 221, Figure 5.

APPENDIX

CARVED, WATER GILDED AND PAINTED TABERNACLE FRAME WITH LUNETTE

Italy, c.1450–1475
Probably the original frame for the polychromed stucco relief of The Virgin and Child after
Domenico Rosselli (c.1439–1497/8). The lunette is painted with the Dove of the Holy Spirit
Bought in Florence (Bardini) for £118
6-1890 (Sculpture Collection)

1219 mm

711 mm

Dimensions (mm)
H: 1219; W: 711 (overall maximum)
Relief: H: 610; W: 445

Ornament

Fluted pilasters with Corinthian capitals and bases support a generalised entablature of architrave, frieze and cornice and a semi-circular arched pediment. The entablature frieze is painted with a scrolling leaf pattern and decorated with punch work. The predella frieze is painted with a barely legible inscription. The inscription is described as reading 'Ave Maria Gratia Plena' (Hail Mary Full of Grace) by Pope-Hennessy.[1]

Structure and Decorative Finish

This frame was not accessible for detailed examination at the time of writing. However, it provides a useful comparison with Frame 1 (5-1890), which was originally water gilded and may therefore have had a similar appearance.

Observations and Conclusions

The sight edge has been cut away to accommodate the Virgin's halo at the top and robe at the

bottom as well as the cushion on which the Christ Child is standing. Frame 4 (57:2-1867) has been cut away in a similar manner. This is a common feature and may have been a device to bring the Virgin and Child into our world. The cutting away of the sight edge around the Virgin's head-dress and the Christ child's head gives the impression of the figures emerging through the window of the frame. It is interesting to note that in paintings of this period, half figures are depicted with parts of the body coming forward overlapping a painted window frame. It is possible that the intrusion of the figures in the relief on to the sight edge is simulating this device.[2]

Comparable Frame

Tabernacle frame, Italian, original frame with similar form for Jacopo del Sellaio's relief of the *Madonna and Child* (Museo d'Arte Sacra). See Sabatelli, F. *La cornice Italiana dal Rinascimento al Neoclassico*. Milan: Electa, 1992. pp. 30 and 33, Figure 31.

Previous Citations

This frame is described as the original frame for the stucco relief in Sabatelli, F. *La cornice Italiana dal Rinascimento al Neoclassico*. Milan: Electa, 1992. pp. 30–32.

The frame is described as contemporary with the stucco relief in Pope-Hennessy, J., assisted by Lightbown, R. *Catalogue of Italian sculpture in the Victoria and Albert Museum*. London: Her Majesty's Stationery Office, 1964. pp. 149–150. Catalogue No. 125.

References

1. Pope-Hennessy, J., assisted by Lightbown, R. *Catalogue of Italian sculpture in the Victoria and Albert Museum*. London: Her Majesty's Stationery Office, 1964. p. 149.

2. Dunkerton, J., Foister, S., Gordon, D. and Penny, N. *Giotto to Dürer: early Renaissance painting in the National Gallery*. London: National Gallery Publications, 1991. p. 208.

GLOSSARY

A

Abacus flat top of the capital of a column in classical and Renaissance architecture, usually supported by an entablature.

Acanthus a Mediterranean plant (*Acanthus mollis* and *Acanthus spinosus*) whose deeply serrated leaf was stylised by the Greeks and the Romans to become one of the principal ornaments of classical architecture. It identifies a Corinthian capital.

Acroterion (pl. acrotaria) block or pedestal, with or without ornament, that rests on the top or ends of a pediment.

Aedicule small temple-like structure usually sheltering a shrine. Columns support a pediment structure over a niche or window.

Antefix decorative addition above a pediment, usually of palmette and rosette.

Antependium term derived from that of a cloth hanging in front of an altar. Used to describe the lower section of a tabernacle frame below the predella.

Anthemion (pl. anthemia) an ornament based on the honeysuckle or palm. Also known as a palmette.

Architrave in Renaissance orders the beam, the lowest division of the entablature, which stretches from column to column.

Auger flame a twisted spiral ornament like an auger shell, used as a finial.

B

Back edge the outer edge of the sides of the frame, sometimes referred to as the 'return'.

Back frame the joined structural frame to which decorative moulded and carved parts of the front frame are attached.

Base the bottom part of the column and the pilaster, made up of mouldings.

Bead-and-pearl an astragal carved with a pattern of alternating pearls and elongated beads.

Bead-and-reel an astragal moulding made up of elongated beads and discs.

Beads see Pearls.

Bezant a coin-shaped ornament.

Bifurcated separated into two parts or branches.

Bole a clay-based paint that can be coloured by pigments.

Bolection moulding a bold moulding of double curvature raised above the general plane of the framework of a door, fireplace or panelling.

Build-up wood attached to the back of a frame to increase its depth, often a later addition added to accommodate the depth of the object to be framed.

Burnisher tool for burnishing water gilding.

Burnishing the process by which leaf is pressed to conform to the surface underneath, making it glossy and reflective.

C

Cabochon a round or ovoid device with a convex surface, often elaborately framed.

Candelabrum (pl. candelabra) decorative motif based on the form of classical branched candlesticks or lamp stands. Often used to decorate pilasters and enriched with grotesque decoration.

Capital   the crowning member of a column or a pilaster.

Cardinal compass points   on tondo frames, points at the centre top (north), bottom (south), left (west) and right (east), sometimes punctuated with patarae.

Carta pesta   a general term used to describe crushed paper mixed with glue or glued paper applied in layers in a mould.

Cartouche   a shield or ovoid form often bearing inscriptions and devices in relief, frequently set in an elaborate scroll frame and bordered with ornament.

Caryatid   a sculptured female figure, sometimes used in place of a column, singly, or in series to support an entablature.

Cassetta   a square or rectangular frame comprising a simple, lap jointed back frame. The mouldings are derived from the tabernacle entablature, with sight and back edge mouldings separated by a frieze.

Cauliculus (pl. caulicoli)   an architectural term for the eight small curled acanthus stalk supporting volutes on Corinthian capitals. Also used to describe a scrolling acanthus leaf.

Cavetto   a concave moulding with the profile of a quarter round or close to it.

Chamfer   bevelled/angled edge on wood.

Cherub (pl. cherubim)   a celestial being in the angelic hierarchy, appearing in many Old Testament stories, and having the attributes of wisdom and knowledge: depicted as a human figure with wings at each shoulder which sometimes cover the feet. The word cherub also describes the winged head of a young child, a familiar religious motif. Several of the frames contain winged heads and these are referred to as cherub heads. The term cherub is sometimes confused with putto.

Ciborium (pl. cibori or ciboriums)   in religious art, any receptacle designed to hold the consecrated Eucharistic bread of the Christian Church. The ciborium is usually shaped like a rounded goblet or chalice, having a dome-shaped cover. Its form originally developed from that of the pyx, the vessel containing the consecrated bread used in the service of the Holy Communion.

Clasps   strap-like ornament that encircles a moulding.

Coffer   derived from a sunken panel in a ceiling or soffit. It consists of a rosette surrounded by four lengths of moulding. Coffered indicates that the ceiling is ornamented with sunken panels.

Coin decoration   also known as money moulding: a series of overlapping discs, with and without central holes, resembling a continuous band of coins.

Column   a vertical member, circular in plan. In classic architecture it consists of a base, shaft and capital supporting an entablature and designed in accordance with the rules of one of the five orders of architecture. When up to a quarter of the shaft is incorporated with or concealed by the surface behind, the terms 'attached column' or 'engaged column' are used. A column also represents the trunk of a tree.

Console (or modillion)   a decorative bracket in the form of a scroll supporting the upper members of a cornice or lower part of the frame.

Corbel   a support, plain or carved, projecting from a wall or vertical surface.

Corinthian capital   Corinthian order, Augustan period, seldom used by Greeks, extensively used by Romans and in the Renaissance.

Cornett (pl. cornetti)   an early brass instrument, dating from the Medieval, Renaissance and Baroque periods.

Cornice   projecting upper part of entablature.

Cornucopia   also known as a horn of plenty, a goat's horn overflowing with fruit, grain, ears of corn and similar items.

Crucifix   a cross depicting or symbolising the Crucifixion of Jesus Christ on the cross.

Cudgel   a club that is used as a weapon.

Cyma recta or ogee   a moulding with an S-shaped curve, concave over convex.

Cyma reversa or reverse ogee   a moulding with an S-shaped curve, convex over concave.

D

Dentil   a small rectangular block, within a band or course, resembling teeth, and forming part of a cornice.

Denticular   enriched with dentils.

Dolphin   this sea mammal was used as an ornamental and symbolic motif in the ancient world, often combined with sea deities.

Doric column   one of the five orders of columns, with a simple capital consisting mainly of an abacus and echinus.

Dragon's blood   a bright red natural resin.

E

Egg-and-dart   also called egg-and-tongue, egg-and-leaf or egg-and-anchor, all variations of the basic pattern of a series of alternating eggs and points: the pointed shape may be sharp like an arrow, dart or narrow tongue, or in leaf form. The ornament was used as enrichment for mouldings in architecture and furniture, particularly on the Greek ovolo, and is often called echinus.

Enrich   to add to, in the case of frame mouldings, with carving.

Entablature   in classical architecture, the beam-like division from above the columns of a temple to the rafters comprising architrave, frieze and cornice.

Entasis   the slightly convex tapering of a column. Used to counteract the optical illusion of a parallel column appearing slightly concave.

Escarpa, sometimes called a swag   ornament in the form of a swag of fabric: common in Sansovino frames.

Eucharist   Christian religious sacrament of taking bread and wine, representing the body and blood of Christ, commemorating the action of Jesus at the Last Supper before his Crucifixion with his disciples, when he gave them bread and wine, saying, 'This is my body' and 'This is my blood'.

F

Fascia   plain wide band across the bottom of the entablature directly above the columns.

Festoon   a garland made of fruits, flowers, leaves or husks and hanging in a curve.

Fillet   small flat moulding, rectangular in section, separating one moulding from another.

Finial   ornament formed at the apex of a gable or pinnacle.

Fleuron   a small flower-shaped ornament usually found on the abacus of a Corinthian column.

Flute   a concave groove or channel running vertically on a column or pilaster shaft. Also found in enriched mouldings, collectively called fluting. Radial fluting is used to describe the angled fluting often found on Sansovino frames.

Frieze   the middle horizontal member of an entablature above the architrave and below the cornice. Often decorated with a run of scrolling or undulating foliage and grotesque decoration.

Front frame   the carved and decorative elements of a frame that are applied to the back frame.

G

Gadroon a convex round ornament, round at the upper end and tapering to a point at the other. Always found in a set and for that reason often called gadroons.

Garland an intertwining of fruits, leaves, flowers or husks.

Gesso (gesso grosso and gesso sottile) white ground applied to the wood before painting or gilding.

Gilding (oil or mordant gilding and water gilding) application of gold leaf.

Grisaille term for painting executed entirely in monochrome, usually in shades of grey or brown.

Grotesque intricate and fantastic ornament originating from grottoes, caverns, vaults and baths of Ancient Rome. Widely used in Renaissance period when it assumed a fanciful and fantastic character, embodying intricate patterns of animals, birds, festoons and stylised foliage. The term also describes a distorted, deformed or hideously grinning figure or mask.

Guilloche an ornament composed of continuous, interlaced, curving lines. When there are two linked patterns, it is known as a double guilloche.

H

Halbard a staff weapon with an axe-like head balanced by a fluke, surmounted at right angles by a central spike. Carried and used as weapons by footsoldiers from the late fourteenth to the early seventeenth century.

Herm bust of a man or a woman on a pedestal used for decorating classical and Renaissance architecture, derived from Greek deity Hermes.

Hippocamp a fabulous marine monster, with the head, body and forelegs of a horse, and the tail of a fish, often a dolphin: the tail is tufted, the hooves tufted or webbed, and the creature may be winged.

Housing A trench with right-angled sides, usually cut across the grain of the wood to receive another inserted piece of wood.

I

Imbricated a pattern of overlapping leaves or scales, usually of bay leaves, oak leaves or bezants.

Impost the capital, bracket, entablature or pier from which an arch springs. This term has been used to describe the protruding blocks in the entablature frieze above each capital and pilaster.

Impresa (pl. imprese) the use of an object, figures, animals or plants to symbolise an individual or lineage.

Ionic one of the five orders of columns, recognised by its capital of volutes or helixes.

K

Key a tapered piece of wood with chamfered sides inserted into a channel of a dovetail shaped profile or section, across the corner joints of a frame.

L

Lambrequin (lambrecated) shaped lappets, imitating textile fringes, often with tassels.

Laurel a motif of classical origin. In ancient Greece, the laurel and leaf, sacred to Apollo, signified artistic achievement and in the form of a crown, victory at the Delphic games: a Roman symbol of victory. Laurel crowns were worn by the Roman emperors when celebrating a triumph.

Leaf-and-dart a repetitive band made up of a stylised leaf and a dart.

Leaf-and-tongue   a variant of egg-and-tongue, in which the oval form is replaced by foliage: occasionally the tongue is omitted altogether, and the enrichment consists of a series of leaves.

Lotus   stylised leaf derived from the lotus plant.

Lozenge   object in the shape of a diamond.

Lunette   area within an arched pediment.

Lunette moulding   enriched with half moon shapes.

M

Mask   in Renaissance decoration the mask frequently appeared as a grotesque face or a caricature, such as the gorgeneion or medusa head. The masks and heads on some of the frames are often similar to the head of a Green Man and Woodwose figures. The Green Man has a head with foliage coming out of face and possibly derives from Oakinos, god of the sea, with seaweed sprouting from the face. The Woodwose is a wild man with fur on his body.

Metope   a square panel between triglyphs on a Doric frieze, often decorated with a relief.

Mirror plate   modern fixing, often made of brass, to attach a frame to a wall.

Modillion   a small bracket used in rows under the corona of a cornice and extending from the bed mould. It frequently takes the shape of an ornamental double volute.

Moulding   plain or decorated profiles, either rectangular or curved and either above or below the surface. Their purpose is to provide a transition or to produce light and shade.

N

Niche   a recess in a wall, usually with a semi-dome, designed as a place for a statue.

O

Orders of architecture   an order consists of a column with base (except in the Greek Doric), shaft and capital and its entablature. Each order has its own formalised ornament. The orders are the basis of architectural design in the classical tradition, providing lessons in proportion, scale and the uses of ornament. The five orders are Tuscan, Doric, Ionic, Corinthian and Composite.

P

Palmette   see Anthemion.

Pastiglia   cast applied ornament.

Patera (pl. paterae)   a flat, circular or oval ornament. The word is derived from the *patera*, a shallow saucer used as a drinking and sacrificial vessel in Roman times. See Rosette.

Pearls   a small half spherical moulding resembling a string of pearls.

Pedestal   the base supporting a statue or column.

Pediment   in classical architecture, the triangular portion of wall enclosed by raked cornices above an entablature and which supports the roof. Renaissance architecture also featured broken triangular, semicircular and broken pediments: the wall ending for any roof.

Pilaster   a flat column of shallow and rectangular projections of the same design as the order that is used.

Plinth   a square block at the base of a column.

Pod and pea or seed pod   sixteenth century development of the arabesque ornament. It is characterised by formalised naturalistic motifs, curving and twining stems, bouquets, groups of flowers and foliage and small ovoid shapes.

Poppy head   intricately carved poppy seed head surrounded by flowing, formalised foliage.

Porphyry   an igneous rock with large grained crystals dispersed in a finer matrix. Purple porphyry was used in Imperial Rome and is often imitated in paint.

Predella   the base of an altarpiece or a tabernacle frame.

Punch work   tool indentation marks applied to gilding.

Putto (pl. putti)   putti are figures of chubby infants, often male, depicted naked with wings. They were frequently used in carved ornament and decorative sculpture during the Renaissance period. Putti are a classical motif, found primarily on child sarcophagi of the second century, where they are depicted fighting, dancing, playing sports, etc. They are also referred to as amorini or winged cupids. Putti are often confused with cherubs; however, putti are secular, human babies as opposed to celestial cherubs.

Q

Quirked moulding   a small channel or recess between mouldings.

R

Rebate   recess beneath the sight edge of a frame intended to receive the framed object.

Reed   a bead or beaded moulding, i.e. a small half round. When used in clusters, it is called reeding.

Restello   typically consists of a wall mirror set into a frame, with hooks from which articles for the toilette were hung.

Ribbon   an ornament in imitation of a cloth ribbon.

Ribbon and stick   a ribbon spiralling around a stick or rod.

Rinceau   a symmetrical swirling ornament of leaves, customarily those of the acanthus.

Rosette   a formalised rose with petals radiating outwards in zones from the centre. Called patera when enclosed in a circular band.

S

Scallop   an ornamental motif, derived from the rounded, ribbed shell of the mollusc pecten, commonly called the cockleshell. In Graeco-Roman times the device was a favourite symbolic and decorative motif, associated primarily with the sea, Aphrodite and fertility. Also an ancient heraldic charge: the emblem of St James the Great.

Scarf joint   also known as a spliced joint. Used to extend the length of one piece of wood by attaching another length, the term includes a range of joints.

Scroll   a curvilinear motif based on a C-curve, the ends terminating in spirals with central circles. Used singly or in series when a pattern of continuous scrolls forms an undulating band of spirals, each flowing from and into its neighbour. The scrolls may all run in the same direction or be reversed and embellished with a continuous curving meander or ornamental foliage, notably the acanthus. Large scrolls are often found on Sansovino frames.

Segmental   the portion of a circle, less than a semicircle, defining the shape of an arch or a vault.

Shaft   the trunk or the longest part of a column between the base and the capital.

Shank   the long part of a metal nail.

Shell   as a decorative motif, the scallop and nautilus have been used since Graeco-Roman times. See also Scallop.

Sight edge   the aperture of the frame that displays the framed object.

Sight edge moulding the moulding at the aperture of the frame.

Slip a moulding, often very plain, even rectangular in profile or section, inserted into the sight edge rebate and projecting into the aperture of the frame.

Spacer a rectangular section length of wood placed behind glazing in the rebate to hold the glass in place to create a space or separate the glass from the surface of the framed object; a modern addition on Renaissance frames.

Spandrel in architecture placed either side of an arch, a triangular space bordered by the curve of an arch, a horizontal line through its top and a vertical line rising from the impost or springing of the arch. Also found on rectangular frames bordering arched or circular objects.

Stopped fluting where the flutes or channels of a column or pilaster, or any grooves, have been filled with rods or rods topped by acanthus.

Strap work intricate patterns of interlaced lines and scrolls.

Swag cloth drapery fastened at both ends and hanging down in the middle.

T

Tazza term used to describe the cup or bowl holding fruit and foliage.

Term, terminal figure also called a herm or therm, this is a column or pedestal, round or rectangular, tapering towards the base, surmounted by a carved head or bust of a man, woman or pagan figure.

Tongue tongue-shaped moulding; fluted tongue: with hollowed interior.

Top edge moulding the uppermost moulding on the profile or section of a frame.

Torus a large convex moulding, sometimes called a round, generally used in column bases.

Trident a three-pronged spear, borne as a sceptre in representations of the Hindu god, Shiva, the Greek god Poseidon and Roman god Neptune: used as a heraldic and decorative device symbolising dominion over the sea.

Triglyph a projecting block with three channels forming part of a Doric frieze.

Trophy a decorative group of weapons, armour, musical instruments or floriated motifs, with ribbons and garlands.

Tympanum surface enclosed within the upper and lower cornices of a pediment.

U

Undulate band a decorative band consisting of a continuous flower, fruit or foliage device with the main stem of the plant running along the centre of the band in a gently curving wave-like form. See also Vertebrate band.

Urn originating from Graeco-Roman practice of cremation and displaying the urn-shaped vessel containing the ashes in a house or on a monument. The device was widely used in architecture or furniture, notably as a terminal ornament on pedestals and finials.

V

Vase a broad vessel with a narrow neck. In classical times, a domestic utensil associated with burial rites.

Vertebrate band a decorative band, consisting of a continuous flower, fruit or foliage device, with the main stem running horizontally down the centre like a straight spine.

Vine leaf decorative motif of great antiquity and universal use. In Egypt it was combined with the lotus, ivy and papyrus as an adornment to capitals and a decoration on tomb ceilings. Originally sacred to Dionysus (Bacchus), the vine, with ivy, was the Roman sign for a tavern. Formalised vine ornament was used throughout Graeco-Roman, Byzantine, Gothic and Renaissance decoration. Combined with ears of wheat, it is symbolic motif of the Eucharist.

Virgin and Child Christian imagery of the infant Jesus Christ and his Mother, the Virgin Mary.

Vitruvian scroll a continuous series of undulating convoluted scrolls, having the appearance of a regular line of curving waves: derived from the Roman architect Marcus Vitruvius Pollio.

Volute architectural term for the spiral scroll ornaments flanking an Ionic capital. A smaller version appears on Corinthian and Composite capitals and the device is also used to decorate consoles and brackets. The form may be derived from the outward curling sepals of the Egyptian lotus, a shell or an inward curving animal horn. Also found on Sansovino frames.

W

Wheat ears of wheat combined with the vine form a symbolic motif of the Christian Eucharist.

Wreath a festoon of fruit and flowers or foliage, fastened at both ends, hanging down in the middle.

References

1. Cole, J. Y. and Reed, H. H. *The art and architecture of the Thomas Jefferson Building*. New York: W.W. Norton, 1997.
2. Curl, J. *Encyclopaedia of architecture terms*. Lower Coombe, Shaftesbury: Donhead Publishing, 2003.
3. Newbery, T., Bisacca, G. and Kanter, L. *Italian Renaissance frames*. Exhibition Catalogue. New York: Metropolitan Museum, 1990.
4. Readers Digest. *Great encyclopaedic dictionary, Volume 3*. 3rd ed. London: Readers Digest Association, 1978.
5. Ware, D. and Stafford, M. *An illustrated dictionary of ornament*. London: George Allen & Unwin, 1974.

BIBLIOGRAPHY

Materials and Techniques

Anon. *Specialized Joinery*. Classic Reprint Series. Algrove Publishing, Almonte, Ontario, 2002.

Baldi, R., Lisini, G., Martelli, C., Martelli, S. *La cornice Fiorentina e Senese: storia e tecniche di restauro*. Alinea, Florence, 1992, pp. 40–41.

Berrie, B.H. *Artists' Pigments: A Handbook of Their History and Characteristics, vol. 4.* National Gallery of Art, Washington, DC.

Bomford, D., Dunkerton, J., Gordon, D. Roy, A. *Art in the Making: Italian Painting before 1400.* Exhibition Catalogue. National Gallery, London, 1992.

Brettel, R., Starling, S. *The Art of Edge: European Frames 1300–1900.* Exhibition Catalogue. Art Institute of Chicago, Chicago, IL, 1986.

Cennini, Cennino d'Andrea (trans. Thompson, D. V.). *The Craftsman's Handbook, 'Il libro dell' arte',* Dover Publications, New York, 1960.

Currie, S. & Molture, P. *The Sculpted Object 1400-1700.* Aldershot: Scholar Press, 1997.

Dunkerton, J., Foister, S., Gordon, D., Penny, N. *Giotto to Dürer: Early Renaissance Painting in the National Gallery.* National Gallery Publications, London, 1991, pp. 152–204.

Eastaugh, N., Walsh, V., Chaplin, T., Siddall, R.A. *Pigment Compendium: A Dictionary of Historical Pigments.* Elsevier Butterworth-Heinemann, London, 2004.

Feller, R.L. (Ed.). *Artists' Pigments: A Handbook of their History and Characteristics, vol. 1.* National Gallery of Art, Washington, DC, 1986.

Fitzhugh, E.W. (Ed.). *Artists' Pigments: A Handbook of their History and Characteristics, vol. 3.* National Gallery of Art, Washington, DC, 1997.

Galassi, A.G., Fumagalli, P., Gritti, E. *Conservation and scientific examination of three Northern Italian gilded and painted altarpieces of the sixteenth century.* In: Bigelow, D. (Ed.), Gilded Wood Conservation and History. Sound View Press, Madison, CT, 1980, pp. 193–203.

Gettens, R.J. *A visit to an ancient gypsum quarry in Tuscany.* Stud. Conserv. 1 (4), 1954, pp. 190–192.

Gettens, RJ., Mrose, M.E. *Calcium sulfate minerals in the grounds of Italian paintings.* Stud. Conserv. 1 (4), 1954, pp. 174–189.

Gettens, R.J., Stout, G.L. *Painting Materials: A Short Encyclopaedia.* Van Nostrand, New York, 1947.

Gilbert, C. *Peintres et menuisiers au debut de la Renaissance en Italie.* Rev. Art. 37, 1977, 9–28.

Hoadley, B. *Identifying Wood.* Taunton Press, Newtown, CT, 1990.

Joyce, E. *The Technique of Furniture Making.* B.T. Batsford, London, 1987.

Mactaggart, P., Mactaggart, A. *A Pigment Microscopists's Notebook, 7th rev.* Published by the Authors, Somerset, 1998, p. 43.

Martin, E., Bergeon, S. *Des bleus profonds chez primitifs italiens.* Techné 4, 1996, pp. 74–89.

Michalski, S. *Crack mechanisms in gilding.* In: Bigelow, D. (Ed.), *Gilded Wood Conservation and History.* Sound View Press, Madison, CT, 1991, pp. 171–181.

Nadolny, J. *Some observations on northern European metalbeaters and metal leaf in the late Middle Ages.* In: Rushfield, R., Ballard, M. (Eds.) The Materials, Technology and Art of Conservation: Studies in Honor of Lawrence J. Majewski on the Occasion of his 80th Birthday, February 10,

1999. Conservation Center, Institute of Fine Arts, New York University, New York, 1999, pp. 134–160.

Newbery, T., Bisacca, G., Kanter, L. *Italian Renaissance Frames* Exhibition Catalogue. Metropolitan Museum, New York, 1990.

Olga, R., Wilmering, A. *The Gubbio Studiolo and its Conservation*. Metropolitan Museum of Art, New York, 2001.

Pandolfo, A. *Aspetti technici e conservative della scultura lignea policroma*. Kermes 1 (1), 1988, pp. 9–14.

Ravenel, N.C. Painted Italian picture frames in the Samuel H. Kress foundation collection at the national gallery of art. In: Dorge, V., Carey Howlett, F. (Eds.), *Painted Wood – History and Conservation*. American Institute for Conservation of Historic and Artistic Works, Wooden Artifacts Group. Symposium Proceedings, Williamsburg, VA, November 1994, Getty Conservation Institute, Los Angeles, 1998, pp. 100–109.

Roy, A. (Ed.). *Artists' Pigments: A Handbook of their History and Characteristics, vol. 2*. National Gallery of Art, Washington, DC, 1993.

Sabatelli, F. *Le cornice italiane dal Rinascimento al Neoclassico*. Electa, Milan, 1992.

Selwyn, L. *Metals and Corrosion: A Handbook for the Conservation Professional*. Canadian Conservation Institute, Ottawa, 2004, pp. 89–112.

Skaug, E. *Preliminary Report on a Collection of Punching Tools Formerly Belonging to Icilio Federico Joni Recorded 1983*. Fellow Villa l Tatti Norsk Folkemusuem, Oslo, 1988/89.

Skaug, E. *Punch Marks from Giotto to Fra Angelico. Attribution, Chronology and Workshop Relationships in Tuscan Panel Painting*. IIC Nordic Group, Norwegian Section, Oslo, 1994.

Smith, A., Reeve, A., Powell, C., Burnstock, A. *An altarpiece and its frame: Carlo Crivelli's 'Madonna della Rondine'*. National Gallery Tech. Bull. 13, 1989, pp. 28–43 London: National Gallery Publications.

Spring, M., Higgitt, C., Saunders, D. *Investigation of pigment–medium interaction processes in oil paint containing degraded smalt*. National Gallery Tech. Bull. 26, 2005, p. 63. National Gallery Publications, London.

Stege, H. *Out of the blue? Considerations on the early use of smalt as blue pigment in European easel painting*. Z. Kunsttechnologie Konservierung 18, 2004, pp. 121–142.

Thompson, D.V. *The Materials and Techniques of Medieval Painting*. Dover Publications, New York, 1956.

General

Ajmar-Wollheim, M., Dennis, F. *At Home in Renaissance Italy*. V&A Publications, London, 2006.

Ames-Lewis, F. *Early Medicean devices*. J. Warburg Courtauld Inst. 42, 1979, pp. 122–143.

Baldi, R., Lisini, G., Martelli, C., Martelli, S. *La cornice Fiorentina e Senese: storia e tecniche di restauro*. Alinea, Florence, 1972.

Bigelow, D. (Ed.). *Gilded Wood Conservation and History*. Sound View Press, Madison, CT, 1991.

Bock, E. *Florentinische und Venezianische Bilderrahmen aus der Zeit der Gotik und Renaissance*. F. Bruckmann, Munich, 1902.

Bode, W. *Italian Renaissance Furniture*. William Helburn, New York, 1921.

Cecchi, C., Blamoutier, N. *Les cadres ronds de la Renaissance Florentine*. Rev. Art. 76, 1987, pp. 21–24.

Cole, J.Y., Reed, H.H. *The Art and Architecture of the Thomas Jefferson Building*. W.W. Norton & Company, New York, 1997.

Curl, J. *Encyclopaedia of Architecture Terms*. Donhead Publishing, Lower Coombe, Shaftesbury, 2003.

Evans, M. *The Painted World from Illumination to Abstraction.* V&A Publications, London, 2005.

Fossi, G. *The Uffizi.* The Official Guide. Giunti, Prato, 2005.

Gilbert, C. *Peintres et menuisiers au debut de la Renaissance en Italie.* Rev. Art. 37, 1977.

Gombrich, E.H. *Norm and Form: Studies in the Art of the Renaissance.* Phaidon, London, 1966. pp. 122–128.

Grimm, C. *Alte Bilderrahmen: Epochen, Typen, Material.* Callwey, Munich, 1979.

Grimm, C. *The Book of Picture Frames.* Abaris Books, New York, 1981.

Guggenheim, M. *Le cornici Italiane dalla metà del secolo XVº allo scorcio del XVI; con breve testo riassuntivo intorno alla storia ed all'importanza delle cornice.* U. Hoepli, Milan, 1987.

Hasluck, P.N. *Manual of Traditional Woodcarving.* Dover Publications, New York, 1977.

Heydenryk, H. *The Art and History of Frames; an Inquiry into the Enhancement of Paintings.* J.H. Heinemann, New York, 1963.

Hughes, P. *The Wallace Collection Catalogue of Furniture.* Cambridge University Press, Cambridge, 1996.

Hunter, G.L. *Italian Furniture and Interiors, vol. 1.* William Helburn, New York, 1920.

Jeffries, J., Romano, D. *Venice Reconsidered: The History and Civilization of an Italian City State.* Johns Hopkins University Press, Baltimore, 2000.

Kaminski, M. *Venice. Art and Architecture.* Könemann, Cologne, 2005.

Kauffmann, C.M. *Victoria & Albert Museum Catalogue of Foreign Paintings before 1900.* Eyre & Spottiswoode, London, 1973.

Lepke, R. *Nachlass Adolf von Beckerath, Berlin.* Kunst-Auctions Haus, Berlin, 1916.

Lessing, J. *Vorbilder-Hefte aus dem KGL. Kunstgewerbe-Museen Rahmen: Italien und Deutschland XVI Jahr hundert.* Verlag Von Ernst Wasmuth, Berlin, 1888.

Lodi, R. *La collezione di cornici.* Galleria Roberto Lodi, Modena, 2006.

Lodi, R., Montanari, A. *Repertorio della cornice Europea: Italia, Francia, Spagna, Paesi Bassi: dal secolo XV al secolo XX.* Galleria Roberto Lodi, Modena, 2003.

Maclagan, E., Longhurst, M.H. *Catalogue of Italian Sculpture Text.* Victoria and Albert Museum, London, 1932, pp. 22–23.

Mariacher, G. *Specchiere Italiane: cornici da specchio, dal XV al XIX secolo.* Görlich Editore, Milan, 1963.

Mitchell, P. *Italian picture frames, 1500–1825: a brief survey.* J. Furnit. Hist. Soc. 20, 1984. pp. 18–27.

Mitchell, P., Roberts, L. *A History of European Picture Frames.* Merrell Holberton, London, 1996.

Mitchell, P., Roberts, L. *Frameworks.* Merrell Holberton, London, 1996.

Newbery, T. *Frames in the Robert Lehman Collection.* Metropolitan Museum of Art in association with Princeton University Press, Princeton, NJ, 2007.

Newbery, T., Bisacca, G., and Kanter, L. *Italian Renaissance Frames* Exhibition Catalogue. Metropolitan Museum, New York, 1990.

Odom, W.M. *A History of Italian Furniture from the Fourteenth to the Early Nineteenth Centuries. Volume I: Gothic and Renaissance furniture.* Archive Press, New York, 1967.

Ojetti, U. *Dedalo: Rassegna D'Arte, vol terzo.* Casa Editrice D'Arte Bestettie Tumminelli, Milan–Rome, 1921.

Olga, R., Wilmering, A. *The Gubbio Studiolo and its Conservation.* Metropolitan Museum of Art, New York, 2001.

Pedrini, A. *Il mobilio; gli ambienti e le decorazioni del Rinascimento in Italia, secoli XV e XVI,* second ed. Stringa, Genova, 1969.

Penny, N. *Frames.* National Gallery Pocket Guides. National Gallery, London, 1997.

Penny, N. *The Sixteenth Century Italian Paintings National Gallery Catalogue, vol. 1.* National Gallery, London, 2004.

Perez-Hita, H. *The Collection: Alorda Derksen: Frames from 16th–18th Centuries.* Alorda Derksen, Barcelona–London, 2006.

Pope-Hennessy, J., assisted by Lightbown, R. *Catalogue of Italian Sculpture in the Victoria and Albert Museum.* Her Majesty's Stationery Office, London, 1964.

The Readers Digest *Great Encyclopaedic Dictionary, vol. 3.* third ed. Readers Digest Association, London, 1979.

Roche, S. *Cadres Français et étrangers XVième siècle au XVIIIième siècle: Allemagne, Angleterre, Espagne, France, Italie, Pays Bas.* E. Bignou, Paris, 1931.

Sabatelli, F. *La Cornice Italiana dal Rinascimento al Neoclassico.* Electa, Milan, 1992.

Schöne Rahmen aus den Bestanden der Berliner Gemäldegalerie. Exhibition Catalogue, Gemäldegalerie, Staatliche Museen zu Berlin, Berlin, 2002.

Schottmüller, F. *Furniture and Interior Decoration of the Italian Renaissance.* Hoffman, Stuttgart, 1928.

Strange, A., Cremer, L. *Alte Bilderrhamen.* F. Scneekluth, Darmstadt, 1958.

Ware, D., Stafford, M. *An Illustrated Dictionary of Ornament.* George Allen & Unwin, London, 1974.

Wilk, C. *Western Furniture in The Victoria & Albert Museum 1350 to the Present Day.* Philip Wilson Publishers, London, 1996.